the GRIM REAPER

the GRIM REAPER

THE LIFE and CAREER of a RELUCTANT WARRIOR

STU GRIMSON

VIKING

VIKING

an imprint of Penguin Canada, a division of Penguin Random House Canada Limited

Canada • USA • UK • Ireland • Australia • New Zealand • India • South Africa • China

First published 2019

www.penguinrandomhouse.ca

LIBRARY AND ARCHIVES CANADA CATALOGUING IN PUBLICATION

Title: The grim reaper : the life and career of a reluctant warrior / Stu Grimson
Names: Grimson, Stu, 1965- author.
Identifiers: Canadiana (print) 2019010113X | Canadiana (ebook) 20190101148 |
ISBN 9780735237247 (hardcover) | ISBN 9780735237254 (HTML)
Subjects: LCSH: Grimson, Stu, 1965- | LCSH: Hockey players—Canada—
Biography. | LCGFT: Autobiographies.
Classification: LCC GV848.5.G79 A3 2019 | DDC 796.962092—dc23

Book design: Five Seventeen
Cover design: David Gee
Cover image: Mark A. Hicks

All photos are from the personal collection of Stu Grimson,
with the following exceptions. Every effort has been made
to contact the copyright holder of all uncredited images.
Image of Stu Grimson and Dave Manson: Ray Grabowski, GrabowskiPhoto.com
Image of Western Conference Champs: Mark A. Hicks
Image of Stu and Jennifer Grimson skating: John Russell

Printed and bound in Canada

10 9 8 7 6 5 4 3 2 1

Penguin
Random House
VIKING CANADA

To my sweet children Erin, Hannah, Kristjan, and Jayne.

*To my mother and father, who instilled in me the value of
hard work: the gateway to a life I never expected to live.*

And to the love of my life, Jennifer.

Battle is the most magnificent competition in which a human being can indulge. It brings out all that is best; it removes all that is base. All men are afraid in battle. The coward is the one who lets his fear overcome his sense of duty.

—General George Patton

CONTENTS

foreword
by **PAUL KARIYA**

When I first met Stu Grimson, he was eating a bowl of oatmeal at the Disneyland Hotel restaurant. It was September 1994 and I was attending my first NHL training camp with the Anaheim Ducks.

Stu was one of the Ducks' leaders and when I walked in that morning looking for breakfast, he motioned for me to join him. I remember being struck by how big he was as I sat down. He was an imposing figure, a massive man with huge hands and broad shoulders. But my second impression of Stu was that his personality was 180 degrees different than I thought it would be.

He was one of the league's toughest enforcers, but that was only a small part of who he was. He had tremendous intelligence, and a wisdom that extended beyond anything we were trying to accomplish on the ice. His off-ice persona is the opposite of the way Stu was on the ice. On the ice, opponents feared Stu. Off the ice, people enjoy his company because he is interesting, witty, and insightful.

From that day forward, Stu and I have become fast friends. I thoroughly enjoy his sense of humour. We had our hair cut at the same place, and Stu once addressed a photo to our hair stylist, Dave Mazza, that read: "I trust my hair to anyone that can make Paul Kariya look presentable! Your friend, Stu Grimson."

Stu being Stu is always priceless.

When I played on the Ducks with Stu in 1994–95 and 1998–2000, I believe he was the toughest guy in the league. He was such a force; his presence in the lineup could affect what was happening on the ice.

We used to all laugh in Anaheim when the play would get a little dicey on the ice and Stu would just stand on the bench and everything would calm down. He would rise like he was Viktor Tikhonov on the Russian bench, intense and focused. He would stare out over the ice and inevitably our opponents would start behaving themselves. It was fascinating to watch the impact his presence could have.

Very few people were willing to tangle with Stu. Anytime something erupted on the ice, he'd come in first with a snide remark and immediately most opponents would back off. He was so intimidating that his glare was as terrifying as his fists.

I remember during my rookie season one game got very heated, so much so that coach Ron Wilson used me at centre with Stu and another tough guy, Todd Ewen, as my wingers.

At no time in my career did I ever have more room on the ice than I had playing with those guys. I remember skating down the ice and feeling completely alone. I'm thinking, *Where is everybody? Am I in a dream?* No one came anywhere near me. Stu and I still laugh about the time we played on a line together. I never felt safer in my life. No tough guy understood his role more than Stu.

In today's NHL, fighting doesn't play the same role it did during my era of playing. But I can tell you that anyone who ever played with Stu understands that we owe him a debt of gratitude for how he helped our teams. Nobody looked after teammates better than Stu did. Stu's former teammates all respect the selfless contribution he made.

A favourite "Stuism" was that he believed his job was "to create a safer working environment for my teammates." Just the way he phrased that sentence was classic Stu. It's not surprising that he became a lawyer.

What people didn't realize about Stu was that he owned one of the NHL's hardest shots. He could hammer the puck. It did take him an hour to release it, but it was a howitzer, a bomb. Ducks goalie Guy Hebert really didn't want anything to do with Grimson's shot in practice.

As soon as Stu realized this, all in good fun, he would mercilessly torture Guy with his shot. In warm-up, he would wind up for a big slapshot from the hash marks.

Guy would sometimes just abandon the net. It was a funny scene.

When Stu is around, there are no dull moments. Stu is such a personable guy that he is popular with everyone he has ever met. In the Ducks' first couple of seasons, we were known as a very tough team and Stu was the face of the team toughness.

I invited Stu to come my jersey retirement ceremony. We had a gathering at a restaurant, and there was genuine excitement when he walked in. Everyone was so happy to see him because he is always the life of the party.

He was a presence in the dressing room. In Anaheim, he was a leader on and off the ice. Even though he wasn't a top offensive player, he wasn't afraid to speak his mind. When the team wasn't playing well, he always had something to say. And we all listened.

Stu could also lead in a more understated way. He was on the bike, always working out. His dedication to his fitness off the ice was a tremendous example to the rest of us.

I always looked up to Stu for the man and player he was; we all did.

Even though Stu, in his role, didn't log a ton of minutes, he was as popular with teammates and with Anaheim fans as any player on the team. He was one of the best teammates I ever had during my hockey career.

Today, Stu is fifty-four and still a physical specimen. He has shed the extra pounds he needed as a heavyweight NHL fighter in favour of a leaner physique. Because of his long arms, I joke with him that he looks today like a competitive swimmer.

Having said that, this is one swimmer you probably don't want to tangle with.

1

THE RELUCTANT WARRIOR

My nickname was "the Grim Reaper." Not a bad way to be known for an NHL tough guy.

No one ever wondered what my job was in the National Hockey League. I played 729 regular-season games over fourteen seasons for seven different organizations. I registered seventeen goals and twenty-two assists. That's roughly one goal every forty-three games and one assist every thirty-three games. But my name showed up on the scoresheet regularly nonetheless. I totalled 211 regular-season fighting majors over my career. That's a fight every 3.45 regular-season game. My mandate was clear. Teams were not paying me for my offensive artistry and magic.

Between 1988 and 2002, I averaged under five minutes per-game playing time and earned $5,625,930 to be an NHL fighter. That's over $1500 per minute on the ice. Or more than $2600 for

1

every minute in the box, if you want to look at it that way. (Another way of looking at it: I was paid about $26,000 per fight.) Not that I looked at it that way. But I did look at it as a job.

An enforcer's job description is more complicated than people realize, but you won't be able to put its finer points into practice if you can't kick ass and take names. You need to be able to do that just to get in the door. And I was skilled at my craft. I respected my opponents. Any true heavyweight back then could best any other heavyweight on any given night. He wouldn't have been in the lineup if he couldn't. But I estimate I recorded a win or a draw in 80 percent of my fights. I was good at what I did for a living.

I took it seriously. A hockey fight usually lasts under forty seconds, but I wanted it to feel like an eternity when you were fighting me. I was six-feet-six-inches tall and weighed 250 pounds at my heaviest. When I landed one, you knew it. That is to say, I hurt people.

Of course, I didn't hurt just anyone. I hurt guys who had a fighting chance of hurting me. I hit St. Louis Blues enforcer Reid Simpson hard enough that two guys were required to carry him off the ice. I stepped over his crumpled body to return to the bench before help arrived.

The meek did not inherit the earth in my world. My job was to intimidate guys who by definition are hard to intimidate. If you're easy to stare down, you're probably not playing in the NHL. And you're certainly not taking a shift when the other team's enforcer is on the ice. When I went over the boards, I knew that whoever I was lining up against could handle himself, and I had to be ready.

While other hockey players were honing their shot or their

stride, I was making sure I had the stamina and left jab necessary to stay near the top in the NHL fight game.

Some tough guys were harder punchers than me. Others were more ferocious. But I could stand toe-to-toe against any fighter in the NHL. I never backed down from anyone and I got the better of most of the league's heralded heavyweights at one time or another. I owned multiple wins against Bob Probert, and one or more wins against Dave Brown, Marty McSorley, Shane Churla, Matt Johnson, Darren Langdon, Craig Berube, Donald Brashear, Georges Laraque, and Peter Worrell, to name a few.

It was a stressful job, but an important one. I took considerable pride in being my team's "policeman," the guy who set things right when players were misbehaving on the ice. My father was a Mountie for thirty-one years, and it felt fitting that my primary purpose was to protect my teammates. Fans in every city feel the same way about the heavyweights on their team. They're often as popular as the team's leading scorer. When I played in Chicago, fans chanted, "Stuuu, Stuuu, Stuuu" after all my fights. There aren't many things you can do for a living that feel better than hearing that.

I enjoyed the strategy of the fight game, particularly making determinations about when my team needed me to fight and when they needed me to turn the other cheek. You needed brains as much as brawn to be a tough guy. A good heavyweight can control the momentum of a game if he understands the nuances in it and his timing is effective. But woe to the fighter who makes poor decisions about when to drop the gloves.

The truth is, I look back with fondness on my career as a tough guy. I enjoy a strong sense of fulfillment because I played so long. When I meet guys I fought years ago, I greet them like comrades or buddies from high school.

I love winning. I loved the fans. I loved doing the right thing for my teammates. So it's odd for me now to remember that when I was nineteen I was ready to throw all that away.

—

Ask any NHL heavyweight how he ended up as an enforcer. You'll hear the same story from just about every guy. They all took a regular shift in minor hockey. They were all skill guys, captains, leaders. They all dreamed of scoring the overtime Cup-winning goal, just as NHL All-Stars did when they were kids. Then, somewhere along the way—maybe they were told by a coach or parent, maybe they figured it out themselves—it became clear that they didn't have the hands, or the vision, or the footspeed, or whatever, to make it as a top-six player. But if they were big enough, and naturally intimidating enough, maybe they'd make it as a guy who could set the tone of a game, or protect the skill guys, open up the ice. That could be the route to the NHL. If they wanted it badly enough. That's how dreams work.

You hear it all the time from penalty-minute leaders: "I would do whatever it takes to play in the NHL."

Not me.

The idea of being an NHL enforcer was so unappealing that I quit the Calgary Flames in the middle of a training camp in Moncton, New Brunswick, in 1985.

One morning, I worked through the chain of command to see Flames general manager Cliff Fletcher. I told him I appreciated the opportunity, but that a career playing the role he had in mind just wasn't for me.

Fletcher looked flabbergasted, not because he was losing a seventh-round draft pick, but because a Canadian-born teenager was in his office giving up on a dream to play in the NHL. He had been in pro hockey for years, and had probably never seen that before. Finally he told me the Flames would book a flight for me. It was a short conversation, mostly because I think Fletcher didn't know what to say.

But given time to mull it over, Fletcher came back at me later. He asked me to meet for lunch with team psychologist Max Offenberger. The Flames were on the cutting edge of training techniques back then, and the presence of a team psychologist was proof of that. Offenberger would come to training camp and help players work through any issue that might be affecting their game. It happens more than you think.

I assumed Offenberger's mandate was to persuade me to go back on my decision to quit. Based on what he told me, the Flames guessed my issue was a girlfriend back home or a case of homesickness. I think I caught Offenberger by surprise when I explained what was really going on.

I was a reluctant warrior.

That's right. The Grim Reaper didn't want to fight for a living.

It wasn't fear. Don't get me wrong—I was definitely intimidated. But I wasn't physically afraid to stand in there with those guys. I knew two things, though. I knew for a fact that I was not *mentally* ready to tangle with those guys night after night. And I also knew that there was too much at stake even to try it. I was a tough guy. Winning fights was who I was. Getting my ass kicked in front of thousands of people was just too much to ask of me.

It wasn't a new feeling. I had gone through exactly the same thing in my first year of junior hockey. Remember, when I was playing midget I was putting up points. I was on the ice for key matchups and special teams. I was a leader. You don't get drafted if you're not a good hockey player. But getting drafted doesn't mean you play big minutes. It doesn't mean you play at all.

Sitting there with Offenberger, I described the resentment I experienced in my first season of junior hockey when I barely played and felt as if I needed to fight every time I was on the ice. I watched a lot of the game from the bench, but at the same time I was expected to sacrifice for other people when a score needed to be settled or the team needed a lift. I'm not saying I deserved to play more that season—I knew just as well as the coaches did that the pace out there was faster than I was comfortable with, and that there were more skilled guys in the lineup than me. If I wanted to play more, it was up to me to play better. But you still feel like a piece of meat when your role means you don't play much.

My reluctance to play the role of enforcer wasn't about the morality of fighting. I believed fighting had an important place in the game. Nor was it about fear of injury. But I *was* afraid of being humiliated by losing a big fight in front of a large crowd. I didn't know whether my ego could take that. Throughout my life, I've always been bothered too much by the way others view me. It's still true today. I didn't bring up my self-esteem and anxiety issues with Offenberger, but I'm sure he knew I had them.

If I was going to accept the job, I wanted to do it well. I needed adrenaline to work up the lather required to be an effective fighter, and it was impossible to manufacture that sitting on the bench.

When you are playing regularly, and circumstances dictate a scrap needs to happen, you already have the anger and intensity you need to drop the gloves. But when you are sitting on the bench, you cool off. Sit there long enough and you may not feel like punching someone in the face anymore. If the tap comes to go over the boards, you may have only seconds to dial up the intensity before the gloves are off and punches are thrown.

It's a stress-filled endeavour. It's not easy to do, and it's even harder to do effectively. I just didn't know whether I had the mental toughness to do that night after night.

Though I hadn't had that problem the year before.

My confidence soared in my final season with the Pats. I arrived at Flames training camp full of hope and self-confidence. By the time I was a third-year junior player, I was a top-six forward. I fought twenty-one times for the Regina Pats that year, but most of those fights arose out of heat-of-the-battle confrontations on the ice. My fighting was just part of playing the game. I had a lot of other ways to contribute, but if someone wanted to mix it up, so be it. Coming off a twenty-five-goal season in Regina, I was excited about the chance to prove myself. Quitting wasn't on my radar. I was going to keep doing what I had been doing.

But within my first forty-eight hours of training camp, I knew my heart wasn't in it. I remembered my first season in junior, when I spent a lot of time on the bench wondering whether I was the lion or about to be fed to the lions. I wasn't sure I wanted a whole career of that feeling. And if deep down you don't want to be there, you have no business squaring off in an NHL rink.

I fought Neil Sheehy in camp out of little more than a sense of obligation. Was there any reason to fight him in a scrimmage? No. But here I am, a physical player. I'm always going to be asked to handle the tough guys. And that was Sheehy. I'd done my homework. He was a Harvard grad—and also a trained heavyweight boxer. He would have had the book on me too. Some snot-nosed rookie looking to make a mark. I was always happy to get things

over with early, and I didn't wait long to issue an invitation to
Sheehy. He was happy to oblige—he had a job to earn too, and
standing his ground was the way to do it. I could feel anxiety
start to wash over me the way it did early in my first year of junior.
I held my own with Sheehy, but my heart wasn't really in it.

Training camp that year was like that. I kept to myself. Veterans
don't really develop relationships with the young guys. I mean,
even calling me a "rookie" is overstating it. I was a prospect.
Those guys didn't even talk to prospects. Guys in similar circumstances tended to run together.

The one guy I hung out with was Mark Lamb. We knew each
other from major junior—he'd played for Medicine Hat. He was an
undersized centre who could put the puck in the net; I was almost a
foot taller and changed the game using quite different skills. We
weren't competing for the same job, so Lammer was someone I
could befriend.

Lamb had played in the American Hockey League the season
before. I remember sitting around in a hotel room listening to
him tell stories about the fighting and mayhem that he witnessed
the previous season. Hearing his tales made me believe I was
light years away from where I needed to be to compete at this
level. To make things worse, a lot of Lammer's stories featured
Joey Kocur *destroying* guys in the minors. He's first year and he's
terrorizing guys. Kocur became a big hurdle for me. I was thinking, *If that's a snapshot of the A, what is the* NHL *like?*

Clearly, it didn't help that I was overwhelmed by the talent I
was matched against in camp. Everyone seemed stronger than
me, tougher than me, faster than me, and fiercer than me. Even
the nice guys seemed meaner than me. Back then, NHL teams
used to share minor-league franchises, and so I was in camp with

Bruins prospect George White. White had us laughing our asses off. He was a genuinely funny guy, and I'd never heard a Boston accent before. The guy was killing us. The room would be in stitches when he made his joke about the "one-handed hanjie." I thought he was the funniest guy on the planet.

Then we hit the ice and he flips a switch. All of a sudden he goes from happy-go-lucky to absolute beast. Where did that intensity come from? I couldn't believe the contrast. It was astonishing. I didn't have that switch.

All the guys were like that. Jim Peplinski. Tim Hunter. Colin Patterson. Al MacInnis. Hakan Loob. Lanny McDonald. Sheehy. The list went on and on. Impressive and intimidating. These were talented guys (in fact, they would be playing in the Stanley Cup Final in a few months). But what stunned me was how these players could be joking around and cutting up in the dressing room one minute and then going at it hammer and tongs the next.

But at the time, what I saw was that I didn't belong in this group. Best-case scenario, I was headed to the minors. And when I got there, I was headed for a replay of my junior hockey experience. I told Offenberger and Fletcher that I just didn't have the appetite for it. I told them I felt like I was standing at the foot of a mountain, anticipating the long climb, and simply not feeling I wanted to make that ascent.

I knew the proper response. Every athlete does: *Okay, Stuart, roll up your sleeves, and let's get after this. We are going to grind our way to the top.* But if grinding your way to the top means putting your body and your entire sense of who you are on the line night after night against another 240-pound tough guy grinding his way to the top, you *really* have to want it. And you really have to believe you can do it. I found myself thinking it was time to follow my dad into law enforcement, and I had a vague idea about establishing my own physical therapy business. At that time, I didn't have it in me to push through my self-doubt.

The conversation with Offenberger lasted for more than two hours. Just explaining my anxiety was exhausting. Much to my surprise, he didn't try to talk me out of leaving. Far from it. He had been listening intently and only wanted to talk about what was right for me, not for the team.

His exact words have slipped away from me through the years, but I remember phrases and the basic message. "If you don't have the right mindset to play this role, there's no sense trying to force a square peg into a round hole," Offenberger said. "At some point, you will self-destruct."

Over the years, I have run into him a few times and I've told him how much he helped me. His task may have been to convince me to stay, but he was honest enough to validate my decision to quit. I think he knew on that day that hockey hadn't seen the last of me. But he knew I needed time away from the game to sort out my issues.

"Fuck 'em," he said. "You need to go back to school. Maybe you will come back to hockey, maybe you won't. But Stu, you've got to do what's right for you."

I'm glad I had those doubts. I'm glad I didn't take the route that others took. I am especially grateful for the perspective that the experience of stepping away from the NHL gave me. I learned a lot from that—and I needed to learn a lot.

One thing I laugh about a little when I think of Offenberger's advice is the idea that a nineteen-year-old Stu Grimson knew what was best for him. Figuring out what's best is hard for anyone, and I was probably a step or two behind a lot of people at that point in my life. You think you know someone by their reputation, or their nickname, or their stats. But those things don't tell you anything. That guy you think you know probably doesn't even know himself. I learned that lesson the old-fashioned way, and I certainly didn't know it when I was coming out of junior.

2

IT'S NOT A PARTY UNTIL STU STRIPS NAKED

The origin story of many NHL players includes the tale of a scout spotting them performing dazzling offensive feats in a charming small-town arena. My journey to the NHL began when a scout spotted me pummelling someone on a public sidewalk.

Regina Pats scout Glen Dirk was driving past the downtown movie theatre in Kamloops, British Columbia, on a Saturday night when he spied me embroiled in a street fight. I remember that fight well. To Dirk, it must have looked like a scene out of a 1950s teen movie. Three of my buddies—Don Simpson, Owen Mattheson, and Randy Rein—and I were walking down one side of the street, each of us wearing our leather-sleeved Sa-Hali High School football jackets. Walking parallel to us, down the other side of street, was a small group of oil rig workers, all in their twenties. We knew the type. Guys who worked long shifts in remote areas of British Columbia and then came to town on the weekend to drink and howl at the moon. We called them "Rig Pigs."

The two groups came together at the movie theatre and I knew instantly that there would be trouble. These guys had been drinking for a while. Their idea of fun was picking a fight with a bunch of high school kids.

"Sa-Hali sucks. Sa-Hali football sucks," one of them taunted.

You can guess what followed. We weren't the type to back down. Instantly, my three friends were paired off with the out-of-towners. I stepped between two of my buddies, waded into the fray, and got the party started by cold-cocking the guy doing most of the talking.

His two front teeth launched skyward and we quickly became the main event. Within seconds, I pinned the trash-talker against the theatre wall and was slamming his head against the bricks. Over and over, and then a few more times for good measure. I left him sprawled on the ground bleeding.

The only damage I suffered was the loss of one of my Stan Smith sneakers during the fight. I never tied my shoes back then. It flew off my foot sometime after I threw my first punch. I located the shoe quickly and bent over to grab it. Big mistake.

My beat-up dance partner drove one of his cowboy boots into my face and split my lip wide open. I was dazed, and he was yapping that the kick to the face squared us up.

I didn't think we were square at all. We'd had a pretty good go the first time around, but I was ready for Round 2. That kick was offside, and I was even more pissed off now. Even more than that, there's nothing like the taste of your own blood in your mouth to awaken the senses. It's the most basic calculation there is. If your opponent lands one, he knows where to find you. If there's one, there could be more. You'd better get busy. I grabbed him. Threw him around. I hammered him again. It didn't take long.

Dirk had seen me play defence for a local midget team. But he hadn't seen me fight before that night. There's not much fighting in midget hockey—even in the Prairies. But from what I was told later, my split lip was a small price to pay. His assessment of my handiwork on that street corner was the reason I received a letter a few weeks later inviting me to the Pats' training camp.

This fight was not out of character for me. I was a rough-and-tumble kid. As a teenager, I was restless, anxious, and bored. I had a habit of drawing attention to myself, and never in a good way.

I was the adopted son of Royal Canadian Mounted Police officer Stan Grimson and his wife, Emgard, known to all as "Em." My sister, Sam, was also adopted. My parents, much to their dismay, were accustomed to their son finding trouble. But my dad was nonetheless shocked to see my heavily damaged face the morning after the theatre fight. I arrived home long after my parents went to bed, and never considered waking up my police officer father to report the incident. He saw the extent of my injuries because he came into my room the next morning to wake me up.

"What on earth happened to you?" he said with a mixture of concern and anger. I didn't look like I'd won. When I explained the sequence of events, he was mad, but not mad enough to stop him from giving me a lawman's advice on how to stay safer in a fight.

"Never, ever turn your back on someone you have fought, whether you think he's done or not," he said.

Because of my dad's job, we moved every two or three years and I always struggled to fit in. I had lived in eight different cities before I was fourteen years old. As a kid, you tend to see yourself the way others see you. I suppose that because the people around me were always changing, I had a harder time than other young people figuring out exactly who I was. Not that I was looking too deeply for those kinds of answers. Mostly what I was looking for was trouble. That's what I ended up finding, anyway.

I don't think I was a bad kid. In fact, what I remember most from that period in my life is the feeling of deep regret over the things I said or, more usually, did. I could be mean. Or uncaring. I would just do whatever I needed to do to provoke a response. I would regret it almost right away, though. And I usually found a way to apologize, but apologies don't always work. I still regret some of the things I did back then.

It may have been what's called the "law of the instrument" in action. You know the saying: When you're holding a hammer, it's tempting to treat everything like a nail. Well, I had two hammers. Moving to a new place is easy when you're a little kid. But as I grew older, it became more traumatic. When I arrived in a new place, I felt as if I needed to do something outrageous to gain people's attention, and wading into a street brawl definitely accomplished that.

I could make friends, but the way I did it wouldn't receive any parent's seal of approval. I believed the best way to make friends was through my outrageous behaviour. I wanted to be the story everyone was telling at school on Monday morning. That meant that I was the guy most likely to take the first swing at a group of jackasses. I was the guy to swing first and ask questions later. I was the guy who made a party memorable. When I was fourteen, a common refrain around school was that "it isn't officially a party until Stu strips naked and jumps in the pool."

That did happen. I actually jumped off a friend's house into the pool, and no, I was not clothed. I'd had a few beers, but I was not drunk. I knew what I was doing. It was about becoming the story. I wanted people to talk about me. I believed that was the quickest way to find acceptance and admiration. That is how I believed the world worked when I was in my teens.

One night, I was driving two of my buddies in my four-door Toyota Corolla when I announced, "It's time for someone else to drive." Instead of stopping the car to change drivers, I told my front-seat passenger to grab the wheel and put his left foot on the accelerator. Then, while we were driving at 80 kilometres per hour down a secondary road, I climbed out the driver's side window, hoisted myself onto the roof, and then crawled over it. My buddy scooted into the driver's seat and I dropped into the passenger seat through the side window. I never even considered how dangerous that was. All I cared about was whether my buddies would tell everyone about my latest stunt.

My parents have never heard that story (until now), and they would have been mortified if they'd heard it in 1981. Maybe I was a thrill seeker, but mostly I wanted to be talked about. I made decisions back then not based on what I thought was right or wrong, but rather based on the following thought process, *How is this group of people going to perceive what I just did? Are they going to tell stories? Are they going to admire me? If people admire me for this, then I'm going to do it.*

I caused my parents considerable grief. It was amazing that I didn't maim or kill myself, or others, during my misguided teen years.

Crusty Kamloops junior hockey coach Joe Tennant was one person who could keep me out of trouble. By the time he was coaching me in midget hockey, he had been a legend in the British Columbia Junior Hockey League (BCJHL) for years. Today, the league's coach of the year trophy is named for him.

Tennant was well into his sixties when he coached us. We viewed him as the second coming of Toe Blake. What an intimidating presence. He was hockey's version of a drill sergeant. Gruff. Tough. Unrelenting. He cussed like a trucker, always wore cowboy boots, smoked like a chimney, and talked in a low, slow drawl.

Knowing that we were all scared to death of him, he would often have to find a way to bring down our anxiety. Sometimes he'd walk to the centre of the dressing room and yell, "It feels like the Tomb of Gloom in here! Somebody say somethin'." Then he'd lift his leg, fart like an old plow horse, roar with laughter, and walk back out of the room.

But the man could coach. He planted many seeds of hockey knowledge that bloomed for years in my head. I took Joe's teaching all the way to the NHL with me. He taught me how to compete at my highest level—always be hard driving, always finish your check, never swing away from the battle, and strive to make the high-percentage play. Good coaches always find a way to stay in your head. Today, I work as a hockey analyst and I still see the game through the lens of what he and others taught me.

Tennant may have kept me out of trouble most of the time, but getting into a little trouble changed the course of my life. Up until the letter from the Regina Pats arrived, my parents and I figured I would be going to school in the United States. My parents, particularly my mother, believed higher education was the path to success. She was pleased when I started receiving letters from

American colleges about scholarships. These were prominent schools, including Ivies. Princeton didn't sound too bad at all.

We had no idea how interested schools really were in my abilities. Those letters likely were sent to more players than were needed. But I was six-foot-four then and still growing, and I had athletic ability. It made sense for U.S. colleges to be interested. My parents and I agreed that National College Athletic Association (NCAA) hockey was the right route for me. I would be able to get a great education while still pursuing a pro career.

That meant that I would be joining the Kelowna Buckeroos of the BCJHL when I left midget. It was a good fit. Kelowna was only 167 kilometres from Kamloops. My mom liked that fact, pointing out that this would be the first time I lived away from home. According to the NCAA rules, I could maintain my college eligibility by playing Junior A hockey. If you played major junior hockey, you were deemed ineligible. The way the NCAA sees it, major junior—the Western Hockey League (WHL), Ontario Hockey League (OHL), and Quebec Major Junior Hockey League (QMJHL)—is professional hockey, while Tier II is not. Obviously, the hockey is better in major junior, but lots of guys planning to head to a U.S. college play Junior A. (Keep in mind, the major junior draft is for sixteen-year-olds—so players going the NCAA route have got to play somewhere before they're old enough to head off to school.)

Even though I was on board for the college plan, I still wanted to go to the Pats' camp. I sold the idea to my parents with the argument that the experience would be good for me. The competition would be more challenging, the players would be stronger. It would be a good way for me to prepare to attend the Kelowna training camp.

Even my mother didn't push back against the idea. My father was originally from Saskatchewan and his mother still lived in Regina. He would make the fourteen-hour drive with me and would have a chance to visit his mother and check in on old acquaintances.

Also, none of us even considered the possibility that I would make the Pats' roster.

I spent a week at the training camp trying out as a defenceman and held my own. I was on my way to six-foot-six and I skated adequately for a big guy.

I don't recall that I fought anyone. But I tried to play physical, believing that I needed to prove to everyone there that I could handle the notoriously tough WHL.

My dad later told me that during one scrimmage a player named Brent Pascal had challenged me. He had played for Regina the season before and was trying to stay on the team. I ran into him and he dropped his gloves while I was skating away. I didn't see him—or it's possible I didn't want to see him—could have been either. At that point, I wasn't really looking to engage in my first hockey fight.

When Pats general manager Bob Strumm called me into his office near the end of my tryout, I thought it would be his equivalent of an exit interview. I thought he would thank me for trying out and give me a no-holds-barred assessment of my strengths and weaknesses. But that isn't how the conversation went.

"We like your potential. We'd like you to stay," Strumm said.

In hindsight, this was one of several roster decisions that Strumm had to make during training camp. This was a routine duty for him. But his decision was life altering for me. This was a stunning development—something I had not seen coming. Was I hoping that the Pats wanted me? Probably. But I didn't truly believe that was possible. The Canadian Hockey League (CHL) is the best hockey in the world for teenagers. So yeah, I wanted to stay.

But if I joined the Pats, I would no longer be eligible to play college hockey in the States. If I wanted to do this, I would have to first persuade my dad and then my mother.

We still had to make the lengthy drive back to Kamloops because my dad had to go back to work. Strumm didn't want me to leave, figuring a trip home would increase the chances that I would say no. He put on a full-court press to convince me to stay.

Before I left for home, Pats players Al Tuer, Dale Derkatch, and Johnny Miner all sat with me and said they hoped I would choose to join the team. Tuer had been on his way to a 500 penalty-minute season before a suspension derailed him. He finished with 486. Derkatch was a five-foot-five pepper-pot centre who had posted 62 goals and 142 points with 92 penalty minutes in 1981–82. He was a dynamic player with a wicked, accurate shot. He could pass as well as he could shoot. If he'd been six-foot-one, he would have been an NHLer. Unfortunately for Derkatch, hockey was a big man's game back then. Miner was a young defenceman of my age.

The three players said they thought I fit well with the team and they liked my game. I knew Strumm had put them up to it, but I didn't care. Given my appetite for attention, it was the perfect way to win me over.

But my dad and I had to make the trip home. Our conversation on the way wasn't as difficult as I'd thought it would be. Even though I hadn't told him what Strumm had said before we left, he sensed what was coming.

"I really want to play in Regina—that's where my heart is at," I told him.

He shrugged his shoulders. "Okay, but let's think about how we are going to present this to your mother because she isn't going to be happy that you are going to be so far away."

When we stopped in Medicine Hat, Alberta, I found a pay phone and called up Strumm.

"Don't give away my roster spot," I said. "I'm coming back."

Dad was a practical man. He understood the lure of the WHL for his son. This was 1982, and at that time, the best path to the NHL was to play major junior in Canada.

In the 1982 NHL draft, nineteen of the twenty-one first-round picks came from the CHL, and seven of the first ten picks were WHL players. Regina forwards Gary Leeman (Toronto Maple Leafs) and Lyndon Byers (Boston Bruins) had both been selected in the second round.

The Pats were expected to be an exceptional team in 1982–83, which was another reason for me to accept a roster spot in Regina. They finished the 1981–82 season with a 48–24 record and they were the WHL's highest-scoring team.

The conversation with my mother was more sad than difficult. I knew she would let me chase this dream. My parents were always supportive of what my sister and I felt we needed to do. But my mother was bothered most by the 1370-kilometre distance between our home and Regina. My parents couldn't pop in on the weekend. And more important to her, she couldn't keep an eye on me. She took some comfort in knowing that my grandmother Annie would be in the city.

Tears were shed over this decision. What made it worse is that I had to fly back to Regina the next day. There was no rescission period for changing our minds. Even if there were, I would not have changed mine.

My parents said my sister didn't come out of her room for a week. She was devastated by my departure. We were very close, and she has told me through the years that it upset her greatly. I may have had a wild streak, but we were a tight family. My memories of childhood aren't just the frequent moves—and the moves probably just made us closer. I remember driving all over B.C. with the family trailer, and fishing. Our family had been stable as four. And now it was three. By leaving, I was taking a quarter of the family with me.

In retrospect, the one issue my family never discussed is what role I would play on the Pats. In my mind, I was going to Regina to be a physical defenceman. It never occurred to me that I might be groomed to be a WHL tough guy. I had never had a hockey fight before going to Regina at age seventeen.

I am not suggesting I was misled or that the Pats' coaching staff forced me into being a fighter. Because I was seventeen, they probably didn't know what they had. Strumm believed I was big and tough, and Tennant had taught me how to play. They were willing to see what happened from there. I'm just saying I never pondered what my role would be in Regina. At that point, I was thrilled to be on the team and I figured the rest would work itself out. But it didn't work out as well as I'd hoped.

My first season in Regina was a struggle, the kind of struggle that you often see with first-year WHL players. I was scratched multiple times, and when I dressed for the game I would play five to eight minutes.

Growing into my extra-large frame, I was awkward in comparison to veteran WHL players. My skating needed to improve and my inexperience showed every time I took to the ice. I totalled 105 penalty minutes, no goals and a single assist in 48 games. And that lone point, by the way, was a gift. The assist belonged to my teammate Al Tuer. The scorekeeper got it wrong after a Pats goal and I told Al as much. "Don't worry about it," he said. "We need to get you going." What a teammate—selfless.

The other issue was that I wasn't really warming to the idea of being a WHL enforcer. I'm sure I wasn't the first guy who had trouble making peace with the role, but preparing yourself to fight knowing that it could happen in any game was really difficult.

I fought mostly because my teammates did; we fought for each other. And I liked the team concept of hockey. We fought for the benefit of the group. I enjoyed protecting my teammates. It felt noble and right. What I didn't enjoy was the feeling that I was *expected* to fight. I didn't like playing a little and fighting a lot.

The idea of having to manufacture adrenaline and intensity before a fight was difficult. I couldn't seem to dial up enough anger in those battles. I could do the job, but I wasn't comfortable doing it.

I also learned that age and experience were important factors when you fought. My first official fight in the league was against Winnipeg Warriors defenceman Guy Paradis. He was seven inches shorter and thirty pounds lighter than me. But he was also two years older, and I would say that was the determining factor when we tangled. It may have been a draw, but it felt like he got the better of me. I sure didn't expect someone that much smaller than me to do as well as Guy did.

It was early in the season, and Winnipeg had a decent lead on us. That's probably why I was on the ice. We collided along the boards. The pushing and shoving started. I figured this was it. Time to get into my first fight on ice.

As much as I'd been thinking about this moment, Paradis still surprised me. It was his intensity more than anything that caught me off guard. He just flipped a switch and came at me, far more combative than I expected. Not that I knew what to expect—I had been wearing a cage my whole hockey life, so I really had no idea what it was like for someone to be firing punches at my face. But I did have the naive assumption that my size and reach would allow me to get the better of him. Not even close.

Balance, technique, and most of all experience made all the difference in hockey at this level. Those elements were exactly what I lacked. Being big and aggressive would only get me so far. I was confident I could have killed Paradis if we were scrapping out on the street, but he got hold of my right arm quickly and tied me up. He knew what he was doing. It was humbling. I remember sitting in the box thinking, *If this guy is any indication, this is a pretty tough league.*

I was feeling pretty good about getting my first fight out of the way, though. And I could hold my head up that I had held my own. My teammates didn't say much about it, but I got a few taps on the shin pads and a few fist bumps. I felt like a bigger part of the team immediately, and I had learned something. But I can't say I was eager to get into my next fight.

It did happen again, though. And again after the next one. And a pattern emerged. If the game was close, I spent a lot of time on the bench. If the score started to get lopsided, I went over the boards. During my first year, neither coach Don Boyd nor Strumm ever asked me to fight more. But Strumm had subtle ways of encouraging me to embrace the role.

He would talk about how much he admired other tough guys, like our Jeff Crawford. Big Crow, as we called him, had rung up 404 penalty minutes the year before I arrived and was probably the toughest man in the league my first year. I always had the feeling that Strumm was making a point of praising players he would like me to emulate.

Strumm would invite us over to his home from time to time, mostly during longer breaks in the schedule or on holidays. Pat Rabbit had played for Strummer in Billings, Montana, and there was a photo of Pat displayed prominently in the Strumm house. This was one of the coolest hockey fighting photographs I've seen. It showed Rabbit's right hand coiled up ready to strike and his opponent was looking awfully vulnerable.

"No disrespect, Stu," Strumm said to me, "but Pat's the toughest son of a bitch that's every played for me."

Strumm always knew how to get his point across to me.

Even though my first WHL season was a disappointing one, the Detroit Red Wings saw something they liked. They took me with the 186th pick in the tenth round of the 1983 draft. That turned out to be one of the most important drafts in Red Wings history—no, not because they took me. They took six future NHLers in their first ten picks, including Steve Yzerman (No. 4), Bob Probert (No. 46), Petr Klima (No. 86), and Joe Kocur (No. 88)—Lane Lambert (No. 25) and I were the others to make it. Batting .600 in your first ten picks is definitely beating the market, particularly given the level of success this group had.

Jim Devellano, the Red Wings' general manager, wanted a tough team and he wanted a player who could look after Yzerman. That's why he drafted three guys who could handle themselves. Looking back, if you're looking for toughness in the draft, you could do a lot worse than grabbing Probert, Kocur, and Grimson. Remember, people jokingly called Detroit the "Dead Wings" back then. They had been kicked around the bottom of the league for a while at that point. They needed to draft skill, and they needed guys who would protect that skill.

Little Caesars pizza king Mike Ilitch had purchased the Red Wings the year before and one of his priorities was to establish his franchise as one of the league's first-class organizations. As part of that process, he flew in each of his team's draft picks and put us up at Hotel Pontchartrain in Detroit.

The morning after we arrived in Detroit, we all gathered in the hotel lobby and it was clear that Devellano had fulfilled a clear objective in the draft of 1983. I was close to six-foot-six and 225 pounds. Probie was six-foot-three, 230 pounds. Kocur was six-foot-one, 215 pounds. Craig Butz, taken in the eighth round, was six-foot-two, 215 pounds, and my Regina Pats teammate Jeff Frank, selected in the eleventh round, was six-foot-three, 225 pounds. We looked more like the offensive line for the Detroit Lions, not players for the Detroit Red Wings. Devellano made it clear; no one was kicking any sand in the face of any Detroit Red Wing going forward. It was pretty clear the Wings were not drafting me for my offensive ability.

While I accepted my first-season struggles as part of the learning process, my family had a more difficult time of it. What I didn't know was that my parents had talked to Strumm about my development. My dad told Strumm he didn't believe a strong enough effort was being made to develop me into a more well-rounded player.

"You're not turning my son into a goon," he said, before walking out of the office.

3

CHASING ATTILA THE HUN

One of the wildest hockey brawls in Western Hockey League history happened because my Regina Pats team called goalie Ron Hextall's bluff.

On March 7, 1984, during my second season in the WHL, we were playing Hextall's Brandon Wheat Kings at home. Any game against these guys was more charged than most. They were among our closest rivals because we saw them frequently. The more you play a team, the more you tend to hate them. And Brandon was a big, tough team. This particular game had been especially physical, and the score was tight at the end of the second period. That always sets the stage for a fierce third. You've already shown each other that you're evenly matched. So now the question is, what else do you have?

But then the Zamboni conked out, and we sat in the dressing room for what seemed like an eternity. After half an hour or so, referee Doug Geiger told us we could come out on the ice to warm up.

Bad idea.

Two factors contributed to the mayhem: we came out of our dressing room first and the Wheat Kings had to skate through our end of the ice to reach theirs. Hockey players are more territorial than wolves. Skating an inch over the red line in the warm-up is a challenge. Skating right through the other team's end of the ice is like tossing a match into a bucket of gasoline. And the Wheat Kings' goalie wasn't just a match. He was more of a hand grenade.

Thirty-six years later, people still debate who should be blamed for the brawl. My take: it was Hextall's fault. No question.

Our coach, Bob Strumm, called Hextall "the eye of the tornado." He said when the referee let the teams back on the ice he saw Hextall's eyes "lighting up like a pinball machine." He led the charge out of the visitors' dressing room and skated through our zone waving his goalie stick over his head like a Viking wielding a battle axe.

In an editorial, the *Regina Leader-Post* referred to Hextall as "junior hockey's version of Billy Smith and Attila the Hun," and noted that "nobody bothers the Pats more than he does."

Our reaction to Hextall was predictable. Several of us converged on him to confront him over his antics. Hextall was wired for some reason and he was trash talking any Pat within earshot. He threatened Lyndon Byers.

Now, "LB," as we called him, was a walking, talking cartoon— a great storyteller, quick-witted, a really funny guy. He was a skill guy too, a second-round draft pick to the Bruins. But the culture on that Pats team was "everybody ropes, everybody rides." That was the way Bill Laforge, the coach who preceded Strumm, put it. Meaning, everybody takes care of himself out there. You fight your own battles. And LB could handle himself. When it wasn't going great for him scoring goals, he kind of fell back on scrapping. As it turned out, his skill game didn't translate at the pro level, so he made himself useful by playing a physical role. For example, when the Bruins needed to send a message to the Penguins after Ulf Samuelsson took out Cam Neely with one of the most infamous knees in the history of the game, they dressed LB. This is the guy Hextall went after. And I followed Hextall as he started skating toward his net. Brandon's Jim Agnew came over to back up Hextall, and a pack of guys formed around him.

Meanwhile, tempers were rising all over the ice. Pushing and shoving evolved into skirmishes. Then Hextall swung his paddle at Allan Acton and caught him square across the back. It was on.

Conspiracy theorists believe the Pats planned all of this, starting with the Zamboni malfunction. The truth is, nobody ever knows how riots start. In this case, we were rivals. We had history. Hextall's personality rubbed us the wrong way. We were a Bob Strumm team. It was the 1980s. And it didn't help that we had lost five consecutive games to the Wheat Kings earlier in the season. In fact, Hextall skated in front of our bench and gripped his stick like it was a machine gun and sprayed us with imaginary bullets after a recent win for the Wheat Kings. We detested Hextall. Do I need to go on?

Trying to explain why that brawl happened is like trying to list the underlying causes of World War II. There were simply too many factors at play. It's clear in my mind that Hextall was the flashpoint. When he chopped Al Acton with his stick it went from a simmering confrontation to a pot that boiled over. In any event, the result on the ice looked like a battle scene from *Braveheart*.

It was a full-scale brawl. Everyone was involved. At centre ice, there was a pile of bodies. I ended up on top of Hextall but couldn't punch him because bodies were layered on top of him. I was mad enough to punch, bite, gouge, or slap him. But I could only curse at him. Everyone was holding on to everyone else's arms. I couldn't move my arms at all. The situation was four stops past chaos.

Strumm said that when he looks back at the brawl now, "I'm just grateful that nobody got hurt." Good point. There were skates, sticks, and bodies clashing all over the Regina Agridome Ice that night. Somebody could have been seriously hurt. Of course, there wasn't a single player in a Regina or Brandon jersey that gave that a thought.

I was impressed by the way that the officials attempted to restore order by escorting the main combatants to the penalty box. When Byers and I were being taken off, we saw Hextall deep in his penalty box.

We tried to go after him again, but it was clear he wanted nothing to do with us. He was white. He had pushed himself to the most remote corner of the Wheat Kings side of the penalty box in order to get as far from LB and me as possible. I imagine it's terrifying to know an army of angry athletes wants to pulverize you. Hextall was tough, but if I had been able to separate him from the mayhem, I would have destroyed him.

The officials kept us away from Hextall. They settled me into the Regina side of the penalty box. But this mess was not yet over nor was my involvement in it. Standing up, with my arms folded across the top of the boards, watching the melee in front of me, I didn't see Brandon's Brad Wells, skating full speed coming up along the boards to my left. Wells wasn't that tall but he was another tough prairie boy, built like a rectangle, and he was one of the primary warriors on the Brandon side. He was like a stealth bomber, flying in low, under my radar, outside of my line of sight.

Before I could even turn to see what was coming up out of my blind spot, he delivers a thunderous sucker punch to the side of my head that topples me backwards. I pull myself back together; I literally shook my head to collect myself. But now my wires are touching. I'm amped up and I am looking for revenge when I pile over the boards and back out of the penalty box.

By the time I track down Wells, I'm exhausted. (I'm sure everyone on the ice felt the same way. This brawl lasted more than twenty-five minutes.)

With no strength left in my arms, I can't punch Wells with any power. Instead, I grab the top of the Plexiglas and I start to body slam him, WWE style, repeatedly into the glass. It was the only option that came to mind. According to the *Regina Leader-Post*, I banged Wells's head into the glass ten times.

It was the craziest hockey fight anyone in Regina had ever seen.

The Wheat Kings' general manager, Les Jackson, stormed down from the press box looking to fight Strumm. Convinced that the brawl was premeditated and started by us, Jackson attacked Strumm, knocking off his glasses.

When he grabbed Strumm by the lapels of his suit coat, Strumm ducked and evacuated his coat in the blink of an eye. Addressing our players later, Strumm joked that his escape from his coat was more dazzling than "Houdini slipping out of handcuffs," and told us, "It's easier to get a new suit jacket than to fix a broken nose."

The game was delayed by more than an hour because of the brawl and the penalties that needed to be assigned. I ended up with two match penalties, a misconduct, a game misconduct, and four stitches where Wells had stung me. Hextall ended up with a match penalty and a game misconduct. Each team ended up with seven game misconducts.

When the dust finally settled, we ended up with a five-minute power play, which suggests that the officials believed that the Wheat Kings were responsible for the mess.

The Pats won the game 10–4 and I told the *Leader-Post* afterward, "[We] probably gained the respect that was lacking— we beat them on the scoreboard and in the fights. I think Hextall more than anything, with his yapping, got things going. He has been aggravating us like that all season."

The WHL didn't appreciate my performance in the brawl. I was suspended for five games. We watched the VHS tape of the Brandon–Regina brawl on a loop for days in our dressing room after the brawl. I think my teammates saw me as one of the stars of the show. Every single Pat was involved in the donnybrook, but I seemed to get special recognition. In truth, I did have a lot of enthusiasm for the project.

If you want a reputation as a guy not to mess with, a long suspension and a highlight reel of rage-filled mayhem doesn't hurt. I sensed that my teammates saw me as a pretty bad dude after that. Or at least somebody that embraced this role wholeheartedly. During one of the countless times we watched the tape, Big Crow, who was a man of few words then, muttered something just audible enough for me to hear: "There's a guy who knows his role."

Yet another obscure message of affirmation on the path to a long career of locking horns on ice. The message was sinking in, bit by bit.

Hextall, of course, went on to a long career in the NHL, where he had the same reputation for stirring up trouble and got into more than his fair share of fights, especially for a goalie. The funny thing is, we played in different conferences for the vast majority of our careers, and our paths never crossed again. I'm sure there would have been sparks if they had.

—

Anyone who witnessed my demented act during this brawl would have believed I was confident in my role as a resident tough guy. But even in my second junior season, I still wasn't comfortable as an enforcer.

What I was sure about was that being a maniacal tough guy now had earned me the acceptance and respect of my teammates. Becoming a WHL player hadn't changed my pattern of tying my self-esteem to being someone whom everyone was talking about. In fact, it probably served to ingrain that type of flawed thinking deeper inside me.

Strumm moved me from defence to forward in my second year, and that switch helped me adjust as both a player and a fighter. It was a simpler position, with a little less responsibility defensively. It is challenging to concentrate on looking after your teammates when you are worried about maintaining your gaps and making sure an opposing forward isn't about to blow past you.

I found playing the wing fit my skill set and made it easier to get involved physically. I started to become more effective, and as a result, I received more ice time. Or was I more effective *because* the coach gave me more ice time? That's always the source of the tension between a coach and a player. In any case, in my second season, I played regular minutes as a third-liner.

The other difference between my first and second WHL seasons was how my fights came about. In the first season, when I was put on the ice, I felt as if I was expected to look for a fight.

In the second season, my fights grew out of the game action. I didn't have to manufacture the anger or adrenaline needed any longer. It was there because I was involved more regularly. Any enforcer will tell you that it's much easier to fight out of emotion and adrenaline that stems from the natural flow of the game than it is to talk yourself into punching someone just because it's the right thing to do for the team. If you're on the bench, you just don't have that emotional engagement. I was on the bench less.

My skills as a fighter also improved in my second year with the Pats. A hockey fight may look like mayhem, but like anything that happens on a hockey rink, it really comes down to skating and balance. Try staying upright and stable on your feet on ice while a 240-pound man is trying to put you on your ass, and you'll see what I mean. If one guy is a better skater than the other, a fight is usually over very quickly, and it's usually not pretty. If the two guys are equal, you're going to have a good old-fashioned hockey fight. Both guys are going to give and get. Early in most fights, you'll see the opponents testing each other's balance. You want to pull him toward you, or back him up with jabs—either way, you want to put him in a situation he doesn't want to be in. I worked hard at the technical side of the game, and regularly honed my footwork and leverage at the White Crane martial arts gym in Kamloops in the off-season. If I was going to tangle with tough guys, I was going to train and attempt to gain every edge I could in this area.

But you wouldn't have known that on the night I fought fellow

Red Wings draft pick Joey Kocur. I put fighters into two classes: reluctant warriors and contract killers. Kocur was a killer.

By Kocur's second year, he was a polished fighter. He had a right hand that landed like artillery shells. He knew his role and he was good at what he did. Plus, he was mean. In my three years of junior hockey, three seasons in the International Hockey League (IHL), and fourteen years in the NHL, he was one of the toughest and nastiest fighters I ever faced.

When we fought for the first time in junior, he held me out at the end of his reach and he clobbered me repeatedly with a right hand. It was like a lightning strike. You see it ripping through the air and then—boom. He won that fight. No question. At that point, I wasn't as competitive as I needed to be. Tactically I wasn't nearly as advanced as Joey at this stage. He was a refined and powerful fighter even at 18 years of age.

Wayne Meier was the Red Wings' director of scouting, the man who'd made the decision to draft me the previous June. He hadn't seen my fight with Kocur, but he had heard about it. When he saw me the next time, he probed me for details.

"Sounds like Joey got the better of you," he said. "Do you think you and Joey will tangle again soon?"

"We'll just have to see what happens," I said.

Wrong answer. I knew it as soon as the words tumbled out of my mouth. He was looking for me to say that I couldn't wait to get another crack at Kocur. He was looking for me to show some fire. Instead, he got a really lame and awkward answer.

I may have been a more willing fighter, but I still wasn't the contract killer I needed to be.

The Red Wings reached the same conclusion. They chose not to sign me. The deadline to offer me a deal came and went, and suddenly I was eligible to be drafted again. It was a demoralizing turn of events, particularly when I knew I'd sabotaged myself with my uninspiring conversation with Meier. Who wants a tough guy who doesn't want a shot at the title? They had their guys in Probert and Kocur.

That stung. Getting drafted is a thrill. Getting un-drafted doesn't feel great at all. However, the disappointment over the Red Wings' snub didn't last long. It seemed to give me an added layer of motivation. I wanted to prove the Red Wings had made a mistake. I was still growing, and I was making progress as a player. I finished my second season with eight goals and eight assists.

I realized that I had made a mistake too. I hadn't made an attempt to set things straight after my loss to Kocur. If you're a physical guy in this game, you have to make amends for something like that. Even in junior, it's all business. You need to demonstrate to the people who control your future that you settle your accounts.

But I wasn't worried about my career. My agent at the time was Don Meehan, and I talked a lot to his colleague Pat Morris. My coaches also settled me down after the initial rebuke. This was the 1980s. The feeling was that a player my size may have a chance at being drafted again or at least signed as a free agent.

The Pats had an exceptional season in 1983–84. Despite losing Gary Leeman and Nevin Markwart to the NHL, we ended up winning our division with a 48–23–1 record. We averaged more than five goals per game.

We even claimed a 3–2 lead in the best-of-seven WHL Final against a talented Kamloops team. We were leading Game 6 by a goal with twelve seconds left in regulation when Blazers forward Dean Evason scored the tying goal. Kamloops player Ryan Stewart scored in overtime to tie the series.

The Blazers then won Game 7 by a 4–2 decision to earn a trip to the Memorial Cup. I've never seen such a dramatic momentum switch like the one that occurred in that series. It was devastating to be twelve seconds away from the Cup and have the series go sideways. We seemed like we were on top of our game one second and then completely rattled the next.

The added disappointment was that we started finger pointing after the Game 6 loss. The blame game undermined our resolve heading into Game 7. We could have made the story about us instead of Evason's goal. We couldn't overcome our disappointment.

We needed someone to step up in that Game 7, and when I look back I wonder if I was one guy who didn't do enough. I didn't play well in that series.

Maybe if I had fought Rudy Poeschek early in Game 7 I could have turned the momentum back in our direction. But at that point in my career, I don't think I had that in me.

I guess I figured our top players, such as Derkatch, Byers, and Taylor Hall, had gotten us that far and they would see it through.

But the sad truth is the Blazers handled us easily in that Game 7. Strumm says he has heard some story, comment, or fact about that Game 6 every month for the past thirty-five years.

—

That game wasn't the only disappointment of my breakthrough season in 1983–84. I really hadn't made much progress in my off-ice behaviour.

One of my sad memories about my Regina years was that my late grandmother Annie, then in her late sixties, saw me at my worst. I would visit her a few times every month, sometimes taking a teammate, and she would feed me a home-cooked meal.

My dad's family has Icelandic heritage, and grandmother Annie made a cured lamb dish called *rúllupylsa* that I can still taste.

But my grandmother lived in Regina and she heard the stories about my carousing. I remember once, when I had to explain the trouble I was in, that the disappointment on her face was worse than any punishment I was going to receive. It was a sullen look, like she could not fathom how someone she cared about could act out in this chaotic way.

My nightlife and carousing habits pushed me into trouble several times when I was in Regina. People will often explain someone's troubles by saying "He fell into a bad crowd."

That was not my problem. If anything, the crowd got in trouble by hanging out with me. Even though I was playing junior hockey, I was still the same lunatic partier I was in Kamloops. I was still a "Hey, look at me" kind of troublemaker.

While I always respected Strumm, believing he had the team's best interest at heart, we weren't always on the same page when I played for him. I tested his patience with my office partying.

Once, when Regina teammate R.J. Dundas and I were out late, we decided to grab a bite to eat at Mr. Sub after a night of drinking. It was well past team curfew, but I wasn't concerned about being caught, because anyone in authority had already gone to bed a few hours before. We completely ignored the reality that Mr. Sub was located on a main Regina road and the restaurant had an all-glass front. At night, anyone who drove by knew exactly who was in there. It was a fishbowl. R.J. and I were halfway through a foot-long clubhouse sandwich when Strumm walked in the front door.

"You just have no idea how small this town is, do you?" he

asked. "Get back to your billets' places now, and I'll deal with this in the morning."

The next day, Dundas and I showed up in our dressing room to find that every piece of our equipment had been removed from our stalls and packed into two shopping carts. We had been demoted to the Regina Pats midget team for one week. I think part of the punishment was having people see us pushing our carts down to the midget dressing room.

That wasn't my last curfew violation. Another time I was with teammates Byers, Taylor Hall, and Kurt Wickenheiser at a combination restaurant-bar just before closing. It's the night before a game.

In walks Strumm.

"I know people all over this town," Strumm says. "I have this town completely wired. Why do you people think you can get away with this?"

We started to believe that Strumm was omnipresent and that it was impossible to do anything that he wouldn't find out about. And that was problematic for me because I had managed to find my share of trouble in Regina.

Public drunkenness. Fighting on the streets. The same nonsense that had landed me in trouble in Kamloops. It sounds like typical boys-will-be-boys stuff, just blowing off steam. But I blew off considerably more steam than most. I ran the risk almost weekly of getting myself into serious trouble. My steam sometimes took the form of confrontation. Sometimes assault.

I was reckless in those days, always in a hurry. I was driving through Regina one evening with R.J. again. We're slowing down in a left-turn lane when the car ahead of us stops short. I have to lock up the brakes to avoid a collision. Looking back, I probably wasn't paying attention to the road. But at the time, I blame the other guy. I put the car in park and get out to have a word with him.

I walk up to the car. Here's my chance for sober reflection. It's a nice car. The driver is about my age, well-dressed. His girlfriend is beside him. The look on their faces should tell me everything I need to know. They're horrified.

The light turns green and the guy takes off. But I'm not done with him. I get back in the car and follow him. I'm right behind. He pulls into a driveway and heads into a house. I don't even try the doorknob. I just kick the door in.

As I step inside, I clock the look on people's faces—and I finally come to realize just how far off the rails I am. I've just barged into a party with the intention of exacting revenge for a minor traffic incident. A bunch of clean-cut young people are staring at me in abject fear. I turn on my heel and we drive away.

Somebody there must have called the cops, and who can blame them? I was charged with public mischief and was given a one-year suspended sentence and had to pay for repairs to the house. Even worse, I felt deep, deep regret. These people did nothing to provoke that response.

And it got worse. I had to return to Regina that summer to plead guilty. That meant I had to explain everything to my grandmother. The look on her face was all the punishment I needed: *This is not the grandson I know.*

—

I wasn't in trouble every day. After I graduated from high school, I worked during the day when I was playing for the Pats. I worked for ABC Engraving, and because the company had a contract with the Pats, I told my teammates I would probably end up our team MVP that season.

42

In my final season, I worked as a salesman for Tip Top Tailors. My manager, Pat Fiacco, ended up becoming the mayor of Regina. Patty treated me like gold and he taught me a lot about men's clothing, which served me pretty well as an NHL player.

Pat, Tim Hubic, Gerry Baumgartner, and all the guys at Tip Top made working there a great time. When the store closed the employees would push back all the clothing racks to create a makeshift soccer pitch. Ties came off. Shirtsleeves were rolled up, and we had some of the funniest and most competitive soccer games I have ever seen. We'd stay an extra two hours after work, just playing soccer. I'd leave the store long after my shift was over and my dress shirt was soaked through with sweat. Not an ideal way to face a Saskatchewan winter night.

My Regina years also produced two lifelong friends in Bob Lowes and Jeff Lawson.

Lowes had been captain of the Prince Albert Raiders when he was traded to the Pats during the 1982–83 season. He became my roommate and we hit it off immediately. He was a highly competitive centre, very businesslike on the ice, a natural leader. Lowes had a knack for knowing when something needed to be said in the dressing room. But "Slob," as we called him, was laugh-out-loud funny and a really caring person.

When Lawson came to the Pats from the Winnipeg Warriors as an overage player, immediately he became a running mate to me and Bob. His family owned Clark's Poultry Farm in Brandon, Winnipeg. He was in his fifth season in the WHL when he joined us. At five-foot-eleven, Lawson wasn't physically imposing, but he was commando-fierce.

One night, the three of us were grabbing a late-night pizza after we'd been out all night. I was in one of those ravenous moods during which an all-you-can-eat buffet would not have satisfied me.

With no consideration for anyone else, I grabbed the last slice of the pie and started wolfing it down. Lawson had just finished his piece and now he was miffed that I had taken the last slice. He attempted to carve a hunk off the piece I was eating.

"Chick," I said, because that's what we called him, "leave it be. You're not getting any of this. I'm starved and I'm not sharing."

He backed off, but seconds later he made a second grab at my pizza.

"Chick," I warned him, "if you come across again, I'm gonna stab you with my fork."

I brandished the fork in his face to demonstrate the seriousness of my threat. But Lawson did not heed my warning. He moved across for a third attempt at the slice, and before he reached my air space, I stabbed him in the jaw with my fork. Blood began to trickle down from the four separate tiny holes in his face.

Lowes looked on in total disbelief. I shrugged. "I told him to stay away from my pizza," I said.

The next two hours were spent walking around outside, with Lawson holding restaurant napkins on his face, trying to get the bleeding to stop. Thirty years later the scars are still visible, giving us reason to retell the story every time we meet. I think we laugh harder every time we tell it. But did we do some goofy stuff back then.

—

At the end of my second season, Strumm told me he believed I would be an important player for the Pats in 1984–85. That's precisely what happened. In my third season with the Pats, I was a full-service player with twenty-four goals, fifty-six points, and

248 penalty minutes in seventy-one games playing on a line with Brent Fedyk and Len Nielsen.

I was even playing on the power play, providing a net-front presence with a few tip-ins and rebound goals. Most power plays are structured so that there is someone in front of the goalie to create a screen, tip in pucks, and jam in rebounds. Today, defencemen try to box that guy out, but back then their job was to move him out, no matter what it took. Not many defencemen are going to move a 230-pound forward, though. I loved those battles, and I was pretty effective in there. A physical guy like Dave Manson would do his level best to move me, and he was every bit as mean as I was. But most defencemen face a two-pronged problem when a guy like me sets up in the slot. If they can't move me, they make matters worse for the goalie by screening him even more. And if they take it too far with a guy who knows how to handle himself, they just might light the fuse. (You don't want to take a penalty when you're out on the power play, but still, the wires are always prone to touching.) At the end of the day, taking liberties with a tough guy does not come naturally to most players. So installing someone in my role in front of the net was a popular strategy if that person could play effective minutes.

By my third season, I had learned to be an effective enforcer. I knew more about how to fight, who to fight, and when to fight. And I enjoyed the notoriety that tough guys had around the league. By then, I was a well-known villain in every road arena. Because it's only 71 kilometres from Regina to Moose Jaw, the Pats became instant rivals with Moose Jaw when the Warriors came into the league.

From our first game, the Moose Jaw fans hated me because I terrorized their team. This was the era of Miller Lite Beer's

"Taste Great vs. Less Filling" campaign, and every small town seemed to create its own version of those television commercials.

In Moose Jaw, fans highjacked the back-and-forth to taunt me. I remember skating through neutral ice with the puck one night, and on one side of that dark old Moose Jaw barn the fans would yell "STU!" and the other side would respond "PID!" "STU!" then "PID!" "STU!" "PID!" There are some moments so funny during a game that you can't help but laugh out loud in the moment even though the play is going on all around you. This was one of those moments.

But the WHL fight club always had subtleties that you could never anticipate, like the time referee-in-training Paul Stewart decided Saskatoon Blades defenceman Trent Yawney should fight me even if he didn't want to.

Yawney didn't fight all that much, but he and I crashed together at the end of a play and we were shoving back and forth. Yawney was pretty comfortable standing nose to nose and chirping me hard while the linesmen was between us. But Stewart had been a tough guy in the NHL. He knew the unwritten rules. If you're going to mouth off, you should have to back it up. Stewart arrived on the scene as Yawney and I were still shoving and barking at each other and he gave the order to both linesmen: "Let 'em go!!"

Imagine Yawney's surprise. The linesmen cleared a path and suddenly he had the fight he said he wanted. Yawney was a good-sized guy, nearly my size. But he's a top-four defenceman—out of his element with a guy like me. I didn't want to hurt him, but I didn't want to get clipped myself. When the gloves come off, it's me or him, survival of the fittest. Trent got everything he asked for in that encounter.

Although I was becoming a top WHL fighter, I was still more reluctant warrior than I was a trained assassin. I didn't like the stress of the role, or the expectation that you had to fight at times when it was uncomfortable for you to do that.

In my third season, Strumm and I had some tension over the fact that I felt I couldn't fight Shane Churla during a playoff series against Medicine Hat.

I had fought Churla earlier in the series and had banged up my hand badly enough that just holding on to my stick was a challenge. I managed to play with my hand heavily bandaged, but it would have been really painful to land a punch. Strumm found a way to make it clear that my team needed me. We were behind in the series and I could tell Strummer thought that another fight with Churla might turn the series back in our favour. Later in my career I would have found a way to fight. In fact, Paul Maurice threatened to pull me out of the lineup in Hartford one night after I cut my right hand badly. I insisted he keep me in the mix and told him I could fight left-handed if it came up. But, in truth, at this stage of my junior career I was grateful to have a legitimate excuse not to fight again.

Strumm was an intense coach, democratic in his tough love approach. He bore down on all of us at one time or another. Sometimes he was hard on all of us at the same time, such as when the Pats went 0–6 on our Western road trip.

Regina, Saskatchewan, to Victoria, B.C., was a twenty-four-hour trip if you drove the bus straight through. That included the ferry hop to reach Vancouver Island to play Victoria and Nanaimo.

In my first season in Regina, we lost to Seattle, Victoria, Nanaimo, Kelowna, Portland, and Kamloops on that trip. We knew Strumm would come up with an innovative way to punish us, and we were right.

The original plan was that we would drive out but the team would fly us home to avoid a second gruelling bus trip. However, Strumm decided there was no better way to punish his under-achieving teenage punks than to cash in the plane tickets and force us to bus it all the way home. On the way out West, the trip was broken up by games in cities along the way.

On the way back, we drove straight through, non-stop, except to stop and eat. We slept in sleeping bags in the aisles and rows on the floor of the bus. Nobody rested well.

Strumm's punishment worked. In my second and third seasons, the Pats were always above .500 on the Western trip. We learned quickly the bus needed to be silent after a loss. You don't want the coach and general manager to think you don't care.

Although Strumm and I had rough periods during my time in Regina, he had an important influence on my career. The WHL was, and still is today, a good path to the NHL. The tough schedule and long bus rides help players learn about the professional culture. You learn how to cope with fans, when to fight and not to fight, even how to behave after a victory and a defeat.

Eventually, I developed a sort of mental checklist. And if the circumstances were right, I'd go out and initiate. First off, is this a divisional rival that has someone who can answer the bell? Is the other team's heavyweight being overly aggressive out there? Is he running around? Is the other team taking liberties with my guys? Has one of our smaller guys just taken a big hit? Does my team need a lift? A fight can almost always change the energy in a building, and a seasoned fighter can sense when the moment requires it. Sometimes I can tell even before a goal is scored that I may need to act, but more often a two-goal difference is the signal that something needs to change. If I sense we're flat, then I'll go looking for something.

For me, I never wanted a coach to have to send me out to do my job. I didn't want that pressure or that kind of attention. So I got to a place where I was hypersensitive to the situations that might require me to fight and I would do it pre-emptively. Before anyone else thought the time might be right.

The guys used to get a kick out of the way I'd manage this situation. It was an advantage to slip out of the sleeve on your dominant hand while you fought. In order to do this, it helped matters if you could remove the elbow pad on that side of your body. When I knew a fight was coming, I'd often slip out of both elbow pads well in advance. Travis Green turned to Marty MacInnis on the bench in Anaheim one night as they were watching me take my turn on the ice. Travis said, "I'll bet you Stu gets into it with Laraque this shift." Marty replied, "Oh yeah, how do you know that?" Travis motioned with his eyes to show Marty my elbow pads tucked neatly under the bench beneath them. They laughed, shook their heads, and waited for the fireworks to start.

There were some nights, I played an entire period without elbow pads, skulking around out there trying to get into it with my counterpart on the other side. You tend to play a little more gingerly (and avoid contact near the boards) when your elbows are exposed in this way!

On the other hand, if the game is looking good for my side, I may have to turn the other cheek even if I'm challenged. Fighting always changes the energy, but it's impossible to control *how* it changes it. Even if I were to win, it could still spark the other team because their guy was willing to sacrifice. If we've got the game in hand, it's better not to let the genie out of the bottle.

—

Strummer didn't teach me the pro culture. But he did teach me the Strumm culture. And his lessons prepared me for the next level. During a very critical period in my life, Strumm was a mentor, a coach, and even a friend. He is an authentic person, someone who can discipline you and still be a friend. Nobody walked that line as well as Bob Strumm did.

The only aspect of professional hockey training he couldn't help me with was getting comfortable with the possibility that I could become a top NHL heavyweight. I had to grapple with that concept all on my own.

That became important because the Calgary Flames drafted me in the seventh round of the 1985 draft, forty-three picks and three rounds earlier than the Red Wings had drafted me two years earlier. After watching me grow into a more polished player under Strumm's coaching, the Flames had interest. The only question now was whether I had enough belief in myself to become the kind of player and warrior they thought I could be.

4

HAVING FUN OUT THERE

When I walked away from the Flames' training camp, I ended up in Leduc, Alberta. That's less than 300 kilometres away from Calgary, but it's about as far from the NHL as you can get.

I had worked on my uncle's dairy farm most summers when I was a teenager. It was hard work, but I didn't mind the spending money I earned. And I didn't have much of a choice concerning what I did for my summers back then. Mom and Dad pretty much insisted I go. There was a lot less trouble to get into on the farm.

I had never worked there in the winter, though. And winter arrives pretty early in Leduc. I walked out of camp in September. By October, the snow can be two feet deep. Dairy animals require your attention twice a day, so I had a lot to do out there in the cold—bedding down and mucking out the stalls, and cleaning manure out of the alleys in the farm Bobcat pretty much daily.

The worst was the feeding. The feed was stored in a silo and would come in by conveyor belt. But of course the system would seize up in the cold, and I was the guy out there in minus-thirty weather getting it going again. Farming is hard work in the best conditions. In the winter, it kicks your ass. It didn't take me long to figure out that a career as a dairy farmer was not in the cards.

The work gave me a lot of time to reflect. The Flames were tearing up the NHL, but I wasn't regretting my decision to tell Cliff Fletcher I was walking away. I was relieved. I was happier shovelling manure than facing the daily pressure to lock horns with guys my size. On the farm, I didn't have that daily sense of doom hanging over me.

Not that I was running away. Not exactly. The other thing I thought about during those long hours out in the barn was how far I could have gone. How far I could still go. I thought about that a lot.

I guess I was thinking along those lines when I wrote a letter to my old teammate Bob Lowes. Remember, there was no texting back then, no Twitter. In 1985, if you wanted to get in touch, you put your thoughts on paper. Bobby was a friend, and I sent him a note to update him on what I was doing and the decision I had made.

He called me almost as soon as he got the letter. Bobby was playing for the University of Manitoba Bisons and had talked to the coach there, Wayne Fleming. Now Fleming wanted to talk to me.

I called Wayne. I don't remember exactly what he said, but I do remember what really caught my attention. He knew the book on me. He knew what kind of player I'd been in junior, and he wasn't looking for that kind of player. He wanted to talk about the upside in my game. And he told me they had a spot for me if I was interested.

I didn't commit right there and then, as I wanted to talk to Mom and Dad. Winnipeg was even farther from home than Regina. But Fleming wanted me on the roster, and I wanted to be there. I had already missed the fall semester, but he could add me to the roster for the second half of the year and I could enroll in classes in the spring semester.

I stayed on the farm until Christmas, then went home for a visit, then headed down to San Diego to meet the Bisons. They were on a tour of California, playing friendlies and having a bit of a break before the second semester started. The guys were great. A lot of them had played major junior: Rick Strachan, Brian Coughlin, Dale Derkatch, Harry Mahood, Chris St. Cyr. The day I walked into the room, there was an instant connection.

The hockey was good, as you would guess from the number of alumni from the WHL. In terms of pure skill level, varsity hockey might have fallen somewhat short of the Dub. But everyone is a little older, a little stronger. Just as fast, and probably a bit smarter. It was pretty physical too.

I was asked to contribute in every way. Power play. Penalty killing. Scoring. Playmaking. Playing an aggressive, heavy contact game was always part of my DNA. I was a complete player for Fleming. He played me fifteen to eighteen minutes per game, and I picked up seven goals, four assists, and 113 penalty minutes in twelve games. (Yeah, 113 PIMs in twelve games *is* a lot. But they were pretty liberal with the ten-minute misconducts in that league. I don't remember getting into a fight that year.)

University hockey was really fun for me. I had no anxiety, worry, or stress. I just played. I never worried that I would have to go over the boards to brawl, simply because there was no fighting in the league. Fighting just didn't determine who won or lost. I was asked to change the outcome of a game, but not by harnessing the energy of the building, and not by taking the whole team on my shoulders.

Of course, I could still throw my weight around. My physical presence in Manitoba showed up in the form of heavy hitting along the boards. As a six-foot-six-inch, 230-pound winger, I could be an intimidating presence without using my fists.

Bisons games were not well attended when I played there, but the players from our football team used to show up and park behind the net where we attacked in the first and the third. They waited there for the forecheck, and they would go berserk when I pasted an opposing defenceman into the glass in front of them. They'd leap to their feet and bang on the glass and roar. The football guys were maniacs; every player was like a one-man crowd. I loved our home games at the Max Bell Center on the University of Manitoba campus; I used to feed off that energy.

I am sometimes struck by how often hockey players talk about "having fun out there." It's almost one of the clichés, like getting pucks in deep and keeping your feet moving. But it's true. You play better when you're having fun. Fun is a signal that you're playing the game right. And hockey was fun playing for Fleming.

My game improved a lot under Wayne. I felt like an important contributor. I felt valued because the team looked to me to help in a variety of ways. I had a hard shot. My puck handling had improved. I was making plays. When you're taking a regular shift and involved on special teams, you can feel your confidence grow almost daily.

Once, Fleming held a session on penalty killing and highlighted a clip of the way I won a battle for a loose puck just inside our blue line and then sent it to the other end. I cross-checked their point man on the hips three times hard and knocked him off the puck. I came in hard but it was clean and assertive. I outbattled my opponent, won possession, and cleared the puck. At the end of that clip, Fleming turned to the group and said, "THAT is how you kill a penalty!!"

Fleming's primary point was about penalty killing, not Stu Grimson. But he might as well have been writing a reference letter for me. That's who Fleming was too. One of his many strengths as a coach was his ability to motivate and inspire players. His meetings frequently ran long, but players always left a Wayne Fleming meeting feeling as if they were eight feet tall. Fleming knew that he would get more out of his athletes if he could affirm them in front of the group as he had done for me on this occasion. Lessons like that stick.

If you want to see who you really are, watching a few shifts of a hockey game can give you a pretty good idea. That was me. Honest, hardworking, willing to do the tough jobs to help the team. Stats don't measure how many times you muscle the puck over the blue line, but it's a crucial job. The whole bench breathes a sigh of relief when you clear the zone. Some guys thrive on doing those unglamorous but essential jobs. I'm one of those guys.

Fleming was ahead of his time in his use of video too. This was the 1980s, when coaches were still diagramming on a white board. One time when we were in a meeting, he showed a video of NHL power forward Rick Tocchet getting tripped in the opposing team's end. Instead of falling and sliding along the ice to embellish the play, Tocchet kept his skates driving forward.

He eventually tracked down the puck and produced a scoring chance.

Fleming showed us the video more than once and kept reminding us what a great play this was by Tocchet. His message: Don't become distracted by the potential of a penalty call. If the referee is going to call it, he's going to call it. If he doesn't, your acting job isn't going to change his mind. "Stay in the moment and battle through everything, including a bad call," Fleming would say.

When I came out of the meeting, I remember thinking how brilliant Fleming was in using Tocchet to make an important point. If he just tells us to keep our feet moving in that situation, the message doesn't stick. But because he used video of a respected NHL player, we remember that message.

Here it is thirty-three years later, and I'm still talking about the point Fleming made in that meeting. I played for many legendary coaches during my career, but no one taught me more about the game than Wayne Fleming.

He also entertained us. Whenever he was giving us instructions on how he wanted us to play in a specific area of the ice, he would always use the phrase "that area right in there."

"Guys, here's a habit I want us to get into," he'd say. "If you're pursuing the puck carrier in that area right in there . . ." He'd point to the area behind the opposition net and continue: "I don't want you to chase him unless you are under a stick length away. Any further away and you're taking yourself out of the play."

Fleming used that phrase "that area right in there" so often that we'd often pretend to coach each other using it over and over and over. "Lowes, keep your head up in that area right in there," I'd say to my roommate. "That's where a D man will clock you if you are not paying attention in that area right in there."

As odd as this may seem, I enjoyed every ache and pain I received as a full-time player. When you are playing regular minutes, you wake up after every game with minor bumps and bruises. A sore shoulder, a hip pointer, or a charley horse are reminders that you were part of the action the night before.

I liken it to watching a baseball game and noticing a player whose uniform is covered in dirt and scuff marks. When you see the player with the filthy uniform, you know he has played a role in determining the outcome of the game. When I was sore the day after a game, I felt like I had done my part. It was always a good feeling if I was nursing a few bruises. Anyone who plays team sports knows what I mean. You give everything you have for the team and in the end you get it all back.

—

The University of Manitoba was a great fit for me. I have to admit, though, that I thought about Princeton every time I lunged across the icy concrete floor of the $85-per-month basement apartment I shared with Lowes. We got what we paid for: a musty fire-trap with only one small window. We nicknamed our place "The Swamp" because the windows leaked, allowing the snowmelt to seep in during the spring. In the winter, though, it was the arctic drafts we complained about when we were showering. It's a wonder the water didn't freeze solid as it poured from the shower head. In those moments, I couldn't help thinking I should have listened to my mother and gone to some Ivy League school.

My dad came to visit me early that semester to bring me my car. He stayed one night with us in the Swamp. I dropped him off at the airport the next day and he told me the following before he boarded the plane for home. "Stu, I have stayed in some real dumps in my time; I am not going to tell your mother where you're living."

—

Not that the old Stu Grimson completely disappeared in a league without fighting.

The sole regret of my University of Manitoba career came in my second season. It was only an exhibition game, but Brandon University's Kelly Kozack and I got into a scrap on the ice and he scratched my neck as the linemen separated us. When I say "scratched," I mean he used both hands, including the nails on all ten fingers, to claw my neck from just under my jaw to my shoulders, and left several really bad claw marks. I wasn't just pissed. I was enraged. Next, two very inexperienced linesmen separated us and showed us off the ice. By no means was that the end of it though. Our dressing rooms were directly adjacent to one another underneath the stands so that when Kelly and I started toward our respective locker rooms, we met each other again face to face. I literally ran at him in my skates and the fight continued in the corridor outside our dressing rooms.

It was ugly. Kelly wanted no part of me there. I hit him several times. Cut him badly and at some point he passed out. All this happened in full view of several hockey fans who had stopped in to see the "friendly" between the U of M and the U of Brandon. They were horrified.

The school suspended me for the six remaining exhibition games, plus the first half of our regular season. I didn't play again until January. But that turned out to be the least of my problems. The local RCMP decided to charge me with assault. At the time, I assumed the police would view it as a hockey fight gone wrong. Not so fast, Barrister . . .

I now realize that the fact we were wearing hockey gear didn't make it any different than two citizens fighting on a public street. I pled guilty and ended up with a year's probation. Ugly. This incident was one of the major regrets of my hockey career. It happened because I was angered and allowed my emotions to get away from me.

The one point I will make in my own defence is that the officials staging this game deserved some of the blame. Anytime you have male athletes engaged in a contact sport at a level as high as varsity hockey, you simply have to take steps to ensure that matters don't get out of hand. That's just standard security in a hockey arena, especially given that our dressing rooms were next to each other. That's not an excuse. But if two guys are going at it on the ice, you don't put them together in the hallway. In any case, I ran into Kelly Kozack weeks later in our rink back at the U of M. I was quick to apologize and our meeting was amiable. He said he didn't harbour any grudge. That was astonishing to me. I wanted to kill him in the hallway that day we fought and almost did. But he was able to smile and forgive.

The trouble was, I had been through that pattern many times, and I had the court appearances to prove it. Some very good people had done their best to keep me on the straight and narrow, and the message just never sank in. I had hurt and disappointed a lot of people. I'd even disappointed my own grandmother. But there was something about Fleming that made me pay attention.

Maybe it was the way he coached. He was understated but very engaging and likeable. He was passionate, but he didn't crack the whip and send us out there to do what he wanted. He was more like a peer. He wanted the same thing as us. Some coaches are generals, sending the grunts into battle. But Fleming felt like one of us. We were all in it together.

I think that's why I was listening when he sat me down in his office. I knew he would give me an honest point of view. He was on my side—and still he made it clear I wasn't doing myself any favours. Did the RCMP need to be involved in a hockey fight? Not in his opinion. But had I crossed the line? Absolutely. Did I need to cross the line?

Absolutely not.

I believe that's when I finally got it. And I credit Wayne Fleming for helping me see what I hadn't been able to see even when it was right in front of my face. You're ultimately defined by the choices you make.

And, over the last several years leading up to this period, I had made a series of really bad choices and injured a lot of people in the process. Hearing that from someone as objective and respected as Wayne Fleming was a sobering experience for me. Wayne held up a mirror to my face in that moment and I was not impressed with what I saw.

Fleming made it to the NHL, too, by the way. None of his players were surprised. He was there for fourteen seasons as an assistant coach with the New York Islanders, Phoenix Coyotes, Philadelphia Flyers, Calgary Flames, Edmonton Oilers, and Tampa Bay Lightning. He was also a head coach for Leksands IF in Sweden, the Landshut Cannibals in Germany, and Avangard Omsk in Russia.

When Fleming died after a two-year battle with brain cancer in 2013, the attendees at his funeral represented the who's who of the hockey world. Ken Hitchcock, Bob Nicholson. Many of his former players were there, including me because it was important that I pay my respects and because I was so grateful for the impact he'd had on my career and more importantly, my life. If it hadn't been for the time I spent at the U of M and with Wayne Fleming, I'm not sure that a career in the NHL would have come to fruition.

I used to see him around the league. It was funny—he made it to the NHL just as my career was winding down, so I'd been in the league longer than he had. I loved running into him. Especially when he was in Phoenix, I'd probably see him every month or so, since we were both in the Western Conference. After the morning skate is always a good time to catch up with friends on the other side. It's early enough in the day that you're still removed from the intensity of game time. I'd always make a point of seeing Fleming, and every conversation began with a laugh—who would have thought the two of us would end up here all these years later? It's an uncommon path for a player, or a coach, to find his way to the NHL by way of Canadian varsity hockey. But Flem and I found a way.

5

MAKING A LIVING

Cliff Fletcher once told me, "Some of the finest people I know never played a day in the NHL." It was a polite way of reminding me that I might not make the NHL. He wanted me to understand it's an uphill climb to reach the show, and if it didn't happen, I shouldn't view it as the end of the world.

Fine—hockey wasn't everything to me. But it was a lot.

While playing for the University of Manitoba, I may have felt like I was in exile from a career in the NHL, but the Calgary Flames had kept track of me and they still owned my rights. After my second year at the U of M, they tried to entice me back to camp. But I hesitated—I was still unsure about climbing this mountain all over again. I had slogged through three years of junior before I finally carved out some playing time. I wasn't sure if I had the appetite to start that cycle all over again in an attempt to make it to the NHL.

I was stuck in that state of mind until our season ended and we were all at the rink doing exit interviews with Fleming. I had a conversation with my teammate Dan Bourbonnais. He was one of the more respected players on the team. Bourbs had played fifty-nine games for the Hartford Whalers before he ended up at the U of M. Unsolicited, Bourbonnais pulled me aside and sat with me in the dressing room on our last day. All the guys knew that Calgary had expressed renewed interest in me. Bourbs seized the opportunity to tell me that he believed I should give it a shot.

"Stu, you have what it takes to play at the next level," he said. "You really need to think about it."

Dan was outside the circle of my close friends and family. He had no reason to encourage me other than a genuine desire to help me reach the best decision. That gave his opinion that much more weight. He was a knowledgeable, neutral observer. If he believed I could play in the NHL, that meant something. I've always been thankful that Bourbonnais decided to speak up. I might never have given taking another shot the kind of careful consideration I did were it not for Dan.

That conversation greatly affected my outlook about the whole notion of turning pro. And everyone in my circle of influence was on board by the time I agreed to terms with Calgary on my first pro contract. The Flames didn't hold it against me that I had quit on them two years before. They gave me a $25,000 bonus, invited me to NHL training camp, and asked me to attend Audrey Bakewell's skating camp a few weeks before camp.

When I arrived at the skating camp, I could feel my anxiety starting to rise. I was right back where I didn't want to be—in more or less the place I had run away from only a couple years before. Gary Roberts, Craig Coxe, Brian Curran—all current and future NHLers—were at this camp. These guys were *good*. Being with them felt the same as I'd felt when I was at the Flames' regular training camp two years before.

I started to second-guess my decision to try this again. Did I really want to be a hired gun? Did I want to be a player who sits on the bench until it's time to fight? A few days into this skating camp, I became ill with flu-like symptoms. Looking back, I wonder if I made myself sick through my constant worrying. If you want to know how hard it is to be a tough guy in the NHL, picture a six-foot-six, 240-pound man lying in his hotel room convincing himself he's too sick to skate, like a kid trying to get out of going to school.

But I didn't give up that easily. When I showed up at Flames training camp in 1987, I was not the same person or player I was when I walked out in 1985. I knew the Flames weren't courting me for my soft hands. But if Wayne Fleming and the U of M Bisons had taught me one thing, it was that I could play the game. I accepted that fighting would need to be major part of my contribution to the team if I was going to make the NHL, but I believed I could do more. I had shown that I could crash, bang, and grind, and also chip in with an occasional goal. One of my objectives at the Flames' training camp was to prove I could play more than a few minutes per night.

I left camp with a full-time job, by the way. I was headed to Salt Lake City in the International Hockey League (IHL). I'd made the team.

In fact, I signed a contract well before camp even started. The way I saw it, I was going to give it three years. The last thing I wanted was to be a career minor-leaguer. I figured three years would be enough to find out whether I had what it takes. (As it turned out, it wasn't. I cheated.) I had three years to go as hard as I could.

My first NHL exhibition game was a road game against the Los Angeles Kings. The Kings dressed both of their heavyweights, Marty McSorley and Ken Baumgartner. I remember the Forum felt like the Roman Coliseum that night. I was overwhelmed.

Up to this point I'd spent my career on the buses on the Prairies, playing in barns that seated no more than four thousand people. Fast forward, and here I am, a member of one of the top teams in the league, flying into Los Angeles and checking into a four-star hotel. The leaves have fallen back home and it's seventy-eight degrees in L.A. I'd been to California before, but never on business. I felt like I was stepping onto another planet.

Everything was familiar but off kilter. I'd been to a lot of NHL games with my dad. But now, when I'm walking into the building, I'm part of the show. I'm part of the reason those eighteen thousand fans are here. Looking down the Kings' roster, I see guys I've been watching for a good part of my life. I see Ken Baumgartner in the warm-ups, but it's not Ken Baumgartner the Prince Albert Raider, a guy I've fought many times before. He seems bigger now. He's Ken Baumgartner, teammate of Wayne Gretzky and Kelly Hrudey and guys like that. He's on the other side of the threshold. If I'm going to get to that side, if I'm going to make it, I realize, I have to make the other team life-sized. They're just hockey players. I just have to play my game.

I didn't go out of my way to engage Baumgartner or McSorley. I played somewhat tentatively. I pretty much stayed in my lane. But my lane could be pretty wide sometimes. I do recall crashing the Kings' net and bowling over their goalie. When the whistle blew, four or five bodies, including mine, were sprawled in the blue paint and the net was off its moorings. When I got back to the bench, Calgary coach Terry Crisp was laughing about the traffic accident I had caused.

"Stuey," he hollered. "Now *that's* the way you go to the net!"

I was physical and noticeable without dropping my gloves. Those were the kind of plays I wanted to make to draw the coaches' attention. When you run a goalie, you have to know that retribution is probably coming, and I thought I might face the Kings' heavy artillery. But if McSorley or the Bomber wanted me to answer for it, they were going to have to initiate it. I wasn't going to chase them around. For reasons only they knew, McSorley and Baumgartner left me alone that night. I was thankful.

I knew it didn't matter what I did in the pre-season. I was destined to be sent to the Salt Lake City Golden Eagles in the IHL. Nobody thought I was ready for the NHL. Even my fighting technique was a little rusty after two years of varsity hockey—though I had been training at the White Crane, that's not the same as a real scrap on skates.

I was more than ready for the minors, though. My performance in my first three months in the IHL is evidence of how much confidence I gained playing college hockey. In my first thirty-six games with the Golden Eagles, I registered nine goals, twenty-three fights, and I piled up 268 penalty minutes. I fought everybody.

Unfortunately, I blew out my knee on December 29. My linemate Steve MacSwain and I were attacking two on one, and we misread each other as we tried to criss-cross at the other team's blue line. We ended up on the same set of tracks and MacSwain lost his balance trying to avoid me.

His full weight landed on my planted right leg. I heard, and felt, the knee joint pop. I didn't need the doctor to tell me I was done for the season. I suspected I needed surgery when I couldn't tuck my leg under me to get up. It was the only time in my professional hockey career that I was unable to return to the bench under my own power.

My anterior cruciate ligament (ACL) was completely severed, damaged to the point that the decision was made not to repair it. The medial collateral ligament (MCL) was pulled away from the bone and had to be stapled back to it. Dr. George Vesey called it a total reconstruction. The Salt Lake City trainer, Brian Patafie, attended the surgery, and a few days later he gave me a play-by-play, sparing me some of the ghastlier details.

"Grimmer, I could tell you about what I saw during your surgery," Patafie said, "but the truth is that it was downright medieval. Bone saws and small hatchets. Not pretty what they did to you."

The surgery lasted two hours and forty-five minutes and I had difficulty climbing out of the anesthesia. I had a yellow complexion and I was sweating profusely. I was told later that I was acting wonky—I kept pawing at the air, trying to get out of my bed.

My girlfriend, Pam, happened to be visiting me from Winnipeg. She was so unnerved by my appearance and erratic behaviour that she fainted. She hit the floor and ended up in a hospital bed next to me.

Vesey did remarkable work on my knee. Even though I have no ACL to this day, I played my entire career on that surgically repaired knee. Never had a problem with it. I'm still running daily on it.

Years later, when I was practising law in Nashville, I was defending a local company being sued over a slip-and-fall accident. During mediation, the opposing attorney and I were negotiating the amount of damages his client should receive. We weren't making much progress.

The other attorney's client had suffered a torn ACL, and he was arguing that monetary damages needed to be significantly higher because his client would be unable to participate in athletics for the rest of his life.

"That may be overstating it, counsel," I said. "I know many people who suffered the same injury and still led a substantially normal and active life."

The other attorney wasn't buying it. "Who are these people you're referring to?" he asked, folding his arms across his chest.

"Me, for one," I said. "I played seventeen years of professional hockey on a right knee that has no ACL at all."

Opposing counsel pushed his glasses up the bridge of his nose and took another look at the pleadings in our case. It took several seconds to locate my name in the footer of a case-related document.

The light went on. "You're *that* Stu Grimson?!" he asked.

The result was that we ended up with a settlement that reflected that the victim would be able to live a normal life. That wasn't any consolation back in 1988, though. What I was thinking then was that I was missing out on the second half of what could have been a memorable first pro season. If you project my scoring rate over an entire season, I was headed toward twenty goals and more than five hundred penalty minutes. That would have been a good start to a pro career.

I wasn't completely at ease as a tough guy, but I was definitely getting more comfortable. One thing that made it easier to settle in was that I was playing a regular shift for coach Paul Baxter. At one point that first season, he told me he could tell that I had been well coached by Fleming at the University of Manitoba. I was playing the game the right way. To a tough guy, there is no bigger compliment.

Besides costing me a half season of development, my injury prevented me from playing with the Golden Eagles when they won the Turner Cup championship that season. The Flames boasted a talented team in Salt Lake City. The late Jim Johannson had come in and scored fourteen goals in eighteen regular-season games and then added twenty-three points in eighteen games in the playoffs. Theoren Fleury joined the team after registering 160 points in sixty-five games for Moose Jaw in the WHL.

It shows you what kind of talent most teams have on tap down in the minors. Jimmy was tearing up the minors at that point in his career. He had great hockey IQ and an excellent sense of where to be and when to arrive, he was extremely coachable and paid attention to detail, and he was dominant in the faceoff circle. He never got a sniff in the NHL. There are a lot of guys like that.

In Jimmy's case, maybe he didn't have that extra gear in his skating. For other guys, it's more about character. At the NHL level, everybody plays with a bit of bite. If you come up and you don't have it, you'll be exposed over time as your game starts to shrink because other guys are crowding you out.

Theo Fleury is a classic example of what it takes to succeed. He could fly, and he had a great shot. But then, there are lots of guys like that in the minors. And Theo had another knock against him—he was only five-foot-six. No one thought a guy that size could survive in pro hockey. The thing about Theo was, he would stare down guys my size. I had played against Fleury in the WHL, and I knew he was a fiery competitor. Fleury knew he was on trial when he came to Salt Lake City, and he put on a show. He had seven points in two regular-season games and then netted eleven goals and sixteen points in eight playoff games. Plus, he hacked and whacked every opponent who came within a stick length of him. He was a tough little bastard.

Bob Bodak, a six-foot-two winger, was assigned to play with Fleury and look after him. Bodak was always rotating his head like a traffic cop, trying to make sure no one was coming from any direction. His job was to make sure Fleury wasn't getting into something he couldn't handle. Fleury would two-hand a player at a second's notice, guys who could snap him in half if they had wanted to. Bodie had a handful babysitting Theo. But no one ever said Theo didn't have bite.

Based on how well he played at the 1987–88 season, Fleury believed he would make the Flames in 1988–89. But we were assigned back to Salt Lake City in the same round of cuts. There was a lot of talent on that Calgary team. If you wanted to play there, that meant taking a spot away from a pretty good hockey player. I took the news the same way I'd taken it the previous year. I was disappointed but accepting of the process players have to go through to make the NHL. You go down, work hard, and wait for your chance.

Fleury's reaction to being cut was different from mine. He exited the Calgary Hockey Operations office boiling mad. Tears flowed down his face, and he was clenching-your-fists-and-jawbone pissed. I didn't understand how he could be that upset. He'd only played ten games in the minors. Plus, if he started the season with the Flames he was going to be the NHL's smallest player. To me, it seemed logical to send him down to give him the opportunity to figure out the nuances of the professional game.

He did go to Salt Lake City and played forty games and racked up seventy-four points. He was scoring at will and making plays like a wizard. Still chopping and slashing anyone in sight. Fleury proved he could dominate in the IHL. The next question was: "Does all of this transfer to the NHL level?"

The answer, as we all know, was that he was just as productive in the NHL. It was impossible not to admire Fleury's determination. He was David in a league full of Goliaths. Called up by the Flames at the halfway mark of the season, Fleury was a point-per-game player and was a major factor in the Flames winning the 1989 Stanley Cup in that year.

The Golden Eagles were blessed with a roster full of quality players. Johannson and I hung out often in my first season. Rick Hayward, Rick Barkovich, Steve MacSwain, Chris Biotti, Marc Bureau, Martin Simard; we all ran together that first year.

Johannson was the first person I ever met who didn't have a middle name.

"So you're *just* Jim Johannson?" I asked.

From that point on, he became "Triple J" for "Just Jim Johannson."

I didn't have too many dull moments in Salt Lake City, especially with Johannson and Hayward around. I don't mean that we were partying especially hard, though we did have the occasional blowout at the Dead Goat Saloon. Mostly we just hung out. We were really close, because no one on the team knew anyone in Salt Lake. We were the Flames' primary minor-league team since the Moncton franchise had just been shut down, so everyone there was there for the first time. We had no one to hang out with but each other.

One afternoon, Hayward is telling me and Johannson about some crazy fight he had been in. The climax of the story was that he had pummelled the guy, as he put it, "like a red-headed stepchild." The next day at the rink, Hayward walked up and started spitting out this long-winded apology. "Stu, I had no idea," Hayward said. "I really didn't know. I'm really sorry for what I said."

I was completely puzzled. "Hayzie, what are you talking about?" I asked.

"When I said 'red-headed stepchild' yesterday," he said, "I had no idea about your background."

I said, "Hayzie, I'm adopted. I'm not a stepchild. You know the difference, right?"

"Well yeah, but when Jimmy mentioned you were adopted, we both thought you'd be offended," he said.

It was hard not to imagine these two nitwits sitting around and reaching a conclusion that I would be offended by Hayward's story. It made me laugh aloud.

"Relax," I said. "I'm not mad. But you might want to have this same conversation with all of the red-headed stepchildren out there." I couldn't resist giving Hayward something to think about.

Hayward was notorious for his practical joking. In the 1980s we flew commercial, and plane trips were the perfect setting for Hayward's rookie pranks. Hayward liked the audience a full plane provided him. He loved to give rookies a "shaving cream hat." When a rookie fell asleep on the plane, Hayward would slip into the seat behind him. Hayward was masterful at squeezing shaving cream out of a can without making a sound. The rookie would wake up, scratch his head, and discover a tower of shaving cream on his cranium.

Watching people react to a player walking through the airport with shaving cream on his head was always hysterical.

By my second season in Salt Lake City, I was far more comfortable in my role as a tough guy. I had thirty-six fighting majors in 1988–89, and one of them occurred in my first NHL regular-season game.

The Flames called me up in November, at the start of a six-game road trip. Coach Terry Crisp inserted me immediately in the lineup, on a line with Joel Otto and Tim Hunter, against the Buffalo Sabres on November 9.

Late in the game, I fought Kevin Maguire. I knew who he was—I had done my homework. Maguire was an established tough guy. I knew I needed to do something to impress. In the third, we were down by a goal. Maguire understood my intentions as soon as our eyes met; I opened my stance in a way any tough guy would recognize as an invitation. The gloves were off and away we went. It was a good fight. Dropyourgloves.com rates the fight as a draw, though I would have given Maguire the edge. But I thought I had held my own against a noted NHL brawler.

The Flames vets were great. Afterward, Colin Patterson said, "I know it's just one game, Stu. But you proved you can play at this level." A veteran guy like Patter didn't have to say that to a guy with one game in the league. I really appreciated it. That's the kind of guy he is. Joel Otto took me aside and made sure I knew that when he was breaking in, he was called up and sent down five or six times in his first year. That meant a lot.

The problem was we lost the game 3–2, and Crisp scratched me the next game on the road. In fact, I didn't play again on the road trip and the Flames won all five remaining games. Remember, the Flames were a dominant team that year, on the way to a Stanley Cup. That was a tough roster to crack. I think the Flames concluded they didn't need me. I was sent back to Salt Lake City at the end of that six-game trip.

While I didn't want to be demoted, I enjoyed my time with the Golden Eagles the rest of the season. We won fifty-six games that season and thought we were going to win our second consecutive Turner Cup. Paul Ranheim scored sixty-eight goals in seventy-five games. Fleury had thirty-seven in forty games before being called up. Peter Lappin had forty-eight. Johannson netted thirty-eight. We were a force. I had twenty-seven points and 398 penalty minutes that season.

One of my all-time favourite hockey moments occurred that season when I scored the overtime goal to put us in the Turner Cup Final. We had a 3–1 lead going into Game 5 of the best-of-seven semifinals against the Milwaukee Admirals. We were playing in Milwaukee and I was really feeling it. It was one of those nights when the puck seemed to follow me. I had several quality scoring chances and it seemed just a matter of time before I would score.

The game was tied 4–4 after three periods. We were back in the room before overtime and it became clear that I wasn't the only one who noticed the raft of great chances I had had earlier that night. Out of nowhere our backup goalie, Wayne Cowley, turned to me and said, "Stu, you got this. I got a feeling man, this is going to be you!"

I agreed. "Cowls, you're right! I feel this—I am all over these guys!" I really was in a groove. My line had been all over the Admirals through the first three periods. I was convinced the next goal was coming off my stick.

In the overtime, my teammate Jim Leavins took a puck deep into the corner from the point, drawing the defence to him. I immediately drove the net. Nobody followed me. No one was within five metres of me. Everyone, including the Milwaukee goalie, was focused on Leavins in the deep corner. Jimmy spotted me going hard to the post. He delivered a perfect pass and I slammed it into a mostly empty net. Easiest goal I ever scored and the only OT tally of my career. I was mobbed, buried under a mountain of teammates. An amazing moment and a small affirmation that I might have more to contribute than just being a fighter.

In the Finals, we ran into an absolutely stacked Muskegon team, with guys like Mark Recchi, Kevin Stevens, Jeff Daniels, and Dave McLlwain on the roster. We played a strong series but Muskegon was simply deeper than us. So, we came up just short of winning the League Championship in consecutive years. Another great run, but we hit a wall in Muskegon.

When I was in the minors, I went out to prove that I was a complete hockey player every game. And it was coming together. I didn't mind fighting as long as people saw that I could contribute in other ways also. I wasn't sitting at the end of the bench waiting for the fighting portion of the program. I was playing the game, and if someone wanted a piece of me, I was happy to oblige.

The game and my role within the game was manageable that way.

6

BROWN VS. GRIMSON

Muhammad Ali once knocked out Sonny Liston in the first round of a World Boxing Council Heavyweight Championship bout. Most ticket buyers were not even settled into their seats when Liston hit the canvas in 1965.

I worried that something similarly catastrophic would happen to me the first time I fought Edmonton Oilers tough guy Dave Brown. I believed I might be lying on the ice before anyone realized we had fought.

Known by the handle "Dave Brown and His Fists of Renown," Brownie had a left-hand that hit like a thunderclap. This was an era when most heavyweights could beat every other heavyweight on any given night, but nobody, not even Bob Probert, was more feared than Brownie. Fans seemed to view Probert as the heavyweight champ, but anyone who fought both of them would tell you that Brownie hit much harder than Probert. Night and day harder. When Brown landed a punch, it was like being kicked by a mule.

When I was breaking in, Dave Brown was the meanest, baddest man on skates.

When you were a minor leaguer like I was in 1989–90, every call-up made you nervous. But being called up by the Calgary Flames in January on the front end of a home-and-home series against the Oilers was next to terrifying. The Battle of Alberta was like an active volcano, always a threat to erupt violently whenever the two teams battled.

Nobody had to explain why I was being brought up. It wasn't to add scoring punch on the left side or to shadow Glenn Anderson. I was promoted to deal with Brown. I was twenty-five and he was twenty-eight. I was six-foot-six and he was an inch shorter. But I would be playing in my second NHL game on January 7 and he was in his ninth NHL season. And he had one other important advantage over me.

That left.

There is nothing you do to acquire a left that hits that hard. You simply have that or you don't. And Brown had it in spades.

It wasn't as if the Flames were throwing me to the wolves. By the time I faced Brown, I had seventy-four pro fights on my resumé. I had fought Kelly Buchberger, Ken Baumgartner, Jeff Beukeboom, and Steve Smith in NHL pre-season games, and my IHL fight card included every heavyweight contender. I hadn't been shy about throwing my weight around for the Salt Lake Golden Eagles. But if Las Vegas had put a line out on a Brown vs. Grimson fight, I would have been a 10–1 underdog.

Plus, I still wasn't convinced I had the mental toughness to be an NHL enforcer. No one had to tell me I had the size. And I had the technique and wasn't physically afraid to stand in there. But it takes more than that to go looking for a fight against a guy who makes it his job to brutalize pro hockey players. If you're going to fight that guy, you have to believe you have more to gain than you have to lose. If losing the fight means losing your teammates' respect—if it means losing your *self*-respect—then the pressure is almost unbearable.

I'm not saying I spent the pre-game feeling sorry for myself. And who knows what Brown was thinking about me? But for me, everything was on the line. Everything I had worked for. My reputation. And most importantly, my belief that I could fill a role for this team, that I could contribute in some way and make this team better. That's who I was. That's who I needed to believe myself to be, anyway. That's a lot to wager in hand-to-hand combat with the toughest guy in the league.

I was so anxious in the hours and minutes leading up to that fight I couldn't produce the saliva to spit. More to the point, there was absolutely no way I was even going to consider ducking Brown. This fight was inevitable. This was an opportunity to impress. The spotlight was on me. Every Flames fan was watching. Every Flames fan *cared*. This was the height of the Battle of Alberta. I knew it was up to me to make the most of this moment. Letting it go by would mean wasting years of hard work.

I knew that the path to an NHL career ran right through Dave Brown and this was my moment.

My heart rate was accelerated, and my thoughts were racing. How will I start it? Should I play a few shifts first? How do I get to that damn left without him clipping me? And what if he does clip me? I don't have a will—who will get my car?

The first game of the home and home was in Edmonton, and Brown may have sensed the rookie would be nervous. He skated wide loops during the pre-game warm-ups, crossing onto the

Flames' side of the red line more than once as if to say, "What are you going to do about it?" He looked huge, fierce, menacing. He *was* all of those things. My anxiety was overflowing.

I didn't wait long to face my fears. On the fourth shift of the game, right after a faceoff in the neutral zone, I elbowed him in the chest to get his attention. He threw off his gloves immediately and fired off three left hands that cut the air just above my head as I slipped under and past his outstretched left to grab hold of that lethal left. I managed to grab hold and I sensed that I had him all tied up.

Then I clocked him twice. Right on the button. Down goes Brown. I laid him out. The Edmonton crowd was stunned. I was stunned.

When I skated back to the bench after serving my five-minute major, Theo Fleury was the first to put some perspective on what I had just done.

"Do you have the name of a real estate agent in Calgary?" he asked. "You're going to be with us for a while."

I laughed, as much out of relief as happiness.

Brown spent the rest of the game looking for a rematch, but I had tagged him hard. He was on wobbly legs. He was hurting. Today, he'd never have passed concussion protocol. Back then, though, he wanted redemption. The rematch that came later in the second period didn't amount to much because he still wasn't himself. I knew he still needed revenge.

I can't say it any better than Charles Dickens: It was the best of times, it was the worst of times. The good news was, I just punched out the NHL's heavyweight champ. The bad news was, now I had to fight him again.

And he was angry—probably embarrassed—by the encounter

with the rookie on his home ice. He thought I had jumped him, though I don't know to this day why he thought that. I believe my push gave him ample time to prepare to fight, and he swung first. It wasn't as if I just started throwing punches without warning.

He warned reporters not to be getting coffee early in the rematch in Calgary, or they were going to miss what he assured them would be the main event of the night.

What I learned after the rematch was that Brown had worked with his equipment man to cut his jersey sleeves and then sew them tight around his wrist. He then coated them with a silicone spray to make it impossible for me to get a grip. Brown's experience served him in the rematch.

Even though I expected to face Brown a couple days later back in Calgary, I wasn't as ready as I needed to be. In our first fight, I injured my hand. It was swollen pretty bad. My glove on the right side wasn't slipping off as easily as it would normally. To make matters worse, I was running a fever. I told our trainer Bearcat Murray what was going on. Both of us knew I wasn't 100 percent and both of us knew that I had to go out there and answer to Brown.

Tough guy code.

I was probably half-hoping Crisp would notice my hand and pull me out of the lineup. But that was wishful thinking, not a real possibility. The rematch came early; Crisp rolled me out there on Brown's first shift. He shook his gloves off right off the drop of the puck and skated my way. I got hung up momentarily struggling to slip my puffy hand out of my right glove. Again, I tried to lock down his left hand. But this time, I groped awkwardly and couldn't seem to find it. My hand slid off his left sleeve.

My situation went from bad to nightmarish when he connected with three left-hand jackhammer punches to my face. Down goes Grimson. He hit me with such force that I assumed I was cut. On all fours, I instinctively tried to wipe away what I thought would be blood under my right eye. Instead, I felt a depression under that eye that I'd never felt before. I wasn't as concerned about that as much as I was embarrassed that Brown had beat me badly in my own building.

Naively, I believed I could hide the injury. I'd been banged up before—it's an occupational hazard. However, sometimes you can cover a cut or bloody nose beneath your hand until you reach the penalty box. Then you can administer a little self-repair. I picked myself up and headed to the penalty box.

As I sat in the penalty box, all I could think about was, *I've got to fight him again in this game.*

But as my five-minute penalty ticked away, I started to realize that my injuries might be more serious than I'd first believed. My head began to feel heavier, heavier, and heavier. Barely able to hold up my head, I skated to the bench and started heading down the runway.

"Where are you going?" a bewildered Terry Crisp asked.

Murray told him we were going to see the doctor. I had just informed him that something was very wrong.

Not long after that, I was in a two-and-a-half-hour emergency reconstructive surgery to repair an orbital bone that had been fractured in two places. My skull had been broken above my right eye and below the cheekbone.

A doctor later explained to me that an opening was created above my ear where a surgical instrument could be inserted, inside my skull. The fracture was then tapped out from inside my skull until it was flush with the other section of the bone. It was stabilized with a fifteen-centimetre stainless-steel pin, which was inserted through my cheekbone and then the three bones in my nose. They left a half-centimetre of the rod sticking out of my cheekbone—so it could be extracted after the fracture had healed.

The rod helps set the fracture. It also helps remind you each morning how horrific this injury truly was. That pin was sticking out of my face for five weeks before the doctor pulled it out. I looked like Frankenstein's kid brother for a month and a half, only I had a pin instead of a bolt sticking out the side of my neck. Brown had exacted his revenge. I had suffered the worst beating a guy in my job can receive.

According to dropyourgloves.com, I had 393 fights in my hockey career, counting pre-season, regular season, and playoffs in junior, the minor leagues, and the NHL, and no one hit me harder than Brown did on January 9, 1990. Probert hit me many times during our careers, and no punch Bob threw ever came close to breaking my orbital bone.

My hideous post-surgery face startled a lot of folks for days after. Flames forward Marc Bureau was overcome by emotion when he came up to visit. We had played together in Salt Lake City and were called up to Calgary at the same time. Since we both lived at the Westin Hotel in downtown Calgary, Marc volunteered to bring some of my personal items to the hospital, particularly my shaving kit. Like any good teammate would.

He was not prepared for the ugliness of my injury. I knew it was bad, though. Earlier the same day, I stood in front of the mirror for the first time. I didn't recognize myself. It had only been two days since the surgery. My face was badly swollen, and the colour of my skin was already changing to a deep purple over the right side of my face. The pin sticking out of my face looked like someone had snapped off a tine from a large dinner fork.

Marc took one step into my hospital room and started crying. He made his way to a chair near my hospital bed but he couldn't stop sobbing. So for the next fifteen minutes, the scene is this: two hockey players sitting in a hospital room, and the guy with the purple face is holding the other guy's hand as he sits beside his bed. I'm patting Marc's hand saying, "It's okay, Frenchie. Don't worry, I'm going to be alright. It's not as bad as it looks, Frenchie. I'm going to be okay."

—

Want to know the irony of this injury? Getting my orbital bone crushed by Brown in 1990 was probably one of the best things that ever happened to me. It was certainly the turning point in my professional career. My time lying there in that hospital bed was when I realized—when I really knew—that I could make my living as an NHL tough guy.

It's odd, I know. But first showing up and holding my own against Brown and then the bad beat that came after were the most liberating things to happen to me in my career. My thinking was that the loss to Brown, and the subsequent surgery, were as bad as it gets in that line of work. The epiphany I had while recovering from my injury was that I had faced my worst fears—getting severely pummelled by another player—and had survived to talk about it. People talk about post-traumatic stress, but in fact, the usual response to something awful is post-traumatic growth. That's how we are built. What doesn't kill us makes us stronger.

In my mind, I had nothing else to fear.

I finally understood what it means to confront true fear. I remember thinking, *If I can come back from this injury, there's really nothing left to fear. I can do this job.*

—

After about five weeks, I was playing again—playing for a couple of weeks with that pin sticking out of my face. The temporary visor was just another reminder of how badly Brown had crushed me.

My next fight wasn't until March 24, when I fought Kerry Clark in three consecutive games in the IHL playoffs. Clarkie and I had been teammates in junior, but we were like oil and water when we were on opposite teams. He played a very abrasive, physical game. He would go out of his way to hit you. He was also Wendel Clark's younger brother, if that gives any sense of how much fun it was to play against him.

I don't remember what it was that set me off. I wasn't in any hurry to get punched in the face after my surgery, but I also knew that I couldn't change my game. Was I a little gun-shy? I certainly didn't want to get clipped in the eye. But at the same time, I knew I had to get back in the saddle. And I couldn't have Clarkie running around out there. So we went at it. Then again the next night. And then again. After that, I was better than ever.

Later in my career, I got a glimpse of what that must have been like for Clark. I was playing in Hartford, and Shane Churla was playing for New York. Churls and I used to tangle all the time, going back to junior. But I decided I wasn't going to get into it with him that night because he was coming back from a broken cheekbone. But toward the end of the game, we were up on the Rangers by a few goals, and Churls started running around. It was my job to settle him down, but he wasn't having it. I gave him every chance to avoid a scrap, but he wanted it. It was pretty lopsided in my favour, and in the end his teammates had to jump in to save him. He put us both in a situation I didn't want to be in. But once you're squared off with a guy like that, there are no half measures. He may not have been himself, but he was still a dangerous guy. I couldn't go easy on him. And Kerry Clark didn't go easy on me.

And that's a good thing. That marked the end of my lengthy recovery. I had got past what I'd thought was the worst thing that could have happened to me, and I had more than survived.

My most oppressive physical fear was behind me. No one in the NHL could ever threaten me with a more devastating punch than the one I had recovered from. But then, I had never really been physically afraid. My fear had always been emotional. Before that fight with Brownie, the fear of the humiliation I thought would come with a loss consumed far too much of my thinking. I used to think that people would only respect me if I won fights. Once I had lost so convincingly that my face had to be put back together by surgeons, I realized that wasn't true. The world went on. And no one respected me any less. I saw that I had been afraid of something that wasn't even real.

And the life lesson from all this? There is nothing more rewarding or liberating in life than facing down your greatest fears and moving past them. Because on the other side of those fears waits the reward and the life you seek. If this book is about one thing, it's about the freedom and the peace you find on the other side of fear, both on and off the ice. Had I not come to that important realization, I would never have realized the dreams of my childhood.

To be clear, overcoming that fear didn't make the life of an NHL tough guy a walk in the park. But the anxiety was no longer debilitating; it became manageable. My thinking after I suffered a brutal loss to Dave Brown was *if I can pull myself up by the bootstraps and I can come back from a loss like this, what else is there to fear?* The answer was . . . *Nothing.*

Our fights were featured in Mark Spector's book *The Battle of Alberta*. After Mark's book came out, I ran into Brownie and asked him if he'd had a chance to read it.

"Yeah," he said. "Can you believe he gave us a whole fucking chapter?"

Classic Brownie line. But I do believe it because I'm devoting an entire chapter to it as well. It was a defining moment in my life. Maybe now Brownie appreciates those moments for what they were as well.

7

MIKE'S MADHOUSE ON MADISON

One day, people simply won't believe the way the game was played in the early nineties. Back in the days of wooden sticks, before the lockout, and before the realignment of the conferences and divisions, the ice was patrolled by guys whose names are still spoken with awe. Dave Semenko and Marty McSorley are spoken of in the same breath as Wayne Gretzky and Jari Kurri. And the division named after former Red Wings owner James Norris was easily the toughest of them all.

Teams in the Norris may not have won as much as teams in other divisions (Toronto made the playoffs in 1987–88 with a 21–49–10 record), but no one pushed those teams around. Teams were built to play other teams within their division, and there was an arms race going on in the Norris. Most teams didn't have just one super-heavyweight. It was considered prudent to have two.

The Detroit Red Wings boasted Bob Probert and Joey Kocur. The St. Louis Blues had Tony Twist and Kelly Chase. The Minnesota North Stars had Basil McRae and Shane Churla. Teams drafted and traded for toughness. If you couldn't handle yourself, you might find yourself in a different division. And you might be grateful to be shipped out. Those who played within it referred to it affectionately as the "Chuck Norris Division."

Chicago claimed me on waivers from the Flames on October 1, right before the start of the 1990–91 season. I was heading to the Norris.

The 1990–91 Blackhawks were nothing like the Norris stereotype. We were an exceptional team, finishing the regular season with the NHL's best record of 49–23–8. Steve Larmer, Michel Goulet, Doug Wilson, Eddie Belfour, Dominik Hasek, and Jeremy Roenick were among the players on that squad.

And we had a star coach in Mike Keenan behind the bench. Keenan had plenty of reasons to enjoy coaching this team. And yet the dawn of every new day was reason enough for him to be furious with us. In fact, what went down on the ice in the Norris was nowhere near as crazy as what I saw behind the bench.

I realized during my third game with the team that my working environment had changed radically when Keenan and my old sparring partner Trent Yawney (hockey really is a small world) engaged in a nuclear screaming session while play was going on.

I don't recall exactly what prompted Keenan to launch his salvo of R-rated criticism at Yawney. But trust me when I say that it didn't take much to light the coach's fuse. All I remember for sure is that Keenan didn't like something he saw from Yawney, probably a missed assignment or mental lapse on the ice, and he walked down the bench and lit into him.

That didn't surprise me. Some coaches are like that. The shock came when Yawney returned fire. F-bombs sailed back and forth until assistant coaches and players stepped in to remind everyone that there was a game going on in front of us.

I was dumbfounded. I had grown up in Canadian Mountie Stan Grimson's house, where authority was respected. My father expected respect from his children, and he got it. He didn't demand it in a physical or an abusive way. I had learned through my father and others that in a team setting you honour the chain of command. That's the way it worked on his job and in his household. Mom operated the same way.

My coach in midget, Joe Tennant, didn't take any crap either. In fact, I never even considered talking back. He was a tough coach, hard on his players, and he left a lasting impression on me. He instilled the idea that what a coach says, whether you agree with it or not, is gospel. Your mission is to do your job within the parameters the coach has laid out for you. Insubordination is never an option.

It was a military-like mentality. I believed in it because that's how I was raised. That's how I thought. It made sense to me that if you started second-guessing your coach, especially in front of others, you undermined his authority. It was counter-productive to running a team effectively.

To see a player and coach screaming at each other at the NHL level was mind-blowing. But I soon learned that this was just the way things worked in Mike Keenan's house. Confrontations occurred daily, and people boiled over frequently. Keenan almost seemed to prefer a fractured, contentious relationship with his players.

Coaches can operate in one of two ways to motivate an athlete: they can create positive energy and attempt to bolster an athlete's confidence or they can create negative energy and try to extract more from an athlete who is playing pissed off. Yes, Mike fit squarely in the latter camp.

In three years, I don't remember Mike ever going over a piece of video and saying "good job." Ever. He was not one to praise a player. He frequently turned the screws on the guys. If you lost two in a row, you were going to have an unpleasant experience with Keenan. The locker room could be a verbal torture chamber on those days. It was as if Keenan subscribed to the belief that keeping us on edge made us play better. Some days it was Yawney who showed up on the coach's radar. Maybe it was because he was our seventh defenceman, and didn't always dress, so he was an easy target. Maybe it was because Yawney didn't take shit from anyone, and Keenan wanted to break him down. But it wasn't always Yawney. There was a different victim, and a fresh episode to the soap opera, nearly every day.

Oddly, Keenan leaned on Steve Larmer a lot too. He sat next to me, and Larms and I always joked that we were "cell mates and soul mates in Cell Block Keenan." Larmer wasn't yet thirty when I arrived in Chicago, but the guys called him "Gramps" because he had been there so long. He was stoic, occasionally grumpy, and always seemed older than he really was. But he was also a talented, committed player who scored 342 goals in his first ten seasons in Chicago. Larmer played a methodical, plodding style of game, and so he looked like he wasn't going at top speed. Keenan used to ride him for that. But Larmer was as reliable and consistent a player as you are going to find. He was incredibly dependable and played the same game night after night. The guy played on a line with Wayne Gretzky in the 1991 Canada Cup and led the tournament in goals. Larmer could play. And Keenan coached that team. No one understood why Keenan would pick on Larms. But he did.

Larms played left wing and he was fantastic on the wall in our end. But one night he turned it over and it cost us a goal. Mike called him out in front of the room. In ten battles along the boards, Larms is going to come out with the puck nine times. The one time he didn't, Keenan called him out. The whole team was sitting there thinking this guy deserves more respect than that. Maybe Keenan wanted to show that even the stars didn't get special treatment. Maybe he thought that was how you got more out of a player. But the consensus in the room was that we didn't win *because* of our coach; we won *despite* him. I'll say one thing about Keenan: he brought the team together. We were unified in our dislike of how he treated us.

The one guy Keenan didn't pick on was captain Dirk Graham. I don't recall a single night that he ever called out Duke. Not that there was any reason to. Duke was a reliable, hard-working, hard-nosed guy. He didn't score a lot of highlight-reel goals, but he got things done out there, and he wasn't shy to drop the gloves. Because Dirk was such a soldier, Mike must have realized he couldn't undermine the respect we had for him. If I were a coach, I wouldn't want to undermine that either. They say a lot of teams take on the identity of their coach, but we modelled ourselves after our captain.

I didn't receive much playing time on the Hawks, and I don't fault Keenan for that. At that point, my game wasn't very effective. But Mike needed a tough team to be competitive in the Norris Division, and he respected the contribution that I did make. I believe Mike also appreciated what I brought to the room.

Keenan never asked, or ordered, me to fight an opponent, and I appreciated that. I never wanted to have a coach tap me on the shoulder. I prided myself on having a keen awareness of when I needed to assert myself. When it came to fighting, I was proactive. By how Mike played me, he made it clear to me that I was supposed to manage the physical momentum of the game. He expected me to change tempo if and when that was necessary. Although it was unspoken, it was very clear.

But my role as the team's protector didn't exempt me from Keenan's wrath. Everyone spent time in his dog house.

One night in the Boston Garden, during the 1990–91 season, we held a three-goal lead after two periods, and I stood up between periods and reminded everyone not to grow complacent.

"Let's keep our foot on the gas, fellas," I said. "Stay strong. Boys, we can't afford to play on our heels. We dictate the pace—let's take it to them. Win this last period and let's get out of here." That kind of thing. That was not out of character. I'm a vocal guy by nature. If I feel it is needed, I will say something between periods.

My teammates seemed to be ready to go for that third period against the Bruins. But our three-goal lead evaporated. The way I remember it, we ended up losing when referee Andy Van Hellemond ruled that our potential tying goal went in after time expired. Keenan believed the official timekeeper had helped the Bruins' comeback by monkeying with a few seconds when the home team needed them.

At the end of the game, Keenan was trying to get to the timekeeper's bench. A bunch of us intercepted him before he committed an act that would get him suspended. A YouTube video shows defenceman Keith Brown with his arms wrapped around Keenan and me in front of him. (In fairness to Mike, the video also shows that the tying goal occurred with four seconds remaining.)

If a team blows a three-goal lead in the third, they can expect an ill-tempered coach the next day. But I was surprised when Keenan summoned me to his office back in Chicago. He laid into me. He hadn't liked my comments between periods from the night before in Boston. He thought I had planted a negative seed and it had grown into a collapse.

I was on my heels. I couldn't believe he felt that way. For the next few days, I replayed my intermission speech in my head and none of it seemed out of line. I said what any coach or player usually says in those situations: play smart, remind yourself the game isn't over. It took me a while to realize I was wasting my time trying to figure it out. It was just Keenan trying to stir up the negative energy in yet another innovative way.

The battles with Keenan continued even into the playoffs. Maybe he had good reason to be angry with us in the playoffs. As the President's Trophy winner, the Blackhawks drew the Minnesota North Stars in the first round. At 27–39–14, they had finished thirty-eight points behind the Hawks in the standings. We were expected to sashay into the second round. But the North Stars saw things differently. They beat us 4–3 in overtime in our own building in the first game.

We got back on course by winning Games 2 and 3. But Mike was boiling mad when the North Stars beat us 3–1 in Game 4 at the Met Center in Bloomington, Minnesota, to tie the series.

I should have known to keep my head down after that game. But simply acting like a regular citizen could sometimes get you in trouble with Keenan. As teammate Dave Manson and I left the dressing room, we spotted Cindy Glynn, wife of North Stars defenceman Brian Glynn. Since both Dave and I were friends with Brian, we decided to stop and say hello to Cindy. A common courtesy. Nothing more.

What we didn't realize was that Cindy and the other North Stars' wives were standing directly across from a secondary dressing room that was being used as the Chicago coaches' office. Keenan saw us talking with Cindy. To him, it was fraternizing with the enemy. We must have been too cordial, or laughed, smiled, or looked happy. Whatever we did, Keenan and associate coach Darryl Sutter saw enough of what they considered to be conduct unbecoming a pair of their Blackhawks in that moment.

Before our conversation with Cindy ended, Darryl hollered across the hall while standing in the doorway of the coaches' office.

"Grimson, Manson," he yelled. "Get in here!"

Because we were about to fly home, Manson and I were toting our luggage, garment bags draped over our shoulders. As we entered the room, obviously concerned about why we'd been summoned, we found Keenan pacing in the back of the room. He came to a halt, took a few steps toward us, and started yelling at us. We could see the anger level rising with each syllable. I don't remember his speech word for word. But I'll never forget his anger.

"What the fuck are you guys doing talking to the other team's wives?" he hollered. "We're in the middle of a playoff series here!"

The situation turned uglier when Keenan turned his focus toward Manson, who was a higher profile player than I was. Manson, a defenceman, was an important contributor to our success. His wicked shot helped him score fourteen goals in the 1990–91 season. And Manson was tough: 191 penalty minutes that season. The season before, he totalled 301 minutes in just fifty-nine games. The guys called Manson "Charlie," a reference to the infamous Charles Manson, because our Manson could be a little erratic at times. And Charlie had a short fuse; when he boiled over, somebody got scalded.

I knew that Mike and Charlie had a bit of a history going back to before I got to Chicago. Keenan vs. Manson was no less contentious than the Yawney–Keenan feud. But I had no idea how volatile it was prior to this moment. As soon as Mike started in on Dave, I recognized that the potential for something goofy to happen had escalated dramatically.

"Charlie, you don't care," Keenan said. "Charlie, you don't give a shit."

As Mike was finishing "You don't care . . ." I swear Manson's eyes rolled back in his head like some scene from *The Exorcist*. Dropping his bags, he started walking toward Keenan.

"Charlie, hang on, you don't want to do this," I said. Bags still in hand, I put myself between Keenan and Manson. This may have been the most surreal moment of my career to this point. I was standing between one of my teammates and my coach because my teammate now wanted to tear my coach limb from limb. Ever have a day like that at the office?

To Keenan's credit, he realized that he had pushed Manson too far with that accusation, and he immediately backed off. He actually threw his arms around Manson's waist and told him, "Settle down, Charlie, this is going to be okay. We have to work this out."

When Mike let go, I stayed between the two. Manson was still worked up. In fact, I got back to the team bus after Dave did to find him doing laps around the bus to cool off. Some of the guys saw Manson and me summoned into the coaches' office so they were keen to hear what happened. I heard a lot of "What's up with Charlie?" I gave the guys a complete rundown.

Larms had been listening to the whole story. After I finished he looks at me to say "You got between them?" He pauses. Then, in a completely serious tone: "Why the hell would you want to do that?" In truth, I think everybody on our squad shared the same sentiment. Although nobody said this to me, I still think stopping Manson from annihilating our coach was probably the right thing to do . . . at least for Charlie's sake.

—

Keenan seemed sadistic at times, brilliant at others. He was demanding, negative, and unpredictable. What isn't well known is that Darryl Sutter was all of those things and more. Sutter was Keenan 2.0. As Keenan's associate coach in 1990–91 and 1991–92, he learned the coaching trade craft from Keenan. He could be more Mike than Mike was. He could even be more draconian. By the time he became Blackhawks head coach in 1992–93, Darryl was a fire-breather.

The Sutter brothers, Darryl included, are caring, principled, disciplined, hard-working, and dedicated hockey people. But Darryl could be a cruel dictator.

I remember a Sutter practice, the day after we had our tails handed to us, when he went from player to player and told us why we had been worthless to him in our last game. He was particularly mean to forward Brian Noonan.

"And Noonan, you should get down on all fours and kiss my ass every day you come to the rink and you have a roster spot," he sneered. "There are twenty-three other teams out there that won't take you. We can't trade you. Yet I find a way to keep you in the lineup."

Noonan's head dropped, his shoulders slumped. That's about as demeaning as you can get; we all felt for Noons. But Brian had a hard exterior and a quick wit. He found a way to let it roll off him. And we all knew deep down that Darryl respected him. As players, you develop some pretty thick skin to put up with the flak you catch from coaches and even each other at times. But that doesn't excuse what Darryl said that day; it's possible to go too far in trying to get something more out of an athlete. As a person, Darryl is principled and big hearted. I see him every now and then in retired life. I have a deep admiration for Darryl as I learned a lot from him. But his drill instructor's approach to coaching worked on some of us but not so much on others.

In spite of it all, Darryl did have a pretty good sense of humour. When Keenan was coach and Darryl was associate, the Blackhawks would dress an extra defenceman and forward for the warm-up, mostly to keep us and our opponents guessing about our lineup. After the warm-up, it would be Sutter's job to notify the players who would be the healthy scratches for the night.

One night, Sutter told Bryan Marchment that he was going to sit out. Marchment got up from his dressing stall, stomped into the fitness room, grabbed a thirty-pound dumbbell, and hurled it through a mirror. He then trashed the place. Mush didn't fight a lot (which drove a lot of his opponents crazy), but he was a tough son of a bitch and didn't take anything lying down. He was also used to a lot of playing time, so Sutter shouldn't have been surprised when he got an angry response. It was completely in keeping with Marchment's character.

The next game, in Chicago Stadium, after the warm-up, I descended that long run of steps and re-entered the dressing room to find a dumbbell sitting in my stall. It was Sutter's humorous way of informing me that I wouldn't be playing in the game. It was his way of saying that if I needed to use the dumbbell to express my anger, I should go ahead.

It was a smart move by Sutter. As mad as I was about getting scratched, I had to laugh when I saw the dumbbell. Sutter defused the entire situation.

Despite Mike's and Darryl's antics, I loved playing in Chicago. The relationship I enjoyed with fans made my time in that city special. Chicago fans seemed to appreciate the way I played. They seemed to understand and respect the importance of having someone who could play that role effectively. The Ligas family in particular.

I learned through the Blackhawks public relations department that Joey Ligas was a big fan and that he was battling a rare terminal disease. Soon after I learned of Joey, I went to visit him and his family at a Chicago-area hospital. The expression on Joey's face when I entered the room was overwhelming. What a unique spirit. His love for the game was palpable.

Regrettably, just a week after my visit, the Ligas family reached out to tell me that Joey had passed away. They buried him in my jersey. To this day, that story touches me. I suppose it's a little overwhelming to think you could have that kind of impact on people by way of what you do.

Fans seemed to embrace me, appreciating how I approached my role as the Blackhawks' enforcer. Remember, we did play in the Chuck Norris Division. And before I arrived, they really didn't have much of an answer for the Proberts, Kocurs, and McRaes on rival teams. Not long after I arrived in Chicago, I looked up into the second balcony and saw a sign that read "Stu's Crew."

Later, I would find out that the banner was hung by the Thiry family. These were humble, gregarious, hard-working Midwestern folks who treated me like family. Even after I was traded, they followed my career. When I first met them, they had a young son named Pat. It was young Pat who was the biggest fan in the family to be clear. I got to know Pat pretty well. He would write me faithfully and we stayed in touch for years after I left Chicago. Pat went on to a career as one of Chicago's finest; he's with the Chicago Police Department today. (Thanks for all you do, friend.)

—

Although my "Grim Reaper" nickname started in junior hockey, it never really caught on until I arrived in Chicago. Fans loved it and sportswriters began using it—both at home and away.

I never really had a strong opinion about my nickname either way. I didn't dislike it. But I never did much to promote it either (that is, until I decided it ought to be the title of the book in your hands).

I do believe it gave me something of an aura, though. It probably enhanced my reputation and made me seem tougher than I actually was. I doubt the nickname had any impact on the true heavyweights of the Norris. But when some young scrapper arrived in the NHL and looked at me and saw a six-foot-six, 240-pound player with the nickname "Grim Reaper," I'm sure that it gave him a little more to think about.

How much is that worth? It's difficult to quantify, but I've always thought that the nickname may have made me 10 percent more intimidating. And intimidation is an advantage; I'll take a 10 percent advantage any time. No one takes a heavyweight fight lightly. There's too much at stake. But there is a difference between an everyday tilt against a guy in your weight class and one against a guy you know is a contender. Against some guys, you wade in and get busy hoping that you might overwhelm him. If you're up against someone you think has a good chance of hurting you, if you let the intimidation get to you, now you're not fighting your fight. If you're fighting to survive, you're not fighting to win. That's a different posture. So if you can intimidate a guy before the gloves even come off, you've made your job a bit easier.

I believe one of the primary reasons Chicago fans embraced me was my ability to hold my own against Probert. Many believed Probert was the heavyweight champion of that era. Chicago fans were wary of the Red Wings. That's why Chicago picked me up. They were trying to Probert-proof the team. Remember, Probert terrorized a lot of clubs back then. He wouldn't just go around punching your tough guy. He'd punch your goalie. Probie didn't care.

My job was to do something about it. When fans talk to me about my days in Chicago, they always bring up my battles with Probie. I fought Probert fourteen times in my career. I didn't fight anyone else more than seven.

I was two months older than Probert, but he was already in his sixth NHL season when I brought my four games of NHL experience to the Blackhawks. I knew the book on Probert. He was kind of a wild, unorthodox puncher but really sturdy on his skates and he could last. Probie's fights were notoriously long. He might start slowly, but soon you would find yourself trying to defend against a relentless flurry of punches that didn't lose steam until you could find a way to tie him up. Or until somebody went down.

Bob's power hand was his right. But he was pretty good with both. Hit him in the face if you could—it didn't really seem to faze him early in his career. Tying up his right hand was a good place to start, but good luck with that—he had great balance, so grappling with him was not for the faint of heart. I figured the best strategy was to get busy with my right hand and make him play defence. Not exactly a risk-free approach, because he was busy and good with both hands. But you don't fight Bob Probert and expect not to get clipped from time to time.

I was in Chicago for a month or two before I fought Probie. We'd played each other once or twice, but nothing materialized. Those games were close, and the situation didn't warrant it. But the third time, Detroit was getting the best of us. We were down by a few, and Keenan kept putting me out there. The time was right.

I came off the bench in the third while Probie was out there and I made my way toward him on the ice. As I glided up beside him, it was fairly obvious I wasn't there to exchange brownie recipes. Bob needed no encouragement and we got started. We stayed close to get the right angle for leverage, then stepped back and started firing. Bob got out of his jersey early on—a big advantage to him, because I had nothing to hold on to. At that point I was just trying to control him, looking for opportunity to return fire. I'd say it was a draw. He wrestled me to the ice once, and I had him down once. He landed a few, and so did I.

But there was more to the scrap than the question of who landed on top of whom when we went down. It was an important moral victory for the Blackhawks. Their guy neutralized Bob Probert.

Steve Thomas and I were watching the fight on a loop the next day. Stumpy was a skill guy, but he was a tough kid and he appreciated what goes into a heavyweight bout. We were going through the play blow by blow, and soon other guys were clustering around. I could tell that my stock as a Blackhawk was rising when Steve said, "You did great; that's one of the best in the business!"

—

Chicago fans remember my tough guy moments, but my favorite Windy City experience was my first NHL goal because it was connected to the birth of my first child, Erin.

In today's NHL, it's an expectation that a father will be in the delivery room with his wife even if his team is in Philadelphia, Winnipeg, or Las Vegas. So it's difficult to believe that I was in danger of missing my daughter's birth. In my early years in the NHL, players weren't present for the births of children if the schedule didn't co-operate. I wouldn't have thought to ask Keenan for a couple days off in 1991 as we headed to Pittsburgh because my wife might give birth that day. So that's where I was when I received the call that Pam had gone into labour. Pittsburgh.

What I was supposed to do was go to the rink and try to focus on the possibility that I was going to have to tangle with Jay Caufield, Jeff Chychrun, or someone else for that matter. What I did do was go to the rink and worry about my wife and fret about the possibility of missing my child's birth.

That game was an emotional roller-coaster ride for me as I tried to concentrate on what was going on out on the ice while wondering whether I would get back to Chicago in time. I've never been in a game where the clock moved slower. It ended in a 4–4 tie, and thankfully a tie was a tie in those days. No overtime.

As it turned out, our doctor understood our circumstances and he was able to temporarily slow Pam's labour down. I made it home and was there the day after the game when sweet Erin arrived at Hinsdale General Hospital on October 23, 1991.

But that's only half the story. We played the Calgary Flames the next day. I was drained but still on an emotional high after welcoming our first into the world. Every parent understands the feeling. You are exhausted, overjoyed, thankful, anxious—it's impossible to describe the wide range of emotions that are swirling inside you.

But as an elite athlete you know that even if that's where your head is, your training and focus will kick in. I suppose that's what happened the next night against the Flames. I was playing on a line with my boyhood idol John Tonelli. John passes the puck to our defenceman Steve Konroyd, who took a shot from the point. I happened to be cruising through the deep slot when Calgary goaltender Mike Vernon kicked out a big fat rebound right in front of me. I didn't even have time to think, I just banged the puck through his pads. Lo and behold . . . my first NHL goal comes just 24 hours after my first child is born! There might be something to this whole fatherhood thing.

(Keenan had played me thirty-five games the previous season and I had managed one assist.)

As soon as I had the first-goal puck in my hands, I knew where it was headed. It wasn't going on the mantle. I took it with me to the hospital and placed it on my wife's bed. First gift to my first-born. Pretty cool moment. I think Pam was more moved than I was. Today, my daughter still has that puck.

Retired Blackhawks goalie Darren Pang, a close friend, was working on the Blackhawks radio broadcasts back then. Darren interviewed me live on air after the game and Panger was nearly as excited as I was about this moment. Darren was thoughtful enough to make a cassette recording of the interview. He handed it to me the next day at the rink. The label read "Stu Grimson's Big Day!"

—

The only negative aspect of my time in Chicago was the team's squandered opportunity to win a Stanley Cup in 1991–92.

We were such a confident group by the time we reached the Stanley Cup Final that we never entertained the thought that we might lose to the Penguins. We entered the championship series on an eleven-game winning streak, coming off series sweeps against the Detroit Red Wings and the Edmonton Oilers.

In those eleven games, we had outscored our opponents 45–22. We were feeling invincible. The sweep against the Red Wings was particularly meaningful because we were 1–5–2 against Detroit during the regular season. We weren't just winning—we were dominating. It felt as if we could score five or more goals every night.

Our view of the Penguins was that they were an offensive team that couldn't stand up to our toughness and checking. We had both finished with eighty-seven points in the regular season. They had led the NHL in scoring with an average of 4.28 goals per game. But we ranked No. 2 in the league with a 2.95 goals-against average. We were from Chicago, where Mike Ditka's Bears had won a Super Bowl with a mean, relentless defence. We were going to embrace a similar strategy to win a title in hockey.

As a group, we were gathering steam and building momentum as we drove through the playoffs. We had created a buzz in the city and around hockey with how well we were playing. Rob Brown was playing for Chicago in 1991–92. Brownie had played for Pittsburgh a couple of seasons before and he had lived with the same family that Jaromir Jagr had been living with his first couple years in Pittsburgh. NHL clubs will sometimes place younger players in private homes as they transition from amateur straight to major pro hockey at a young age.

Brownie's former host family relayed some inside intel that had our group buzzing going into the series. Apparently, Jagr had mentioned to his host family that he didn't look forward to playing Chicago in the Finals. According to Brownie, Jaromir was saying the Blackhawks were a very physical team and he doesn't like to be hit. Part of our game plan included playing Jaromir physically in order to get him out of his game.

Spoiler alert . . . guess what? It doesn't matter.

I remember watching us build a 4–1 first-period lead in Game 1 of the Stanley Cup Finals that year. I was on the bench thinking, *Is it really going to be this easy?*

Turns out, it wasn't. Rick Tocchet scored for Pittsburgh, followed by goals by Mario Lemieux and Jagr. That tied the score. Then Lemieux scored again to win the game with seventeen seconds remaining in regulation.

In the throes of that horrific lead reversal, Keenan orchestrated another of the more surreal moments I have witnessed in my career. Moments after the Penguins had tied it at 4–4, Mike was totally exasperated on the bench. "That's it . . . I don't give a fuck. The next five guys who wanna play, go ahead."

As Mike spoke, I was sitting between my two linemates Jocelyn Lemieux and Mike Peluso. I looked right and then left and I hopped over the boards. I knew the old man was pissed and we may not have been his first choice to be out there but I wasn't saying no to a turn in the Finals. Our line had played sparingly to this point in the game.

The face-off is in our end. Who does Penguins coach Scotty Bowmam, send out but the other Lemieux—Mario—plus Ron Francis, Jaromir Jagr, Larry Murphy, and Ulf Samuelsson. Francis strips Jocelyn on the draw clean and the puck goes back to the point immediately. Samuelsson fires a heavy slapper into the traffic at the net and Eddie Belfour makes a great save and shuts the whole play down. The entire ordeal may have taken three seconds to play out. I looked back to our bench and Keenan is motioning for the three of us to get the hell off the ice.

He had either regained his composure or he'd decided his psychological ploy wasn't going to work if our line was going to jump on the ice. In any case, he'd seen enough.

Can you imagine though?! "The next five guys who wanna play, go ahead." In the Stanley Cup Finals!? It's not as glamorous as you think, folks.

Ultimately, our plan to bang away at Jagr missed the mark because we couldn't get anywhere near him. He was just so elusive. His tying goal in Game 1 was spectacular. He weaved and bobbed his way through three Blackhawks before beating Ed Belfour on a backhander. Brent Sutter (yes, Darryl's brother; and yes, Darryl could be hard on Brent too) was one of the NHL's best checking centres, and Jagr turned him inside out on that play.

It was clear early in that game that we weren't going to be able to intimidate him or knock him off his game. He was as strong on the puck as anyone in the game.

Game 2 didn't go any better for us. In fact, it went worse. The Penguins built a 3–1 second-period lead and then shut us down. We managed only nineteen shots on goal against Barrasso.

The Penguins won the game 3–1 and then beat us twice in Chicago to sweep the series. That gave the Penguins eleven wins in a row. I believe hard work can conquer skill if the skilled athletes believe they can win on skill alone. But when I look back at this series, what I see is us overwhelmed by a superior force, a team with more skill than we realized at the time. Lemieux. Jagr. Francis. Paul Coffey. Larry Murphy. Tom Barrasso. Tocchet. Time has proven that team was a full stride ahead of where we were in 1991–92.

That analysis doesn't make the loss any easier to take. You don't get many chances to win it all, and I'm always going to look at that series as one where we failed to make the most of a great opportunity. We didn't return to the Stanley Cup in 1993. In fact, we were swept by the St. Louis Blues in the opening round.

In better news, Hawks' general manager Bob Pulford gave me a new three-year contract that would pay me $300,000 per year starting the following season. I joked to the media that it felt like a "lifetime contract."

After the deal was announced, we played in Vancouver and my former Regina general manager, Bob Strumm, was there, as were my mom and dad. When Strumm saw Stan Grimson in the stands, he went to see him. He remembered that my father had said that he wasn't going to allow Strumm to turn me into a "goon."

"I guess he can't be a tough guy for $125 per week, but he can do it for $300,000 per season," Strumm said with a laugh. Dad laughed too, and they shared a handshake. My dad thanked Strumm for what he did for me.

After the 1992–93 season, Pam and I concluded the Chicago area was a good place to raise a family. We enjoyed living in the Chicago area. I had played seventy-eight games that season and it seemed as if I was as established with the Blackhawks as I could be.

During the previous season, my teammates Troy Murray and Warren Rychel had been traded to the Winnipeg Jets in the trade that brought in Bryan Marchment and Chris Norton. When Murray left town, Pam and I began renting his townhouse for $1000 per month.

We began to think that Chicago would be our permanent home. By then, we had been married three years and had Erin. At twenty-seven, I was finally going to be making NHL money. We were probably overdue to buy a home, and that seemed like the next logical step for our growing family.

It sure seemed as if the Blackhawks viewed me as important to their present and future. Keenan thought enough of me that he had protected me the previous summer during the expansion draft. The Blackhawks lost Mike Peluso to the Ottawa Senators and Dan Vincelette to the Tampa Bay Lightning.

Another expansion draft was coming in the summer of 1993. The NHL Board of Governors approved the Florida Panthers' admission and the Disney Corporation's plan to put a team in Anaheim. When Disney received permission to name the team the Mighty Ducks after the movie, I can remember players laughing about it in the dressing room. Players thought the team would end up the laughing stock of the NHL.

"You can't be serious," I said. "Can you imagine playing for a team named the Mighty Ducks?" I felt as though I could joke about it then because I was fairly confident I would be protected again.

Pam and I wanted to look for houses as soon as the season was over. However, my agent, Buddy Meiers, raised the caution flag. "Don't buy a house yet," he said. "Let's get through the expansion first and then re-evaluate." Best advice I ever got from an agent.

On June 24, 1993, I was lounging at our cottage in Kenora, Ontario, when the phone rang. Buddy Meiers was calling to inform me that I had been selected by the Anaheim Ducks in the expansion draft. My Chicago teammate, defenceman Milan Tichý, was taken by the Florida Panthers.

So much for our plans to buy a home in Chicago.

When the shock of being snatched up by an oddly named expansion team wore off, I began to see my pending move as a great opportunity. When Pam and I had fully analyzed the pros and cons of where I was headed, we began to see the sunshine. We were going to Southern California. Plus, I was going to a new team where, theoretically, everybody was bound to get more responsibility. Anaheim may not have had the depth Chicago could boast, but that meant more ice time. I took note that Peluso had played more when he went from Chicago to Ottawa in the expansion draft. I expected that would be the case for me in Anaheim. As saddened as I was to leave Chicago, maybe my new situation would present a better fit.

However, the Blackhawks' decision to leave me unprotected brought home the reality that tough guys are transient workers in the NHL. It was naive to believe that I had established myself with the Blackhawks to the point of being considered an essential employee. The truth was, and still is today, that enforcers are very expendable, regardless of how well they perform in their job. We're treated like any other third- or fourth-liner, even if we're well known. Fans may fall in love with tough guys, but the truth is NHL GMs view us as interchangeable parts.

You rarely see enforcers enjoy long careers with just one team. I was a loyal employee everywhere I played, always willing to fulfill the expectations of my role, but at the end of the day when my career was over, I had played for eight different NHL teams. I didn't know that when I headed for Anaheim, though. I just knew that I might play more minutes, and that I wasn't going to buy a house.

8

MUSCULAR
WATERFOWL

The average Canadian family eats 3.2 boxes of Kraft Dinner every year (that's Kraft Macaroni & Cheese for my American readers). That's over ninety million boxes a year. So getting your photo on a box of KD may not have the same prestige as appearing on a box of Wheaties. But it's pretty cool.

It's even better if you're wearing a "C" in that photo. When I arrived in Anaheim, a couple of reporters suggested I might be named captain of the new franchise. While I would have loved to wear the "C," I knew that I may not have been the ideal candidate. A captain needs strong leadership skills, plus an ability to set the tone—and I figured I checked those boxes. But he must also be able to lead by example, and that means he needs to be on the ice enough to show those traits and to talk to the refs. I just didn't log enough minutes to fit the job description. Troy Loney was the Mighty Ducks of Anaheim's first captain. It was a good choice. He was one of the older guys on the team, and leadership came easy for him. He spoke up at the right times. I was, however, proud to be awarded an "A" as an alternate captain. It was the only time in my NHL career that I consistently wore a letter on my jersey.

Visual evidence does, however, exist to prove that I was captain of the Mighty Ducks—at least for a brief moment. Unbeknownst to us players, the Kraft company had sent a photographer to one of our pre-season games that first year with an assignment to snap a photo of an identifiable Mighty Duck to include on the back of boxes of Kraft Dinner in Canada.

At that point, coach Ron Wilson had not decided who would be the team's captain. He was rotating the rank among several players, and that night it happened to be my turn. That's the reason why, when Kraft Dinner boxes appeared on store shelves later that season, some of them had a photo of me in my Ducks uniform wearing the "C."

No one enjoyed seeing me on those boxes of KD more than a guy named Bill Tibbs. He has since passed away, but Bill was a good friend. We bonded through our shared profession of hockey. Bill never played in an NHL game, but he was with the Detroit Red Wings' organization in the 1950s. He played in the International Hockey League and the American.

He won the IHL's James Norris Trophy for having the league's lowest goals-against average. He also owned an accomplishment that I wanted and never achieved: Bill had his name engraved on the Stanley Cup in 1952 when he served as Terry Sawchuk's backup.

Backups didn't even sit on the bench in those days. Bill

practised with the Red Wings, but when the games were played he'd sit in the stands. But the Red Wings respected his contributions enough to make sure his name was immortalized on the Cup.

Because of an important connection we shared, Bill was very proud of my NHL accomplishments. In fact, one day found him on his hands and knees in an aisle in the Safeway supermarket in Winnipeg pulling boxes of KD off the bottom shelf.

Bill told this story with a big smile when he was alive. Some of the boxes had my photo on it and others did not. But Bill wanted only the ones with the photo of the Ducks' captain—me. That meant he had to inspect each and every box on the shelf. Apparently, Bill was so caught up in his mission that he didn't notice the crowd of people and shopping carts forming around him. I suspect they thought that if an older gentleman thought enough to drop down on all fours and root through the lowest shelf, there must be something of great value down there.

When Bill rose to his feet, turned around, and saw the crowd, he was a little surprised at the following he'd garnered. "Uhh, I'm a little low on Kraft Dinner," he mumbled, and walked away with an armload of every North American kid's favourite lunch.

What Bill didn't tell the small crowd of shoppers that had formed on this day was that he was my father-in-law.

—

I met Pam Tibbs during my time at the University of Manitoba. We first met at a "social"—a Canadian prairie tradition. When a couple is about to marry, the best man and maid of honour throw a bash. They rent a hall, hire a deejay, charge admission, and offer a cash bar. And all the proceeds go to the soon-to-be-married couple.

I went with my roommate, Lowes, and another teammate named Rick Strachan whom we both knew from the WHL.

Strachan had played for the Winnipeg Warriors. Strachan's sister Angie was there with her close friend Pam, and we all ended up at the same table. The odd thing is that neither Pam nor Bobby nor I knew the bride or the groom. I wouldn't have guessed that the young woman sitting beside me would end up being my wife and the mother of my four children.

We weren't at the social long. The group of us headed out to a little bar just off the U of M campus called Strawberry's. That's where Pam and I really started talking. Like all undergraduates, we talked about our classes. Unlike any undergraduate I'd ever met, her father had his name on the Stanley Cup. So we had a lot to talk about. Then and for the next twenty-six years of our lives together. Pam and I were married at the St. Charles Country Club in Winnipeg, Manitoba, on June 4, 1988.

—

Suiting up for any NHL team is an honour. Working for the Mouse just added a layer of amusement park fun to the experience. Playing for the Disney-owned Mighty Ducks of Anaheim in their inaugural season in 1993–94 was like living in a wonderland. Every day was a fresh adventure. My first year with the Ducks may have been the most enjoyable season I ever had in the NHL. Riding on a float down Main Street at Disneyland. Mickey, Goofy, Pluto, and the gang in the wives' room at the rink. Silver passes allowed the players and our families free admission into the theme park any time we wanted to go. "It seemed like we were on a float every other day," former Ducks general manager Jack Ferreira recalled. "Guys said we had more parades than the Montreal Canadiens."

One time, Disney was opening the new "Indiana Jones" ride and invited the Mighty Ducks to come to the park and test it before it was opened to the public. We must have ridden it ten times. Nobody enjoyed it more than Ron Wilson, our coach. He was like a wide-eyed kid in a candy store, grinning the whole time we were riding.

A hockey nerd and student of the game, Ron would often be seen with VHS tapes, running in and out of offices, really hard working. I liked Ron. If he needed to crack the whip, he could, but he was kind of a peer. He rubbed some guys the wrong way. Video packages of positive stuff. Correction by video, nearly every day in front of the monitor breaking down tape, on its own very helpful; second component, positive pump-up tapes, winning battles, scoring goals, maybe a fight, careful to make sure everyone was featured. Great for confidence during lean stretches. Exceeded expectations. He was younger and this was his first head coaching position. So Ron leaned on some of the vets for leadership.

Anaheim may not have been a traditional hockey market, but the residents of Orange County embraced us right away. Former major league catcher Jim Campanis, the son of noted Los Angeles Dodgers executive Al Campanis, was the sales manager of a Lincoln-Mercury dealership directly across the freeway from the Arrowhead Pond Arena in Anaheim. Jimmy asked me to come in to talk. I proposed to Jimmy that if they allowed me to use one of their cars, I'd be happy to appear in whatever form of advertising they wanted. Jimmy and the dealership were thrilled to work with one of the players from the area's new NHL team.

Better still, they were happy to extend the same deal to some of my teammates. When I brought my new car to the rink, the guys wanted the story. I told one or two of them about my new deal and the word spread around the dressing room fast; hockey players gossip like an old sewing circle. First one guy wanted me to introduce him to Campanis and the rest of the guys at the dealership. Then another. And another. And another still. Everyone in the dealership was so caught up in the excitement of having a new NHL team in the neighbourhood that Campanis and his owner couldn't say no. Before long, there were no fewer than eleven Ducks players driving big Continentals and Town Cars around SoCal. When we would show up for a team meeting or for a team function of some kind, the parking lot was full of the big dark sedans. It looked more like a meeting of the Orange County Mafia than it did a bunch of Ducks.

We had a practice rink a couple of miles from the Pond. We'd dress at the arena, putting on everything but our skates, and then pile into our Lincolns and drive over to the rink. It must have been a comical sight to see a parade of great big men, dressed in full gear, including helmets, driving these big Lincolns down the road in one long line. We had to have looked like a funeral procession out of Bizarro World.

Not that everything was easy. If you find it hard to imagine an NHL enforcer representing a Disney character, you're not alone. Three days after I had been drafted by the Ducks, Mike Kiley, writing for the *Chicago Tribune*, had planted seeds of doubt about whether I was going to fit in. The headline read: "Grimson a Misfit in Disney Picture."

The story went on: "Ex-Blackhawk Stu Grimson isn't the normal Disney material. He hits people until they bleed or fall. No Goofy pratfalls. When this Donald Duck blasts a chipmunk, the chipmunk stays down and sometimes needs medical aid." Lively copy unless you are the Donald Duck in question, worrying about job security.

The story's theme was that Disney was known for its G-rated image and my forty-four fighting majors from the previous two seasons in Chicago were for mature audiences only. The author even included a quote from Disney boss Michael Eisner saying the organization wouldn't be altering its wholesome image to accommodate its new NHL partnership. "No professional wrestling for us," Eisner said. "I don't disapprove of having people be competitive. But we are not going to have people who are insane." I did wonder if Eisner was talking about me.

If so, he might have been thinking about an incident back in Chicago that would never make its way into a kids' movie. The Leafs' Bob Halkidis jumped my teammate Bryan Marchment. Any hockey player will tell you there are some pretty firm rules about when to fight. Now, there had already been a few fights, and there were gloves and sticks all over the ice. And Marchment was no angel. But Marchment was coming back from a broken cheekbone and was wearing a visor. Halkidis ripped off his helmet and went at him.

It was bad enough that Halkidis was going after a vulnerable guy. What made it worse was that he was trying to provoke me—and I was already beyond provoked. Wendel Clark had already speared Steve Larmer and referee Dan Marouelli had prevented me from settling the score. As Keenan and a couple of teammates tried to restrain me from going back into the fray, I could see what was going on at centre ice between Marchment and Halkidis. I was pointing at Halkidis, saying, "Don't touch him." Of course, he went ahead and started in on Marchment. I couldn't tolerate it. I snapped.

I received a ten-game suspension for abuse of officials for my attempts to get at Halkidis. Half the players on the ice tried to intercept me. I took a swing at Lucien DeBlois when he tried to intercept me, and Doug Gilmour tackled me from behind. When I got back up, linesman Ray Scapinello got between me and Halkidis and kept me tied up. After all that, I never did lay a hand on Halkidis.

As ugly as the incident was, you have to agree that my heart was in the right place. I was sticking up for a vulnerable teammate, and that's how my teammates saw it. Back then, the league did not enforce the rule that suspended players had to pay their own fines or forgo salary. If a player was penalized for something he'd done for a teammate, the team had his back. The Blackhawks did the right thing; I didn't lose a cent.

But now the question was, would that night come back to haunt me? Kiley's article gave me reason to be somewhat worried. The Grim Reaper wasn't exactly a hand-in-glove fit with Snow White and her Seven Dwarfs. But I'm primarily a positive person, and when I arrived in Anaheim, I viewed it more as an opportunity than as a downturn in my career. Even though I didn't initially like the idea of naming an NHL team after a kids' movie, I always believed an opportunity with an expansion team would allow me a framework to expand my role. Wearing a letter certainly helped put most of my concerns to rest.

Besides, it wasn't as though the league was going to alter its rules to accommodate the Disney brand. I wasn't the only tough guy in the league. I wasn't even the only tough guy on my team. That's just the way expansion worked then. No new team is going to have top-end skill, because no established team is going to leave top-end skill exposed in the draft. So new teams aren't going to beat anyone by shooting the lights out. If they want to get respect, they're going to have to get it the old-fashioned way.

They're going to have to win puck battles, they're going to have to go hard to the net, they're going to have to work their tails off, and they're going to have to stand their ground. And they're never going to get a night off. That was the way I played the game.

And the room was full of guys like that. Ferreira also made it clear that he was going to have a tough team. "One thing I learned when I was in San Jose is that you had to have an identity," Ferreira said. "The reason I wanted to have tough players is that when you are an expansion team you get no respect. You don't get the best referees. No one pays attention to you. I wanted our identity to be that we were going to be tough. We weren't going to go looking for it, but we were not going to back down." It's not easy to get respect in the NHL. Ferreira recalled that even in the Ducks' third season, a top referee showed up in Anaheim and pointed out it was the first time he had been there. No respect.

That's why Ferreira had drafted me and traded for Todd Ewen. He gave up a third-round pick, a major give for an expansion team, to the Montreal Canadiens to land Ewen and Patrik Carnback. Ferreira believed he needed to create respect for his team by making sure the Mighty Ducks wouldn't be pushed around on the ice.

I wasn't present for the expansion draft of 1993 but when Ferreira announced the Ducks were selecting me with the 28th pick in the draft, the move sparked an audible buzz in the room. The Mighty Ducks were announcing in no uncertain terms that they weren't going to be pushed around in their first year. I mean, Jack took me ahead of guys like Terry Yake—who would go on to be our leading scorer that year.

Disney was proud of its wholesome, family image and required its employees to be the clean-cut public face of this image. But even Mickey Mouse would rather fight and win than get pushed around. Eisner was so careful about giving Ferreira freedom to do what he needed to do that he would call and ask Ferreira's permission before he would enter the dressing room after a game.

Even though the Los Angeles Kings were nearby, we were a fresh market with a fan base that would be learning about the game as we played it. What we know is that the most memorable moments in every game in the 1990s were goals, saves, and fights. I was going to be the man in those fights they were remembering. Even if you don't believe fighting has a place in hockey, you have to admit that no one looks away when a fight starts. Fans love it. Because the role is easily identifiable, I thought fans would embrace me. And they did.

Even if you didn't fully appreciate the finer points of hockey, you understood what it meant to be tougher than your opponent. In that sense, Anaheim fans were no different from fans around the league. I used to love playing in the old Chicago Stadium. It was dark and smoky, and rock-concert loud. The seating was so steep it felt as though the fans were hovering right over the ice, and the ancient pipe organ provided the perfect soundtrack to old-time hockey. But fans jumped out of their seats in the bright, clean, modern Arrowhead Pond when the gloves came off. They may not have been the most sophisticated fans at first, but they understood the game the way I played it. I heard my name a lot from the crowd when things got physical while I was on the ice. It came across as a low roar, and our marketing department capitalized on the phenomenon. The team store produced a t-shirt with an explanation to the uninitiated: "We're not Booing, we're Stu-ing."

—

We played the Detroit Red Wings on October 9, 1993, in the first game in Mighty Ducks history. We lost 7–2. But the game included yet another installment in the Grimson vs. Probert series.

In the first period, I received double roughing penalties for trying to mix it up with Bob. There was no question I wanted to make this night memorable for the fans.

In the third period, we fought, and I probably got the better of Bob in this one. Even fans in our new market knew he was a badass and that he was among the best, if not king of the NHL fighters. I came at him and knocked him down. He had no choice but to engage at that point. We both gave and got, but I landed a couple of rights that I knew our fans appreciated. The Mighty Ducks didn't come away with a W that night, but when the fans walked out of the Pond, they probably remembered that their guy took on the league's heavyweight champ and represented well.

Just as Ferreira planned, the Ducks were a tough team. In our first season, Todd Ewen had thirty-one fights and 272 penalty minutes, while I had twenty-three fights and 199 penalty minutes.

Ewen and I became the best of friends. We sat beside each other in the dressing room and played on the same line. We provided tag-team toughness. Paying homage to the Disney connection, *Calgary Herald/Hockey News* cartoonist Dave Elston did a takeoff on the Disney characters Huey, Dewey, and Louie by creating the rebranded crew of Huey, Stuey, and Ewie. It made us all laugh.

Todd was so unique; there was never a dull day with Ewey in the room. He had a crazy hobby of sculpting with hockey tape. He spent countless hours designing helmets, animals, and player and goalie masks out of tape. I remember one helmet design he did with a detailed Ducks logo on it. You can say it was a quirky hobby, but these were true works of art.

One of the funniest moments of that inaugural season involved Todd and his son Chad, who was about four at the time.

Minutes before game time, we were all sitting at our lockers during the home dressing time. This is the time players do their final game preparation. In the hockey world, this is a sacred and solemn moment. This is a players-only moment. This is a time when the club's leaders are the most vocal. It's their last opportunity to ensure that the group is focused; puck-drop lies just on the other side of this moment.

"We need a fast start; win a draw and let's get down to their end early."

"Keep it simple, finish every check." And so on.

My back was turned away from the door right beside my stall as I was talking with Todd about some aspect of the game. I realized at some point that he was looking right past me. Todd's eyes had turned toward the centre of the room and his head dropped. I turned to see his son Chad standing all alone at the centre of the room with his hand outstretched. "Dad, can I get five dollars for a hot dog?" he asked.

The team came unglued; the entire room broke into laughter. It was the most hilarious dressing room moment I have ever experienced. Todd sheepishly got up, grabbed Chad's hand, and escorted him out of the room.

We later learned that Chad had been working his mother, Kelli, in the wives' room and she wasn't giving him what he wanted. That's when he decided to take matters into his own hands and to go see his dad. Ewen was always a soft touch. And the most logical place for Chad to go to find his dad was right next door to the wives' room, in the team dressing room—where he had been dozens of times before.

I told that story in St. Louis as Terry Yake and I eulogized Todd in September, 2016. Todd's friends and family who had gathered to pay their respects seemed to appreciate a little levity. I believe Todd would have liked that also; he loved his family and he loved to laugh.

He was a wonderful spirit and a free thinker. We miss you dearly old friend.

—

I have a difficult time deciding which of my NHL teams was most meaningful to me because they were all different. But unquestionably my family enjoyed my career the most when I was working for the Mouse.

Pam was pregnant when I joined the Mighty Ducks. When she gave birth to our second daughter, the organization called Hannah "The first Mighty Duckling." She wears this distinction like a badge of honour even today. The organization was so good to us at the time. Pam's hospital room was full of flowers and stuffed animals to celebrate our second child.

Todd Ewen wrote a children's book and Disney published it through its Hyperion publishing company. Everything about the organization was fun- and family-oriented. Disney asked the players to do plenty of promotion for the team and for hockey in Southern California, but the company treated us amazingly well in return.

The fan base in Anaheim treated the players like family. Even today, I still keep in touch with some of the fans I met while I was playing there. Ruth DeSilva had season tickets behind the player's bench from day one.

What she didn't know when she bought them was that they would be "obstructed view" when I was dressed to play. I had a habit of standing behind the bench when I wasn't on the ice. Since I usually spent only a few minutes on ice per game, she had no view of the neutral zone for more than fifty minutes every home game.

If it upset her, she never showed it. She seemed to enjoy the novelty of having me posted up in front of her. Hopefully I at least kept her entertained with my in-game commentary.

She still has those tickets today, and they are no longer classified as obstructed views. I text with her now and then and I stop by her seats to say hi when I'm in town for a game. Ruth is a sweet lady and a dear friend. The Ducks have no follower who is more devoted than Ruth. She is an institution around the Pond.

—

The team's toughness helped us in the standings. We weren't intimidated by any opponent and we ended up winning more games than anyone anticipated.

Our record was 33–46–5—no NHL expansion team had won that many games in its first season. It was a record that stood for twenty-four years until the Vegas Golden Knights had their spectacular expansion season.

One reason why we were better than past expansion teams was that we didn't act like an expansion team. In fact, Wilson instituted fines for any player or coach who used the term "expansion team" to describe us.

Although we didn't talk about being an expansion team, we did rally around the idea that we were all castoffs, players that our previous teams had deemed expendable. The reason we were Mighty Ducks was that our previous team didn't want us.

It's fascinating how playing these motivational tricks can spike performance levels. We talked like we had to prove something every game, and we always seemed to play as if our careers depended upon the outcome. I believe we surprised a lot of teams in terms of how competitive we were—like a November road trip that year when we won four consecutive games against Vancouver, Edmonton, Calgary, and Winnipeg.

The funny story on that trip was that Ferreira was supposed to join us, but team issues delayed his departure from Anaheim. He missed the game in Vancouver. He tried to get to the game in Edmonton, but he couldn't get there on time.

He called Wilson and said, "I will definitely be there for the game in Calgary."

"No, don't come," Wilson said. "I don't want you to jinx us. We are winning without you."

With Ferreira staying in Anaheim, we won all four games. I'm surprised Wilson let him make another trip.

The other factor that made the Ducks special was the players in the dressing room.

The way the draft was set up in 1993 was that all existing teams were allowed to protect one goalie, five defencemen, and nine forwards. All first-year and second-year pros on the reserve list were exempt.

What that means is that the Ducks and Panthers were primarily going to get third-pairing defencemen and bottom-six forwards.

That seems like a bad situation until you consider that most NHL teams fill those positions with hard-working players who are really rich in character. In addition to making sure his team was tough, Ferreira seemed to pick one of the more respected pros on every team.

Sean Hill. Bob Corkum. Bobby Dollas. Joe Sacco. Bill Houlder. Todd Ewen. Ron Tugnutt. Guy Hebert. We didn't have a lot of stars, but we had good, solid pros who knew how they needed to play to help their team win.

Our dressing room was always buzzing on game days as the guys prepared to compete. We won more games than we should have because we were a tight-knit team.

—

During my second season with the Mighty Ducks, the owners and the NHL Players' Association attempted to negotiate a new collective bargaining agreement.

No one expected talks to go well, and they didn't. The owners locked us out. In anticipation of that happening, I moved my family to Winnipeg. We owned a house in the city and had a cottage two hours east of there. Additionally, Pam's family lived in the city so retreating to Winnipeg was a great way to live less expensively and close to family at a time when returning to play was uncertain. There was a legitimate concern that the season may be lost entirely.

Because I was in the last season of my contract, I didn't want to sign another year's lease in Anaheim when it was possible the season could be cancelled.

Plus, I didn't know whether I would still be in Anaheim after this season. My agent, Larry Kelly, and I had preliminary talks with Ferreira about a new deal, and we didn't have the sense that my contract number in Anaheim would be as high as it might be elsewhere. After all, this was the Disney organization, and the Mouse was a well-known penny pincher.

The lockout lasted 103 days. We lost 43 percent of our pay. That was a lot of money for us. And keep in mind, most of the guys on the roster weren't all that highly paid, so we had to button down tight. But the union had communicated well in advance that we should be tucking money away to prepare for life without a paycheque. Also, the union had been preparing a war chest, and we all got a modest stipend of a few thousand dollars a month during the shutdown.

For the first few weeks, everyone stayed in town, hoping we'd be right back to work. But the longer it dragged on, the more anxious the players got. Partly it was the little things, but deep down I knew that some guys were worried about their careers. You've only got so many years in the league, and for most players it's not a lot. The average NHL career is only about five years long. Half of them last fewer than a hundred games. You work your whole life for a roster spot in the NHL. Then you get there and the league locks you out. It can gnaw at you. One day, Pam was talking to Steven King's fiancée. She had just bought a new trash can for their apartment—even back then this was a thirty-dollar item. Steve snapped at her that they already had two trash cans. An NHLer would not have been worrying about the sunk cost of trash cans in his household had he been playing hockey.

There were rumours that the league's stars were attempting to lobby the league through their agents in order to get a deal done. Sitting at home was costing some guys millions. But I can say I never saw any evidence of that type of backchannelling. We didn't have any elite level players with that sort of influence on our roster. But I had a reasonably good sense of what the players were thinking during those months.

I was the Ducks' union rep, along with Bob Corkum. We stayed pretty busy keeping in touch with our teammates, disseminating information and setting up meetings. I wasn't in the driver's seat by any means, but I wasn't just a passenger either. It would not have been healthy to be isolated with nothing to do. But the way it turned out, I found I was more and more engaged with the issues. Being involved as a player delegate to the union during this time was great insight into the way the league and the players' union interacted. Hearing the owners crying poor while franchise values continued to climb really galvanized my interest in union matters.

—

When we finally got back to work, the Mighty Ducks' second season didn't go nearly as well on the ice as the first. The schedule was reduced to forty-eight games, and we won just sixteen of them.

The only good news for the organization was that Paul Kariya decided to leave college early and play his rookie season in the lockout-shortened year. It was clear early on that Paul was going to be a difference-maker. He posted eighteen goals and thirty-nine points in forty-seven games for the NHL's worst-scoring team.

You could tell from the moment he took his first shift, Kariya would be our best player. He had breakaway speed to go with an exceptional shot and sixth-sense passing ability. His skill set stacked up with the NHL's best. But what separated Paul from the field was his focus. On game day, he was locked in. You could not reach him. There was no point in even attempting to talk to him if he was preparing to play. Before a game, he had nothing to say to anyone. You had more hope of conversation from a bag of potato chips than you had from Kariya. He was on his own island on game day and there was no ferry to Kariya Key. Better to save your breath than to run the risk of having a conversation where just one person does the talking.

Kariya's only flaw, if it can be called that, was that he was five-foot-ten, 185 pounds. I made it my business to look after him in his first season. I paid attention whenever he was on the ice. I took notes. I collected names.

But to be honest, Kariya was elusive to the point that he really didn't put himself in a vulnerable position very often. Part of his dominance came from finding seams in the defensive coverage where you couldn't stop him.

He could venture deep into the corners and somehow avoid the heavy-hitting defencemen. He ducked, side-stepped, and eluded everyone trying to stop him. It was if he had a cloaking device.

Once, when we were playing the San Jose Sharks, I decided to warn Kariya about my former teammate Bryan Marchment. Mush liked to crush speedsters in the open ice. Bad-boy Marchment was one of the league's heaviest and meanest hitters. He had also gained a reputation for hitting guys low, putting their knees in jeopardy.

I approached Kariya before the warm-up and advised him that Marchment was to be avoided at all costs. "There's not much I can do to discourage him from acting up," I told Kariya. "He's a pig. He will take you out for no good reason. That's his game. Do your best to stay on the other side of the ice and always be aware of where he is." Kariya didn't say a word. He just nodded, making it clear to me that he understood. And Marchment was never a factor.

Some stars would have avoided my advice, figuring they could dance their way out of trouble. Kariya wasn't like that. He didn't go anywhere near Marchment. He knew I wouldn't have warned him if Mush wasn't a threat. Kariya was as smart as he was talented.

The league needs more players like Paul Kariya, and I would like to think that I was helpful in opening up the ice for him a little. My job was to make it easier for him to play his game without fear of the Marchments of the world taking runs at him. He played the game beautifully, and that made him a magnet for other teams' thugs. I did my best to keep them at bay while Paul and I played together. I was fond of saying that "I created a safer work environment for my teammates." Paul got a kick out of that.

Paul also made his appreciation known. He had a deal with a local tailor, and he had a steady flow of bespoke suits. Paul told the tailor he had enough suits and he wanted the guys who looked after him to be looked after. He took me in with him and that's how I got my first custom suit—sort of the way Joe Montana used to buy gifts for his offensive linemen.

One of my favourite Kariya stories involves a random meeting at the Orange Hill restaurant in Orange, California. While out for dinner with Pam, I was headed to the restroom when I spotted Kariya dining with a date.

Seeing Kariya in public was a rare occurrence. Seeing Kariya in public with a date was an even rarer event. Paul was a very private person. He was as friendly as could be at the rink, but he didn't volunteer a lot of information about what he did away from the rink. He spoke less about who he dated.

I was like a bird enthusiast spotting his first blue-footed booby. I had to move in for a closer look. Grabbing a white cloth napkin from a vacant table, I draped it over my forearm and walked up to the table with the strikingly handsome couple.

"Good evening, my name is Stuart," I said. "I'll be your maître d' for the evening. If there is anything I can do to make your meal more enjoyable, please don't hesitate to ask."

The young lady with Paul had no idea that I was a total fraud, and she was perplexed to see that her date was spitting food because he was laughing uncontrollably.

The following day Paul had the entire dressing room in tears while he was retelling the story of the night before. The post-script of the tale is that Paul Kariya and Valerie Dawson, the young lady at the table in 1995, are still a couple today. Whenever I see them, I'm happy to take credit for "putting" them together. Proof that a quality maître d' at a quality restaurant can completely change your experience for the better.

—

In the second half of the 1994–95 season, Larry planted the seed in my head that our best move might be to seek a trade to a contending team before the trade deadline. That would give me time to establish my value with my new team and maybe parlay that into a multi-year contract. In the coming summer, my current deal was up and I would be a restricted free agent.

For an enforcer, landing with a contending team was a good path to getting fair value. That wasn't an easy strategy for me to embrace right off because I really liked my situation in Anaheim. I was popular with the fans and I was playing more than I did in Chicago. Plus, the playing environment was uniquely fun. I mean, who didn't like going to the rink in shorts in January?

But when Wilson started to play only one tough guy in each game—meaning that either Ewen or I would sit, I decided it might be time for a change. I went to see Ferreira and asked him for a trade. I told him that this had nothing to do with my role, the team, him, or coach Ron Wilson. I enjoyed playing in Anaheim. I tried to make it clear that this was strictly a business decision.

Ferreira was still pretty steamed and didn't want to lose me. "But if you don't want to be here," he said, "I will move you." The Red Wings had called about me the month before, but Ferreira had declined their offer. Given this new development, Jack called Detroit for a second pass at the conversation.

Two days before the April 7 trade deadline, Ferreira moved me to the Detroit Red Wings. The official deal had me, Mark Ferner, and a sixth-round draft pick going to Detroit for Mike Sillinger and Jason York. I should have been thrilled by the news. The Red Wings were the NHL's best team. Their owner, Mike Ilitch, had a reputation for paying top dollar to keep the players he wanted to keep. But I had mixed feelings. It was difficult to say goodbye to guys I had bled and sweated with for a year and a half.

"It put into my mind that there was the option for the team to leverage one of us," I told Robyn Norwood at the *L.A. Times*. "This team is growing, and they get two young players [in the trade]. I knew once they were content to go with Todd or myself this might happen."

Ferreira was classy right until the end, telling Norwood, "Stu does things for your team that don't show up in the statistics." Bobby Dollas thanked me for sticking up for him and for the team. "That earns a lot of respect in my book," he said.

Norwood wrote that I was the "heart, soul, and fist" of the Mighty Ducks. I was leaving a comfortable situation, loyal team-mates, and a fan base that appreciated what I offered. As I was packing up, I couldn't help but wonder if I was making the right decision.

9

SCOTTY THE MAD GENIUS

I never liked it when a coach directed me to fight. I figured I knew as well as anyone how to manage the physical side of a game. As well as anyone, that is, except my wife. As I've already mentioned, my wife, Pam, knew the game well. She had grown up around hockey, and she knew what she was talking about. But she rarely offered advice. Emphasis on "rarely."

As I was leaving for a game one fall afternoon in Detroit, she stood at the door, smiled as she kissed me goodbye, and said, "You think you might want to get into one tonight, Stu? It's been more than two weeks since you had a fight."

She was right. Pam had been a tough guy's spouse long enough to be concerned about my job security when I wasn't fighting much. Her cute advice that I drop the gloves with someone was a loving way to raise the issue about whether I might be traded.

A trade was the last thing either of us wanted. We loved living in Detroit. It was distressing to be wondering whether the team needed my services.

Tough guys didn't receive no-trade clauses. Ducks GM Jack Ferreira could have traded me anytime and anywhere. But he traded me at my own request and chose to send me to the NHL's most skillful team. The 1994–95 season was shortened to forty-eight games because of the lockout. But the Red Wings were considered the Stanley Cup favourite. Jack did me a solid and he was under no obligation to do so.

As much as I enjoyed playing for the Ducks, I viewed my family's move to Detroit as a chance to earn that Cup that I didn't win in Chicago. I was smitten with my new organization—a roster full of skilled players led by a legendary captain in Steve Yzerman and a very eccentric and cerebral coach in Scotty Bowman.

Throughout the 1980s and into the 1990s, the Red Wings had protected their stars with some of the league's roughest competitors. Steve Yzerman received plenty of space to work his magic because opponents quite reasonably feared Probert and Kocur. But Kocur had moved on, as tough guys do. Probie's case was a little different. He wasn't just another tough guy; he was an integral part of that Detroit team. But he was out of control. The Wings gave him all kinds of chances, but Bob had a hard time holding it together. When he crashed his motorcycle with booze and drugs in his system, they finally had to let him go. I know it must have been hard for them, and for Probie too. He signed with Chicago as a free agent in the summer of 1994.

I know Steve Yzerman lobbied management to bring in someone who could take care of things on the ice. When they decided to act, the choice for a tough guy came down to Tie Domi or me.

Bowman is usually a coach who knows who and what he wants. But in this situation, he elected to poll his leadership group from what I was told later. Based at least in part on the players' input, Scotty went out and made the deal for me. Reading between the lines, Domi came with baggage. I suspect I was believed to be a better fit.

I got a lot of affirmation out of it when my new teammates told me that story. In pro hockey, like any other walk of life, reputation matters. Being a good teammate and having a willingness to put the club first goes a long way. Anyone who had bothered to call players or coaches from my previous teams would have learned that I knew my role. I took great pride in being the sort of teammate who included everyone and at the same time, would hold others accountable. By the second half of my career, I was one part big brother and one part an extension of the coaching staff.

And for what it's worth, I know that added a couple years to my career at a minimum.

It's difficult to describe how excited I was to join a dressing room that included Yzerman, Sergei Fedorov, Nicklas Lidstrom, Mark Howe, and Paul Coffey. I believe "smitten" might be the right word. I was smitten with the idea of being on the NHL's best team.

On my first road trip with the Red Wings, Yzerman, the team's captain, went out of his way to sit next to me on the bus to the hotel in Toronto. That's leadership. It isn't always about standing in the middle of the dressing room and making speeches like you're some reincarnation of Knute Rockne. Sometimes leadership is simply about making the new guy feel comfortable. As a leader, you want new players invested in the team as soon as possible. A captain like Steve realizes that a new teammate—especially one that he was drafted with all the way back in 1983—is quicker to make that investment when he feels as though he belongs.

The truth is I didn't need much help getting fired up, though. I joined the team on the road, so I played three or four games before I made my debut as a Red Wing at Joe Louis Arena in Detroit. Remember, previously this was Bob Probert's barn. I wanted the fans to know that I could be every bit as physical as Bob, and aimed to make an impression. San Jose was in town, and I went at it with Jeff Odgers, Jim Kyte, and exchanged a few bombs with Shawn Cronin before the officials broke up what would have been my third bout. The building was absolutely electric; Wings fans love a good tilt. Never mind three from the same Wing in the same game!

But not long after I joined the team, I discovered Bowman was lukewarm about using me as a true weapon. He liked having me as a deterrent, but was reluctant to push the launch button. There were red flags right away. Not long after my trade to Detroit, the Red Wings had a three-game Western road trip to San Jose, Los Angeles, and Winnipeg.

I thought I might have a busy evening against the Kings. They had a tough team. Troy Crowder and Matt Johnson were on the Kings that season and they were both throwing their weight around. Johnson had played just fourteen games and posted 102 penalty minutes.

But under Bowman's orders, assistant coach Dave Lewis came up to me and told me that I wasn't going to play against the Kings. He said I could fly to Winnipeg early and go see my family. We had lived up there during the lockout.

"You'll play in Winnipeg," Lewis said.

I was stunned. I was thinking, *The Kings have these two huge knuckleheads to deal with and you just acquired a tough guy. Why wouldn't you want to have him in the lineup?*

But I'm a loyal soldier. I didn't say a word. I appreciated the opportunity to see my family. But the way Bowman deployed me was peculiar to say the least. I had only two fights in the eleven regular-season games I played for Detroit in 1994–95. During my career, I fretted about coaches ordering me to fight. But I had the opposite problem when I played for Bowman. I had to worry that I would fight when he didn't want me to fight.

One night, we were in Montreal and Donald Brashear was running around. I was making my way over to Big Brash. We were circling each other, ready to go, when I heard the Scotty shouting from the bench.

"Stuey, *don't!*"

It was a maddening situation for a tough guy. Bowman wanted me in that role, but he didn't want me to play that role. It put me in a quandary. How did I protect my teammates, fulfilling my duties, without getting into a scrape with anyone? When I played for Bowman, I could go two or three weeks without a fight. Once, I went a month between fights. In the beginning, if I'm being honest, Bowman's reluctance to allow me to play the way I always played was a welcome respite. I was playing two out of three nights on an elite team that rolled four lines. It was nice, for a short while, not to crack heads every other night.

But when even your wife is getting impatient for you to get back to work, you know the time has come. If it was obvious to Pam, she couldn't have been the only one to notice. It was a reality check.

I didn't get a chance to mix it up that night, as it turned out. But Pam didn't have to remind me. The Red Wings were on the road in New York a few nights later, and this was the type of team I needed to play in order to snap out of the funk I was in. First I got into it with Jeff Beukeboom. Jeff was a big, physical defenceman who could handle himself. He nailed Viktor Kozlov and then took a run at Sergei Fedorov. That was my signal. I connected twice pretty cleanly, and he got up bloody. But that set off a chain reaction, and next up on my dance card was Joey Kocur. Neither of us did much damage, but I figured that at least I had made a case for job security. At best, I had appeased my wife for the time being.

—

You can tell a lot about hockey from my relationship with Bob Errey. Bob and I more or less shared a roster spot. We were never in the lineup the same night. So you'd think that would set us up for a bitter rivalry, when you consider the money and the pride that's at stake. But that wasn't the case at all.

Bob was a great guy. Great sense of humour, a great voice in the room. He came over to the Wings from Pittsburgh, where he had been part of their Cup runs in the early nineties. He and Paul Coffey were really the only guys in the room with Stanley Cup experience, and a lot of the Wings looked to them for leadership. Winning consistently is something a team has to learn; Bob and Paul were great teachers. And it wasn't so much an oral lesson; they did what they did day by day and the rest of us tried to model their example.

Bob wasn't a huge guy, he didn't have the hands of a forty-goal scorer, and he wasn't an elite playmaker. But he played with this hard physical edge that was an important part of our identity. Sure, during this period, the Wings boasted the skill and finesse of several future legends. But another important part of what made us hard to play against was the presence of guys like Errey, McCarty, Konstantinov, Draper, and Maltby.

I'm not sure how it works in other sports, but it seems to me that the relationship between two guys like Bob and me tells you a lot about what it takes to be part of a team. Even though it would seem we had every incentive to be rivals, we never were. It was never a source of tension between me and Bob. For one thing, it's just the right thing to do. That's part of being a pro. For another, if you're viewed as a guy who allows something like that to become a source of tension in the room, no one wants you around. Far better to be inclusive than divisive, in terms of the impact you had inside that room. That's just the way hockey works.

Scotty Bowman could say, or do, things that were brilliant and he could say, or do, things that would make your head spin. More than any other coach I ever had, Bowman knew the value of his assistant coaches. They were his only channel for communicating with his players.

One night versus the Leafs, I was chasing Domi around on the ice, trying to draw Tie into a fight. In spite of my good intentions, I completely ignored my defensive responsibility. I was the left winger in our left-wing lock system but, on this occasion, the left wing came unhinged. I went crashing around deep inside the Toronto zone trying to get a piece of Domi. I knew I was in the wrong positionally but I assumed all would be forgiven if I tore a strip off Tie.

When I get back to my seat on the bench, Lewis is standing right behind me. Bowman is standing next to him. Their shoulders are touching. That puts Scotty about half a metre from me. He could have whispered and I would have heard him.

Most coaches would have tapped me on the shoulder and given me an earful directly about the bad read I had just made. But that wasn't Bowman's style. Instead, he talked to Lewis about me.

"Dave," he says, "Stuey can't do that. That's no good. That's not the play. You gotta tell him. He can't do that again. That's no good."

I'm watching the exchange out of the corner of my eye as Dave Lewis nods. I turn to Dave who, of course, says nothing to me because I'm as close to Bowman as he is. I heard every word.

Unfortunately for me, I'm thinking more about Domi than Bowman. But Domi isn't making it easy for me. I keep chasing him and he keeps saying no. Meanwhile, Bowman's level of frustration is growing because I'm out of position yet again.

When I return to the bench, the same scenario plays out. Lewis is standing behind me and Bowman is right up in Lewis's space now. Both are directly behind me. "Dave," Bowman says, "he did it again. That's it. No more. He can't play anymore. That's no good. If he is going to play like that, he can't play anymore. Tell him, Dave. That's no good."

It was hilarious. He wouldn't talk to me; he would never speak to his players directly. He had to go through Lewis or Smith. And those moments happened every day with all of us. My centre and linemate Tim Taylor and I were constantly cracking one another up doing our best "Scotty" impressions. "Barry, that's no good. Tell him, Barry, he can't do that."

Everybody had a Bowman story. His eccentricities were constant fodder for player conversations. One night during a Wings' home game, I noticed Bowman fidgeting with his belt and looking down every several seconds. Lewis caught me watching Scotty.

"Is he doing what I think he's doing?" I asked Dave quietly.

Lewis nodded yes. "Oh yeah, he's checking his pager. He's checking for messages."

Imagine that. The best bench boss in the game and he's trying to keep up with folks trying to reach him while NHL hockey is racing back and forth in front of him. How you manage line changes and matchups while you're focused on your beeper is beyond me.

Another night, another Wings' home game is just under way, and Bowman is turned around with his back to the ice. I caught him staring into the stands for what seemed like an entire shift of hockey. Scotty eventually leaned over toward assistant coach Barry Smith to tap him on the shoulder. And now, with two thirds of the coaching staff with their backs to the play, Scotty asks, "Barry, who's sitting in my seats? I didn't give my seats away. What's going on up there? Barry, you need to straighten that out."

When I joined the Red Wings, the dressing room was a future wing of the Hockey Hall of Fame. The team had Yzerman, Coffey, Sergei Fedorov, Nicklas Lidstrom, Mark Howe, Dino Ciccarelli, and Slava Fetisov, who would all end up in the Hall. The following October, Bowman added one more when he traded for Igor Larionov.

With Larionov joining Fedorov, Fetisov, Vladimir Konstantinov, and Slava Kozlov, we had our own Russian neighbourhood within our dressing room. That's how the Russian Five was born. The Russians were known for playing five-man units in international tournaments, and Bowman decided the best way to maximize the impact of his Russians was to play them all together. That concept was foreign to the NHL. Still is today.

But it was the right decision for our Russians. Watching them play together was like listening to symphonic music. Their chemistry was perfect, their harmony exquisite. Everyone was on the same page, understanding precisely when it was their turn to claim the spotlight. It goes to show you that hockey is not just a game of beating the other guy one on one. It's about anticipation, and coordination, and the thousand things you do away from the puck.

Larionov was the conductor, and the rest of the Russian Five took their cues from him. He was an understated, soft-spoken, masterful centre. He moved the puck with patience and precision. From my seat on the bench, I marvelled at the way he could control a game.

He would artfully carry the puck out of our zone, into neutral ice, and just before he reached the opposition blue line, he would take stock of what lay in front of him. If he didn't like what he saw, if he didn't think he and his line could gain the offensive zone with possession of the puck, he would double back and start his process over again. Larionov was willing to make two or sometimes three trips back into our zone in order to regroup.

One night, we were playing Edmonton in Detroit's Joe Louis Arena, and Larionov circled back into our zone to claim the puck and start our breakout. He picked up speed as he threaded his way past the checkers in the neutral.

Then, without warning, he just stops playing. He leaves the puck and skates directly toward the closest referee while the play is going on without him.

Larionov reaches the referee, points back at the other team, and says, "They have too many men on the ice."

Everyone looks around—including the referee. We all count the players, and realize that Larionov is right. The Oilers had six skaters on. The whistle blows. Play stops. The Oilers are assessed a two-minute penalty.

Nobody in the arena saw it, including me. Throughout my career, I made it my job to catch opponents with too many men on the ice. I was pretty good at it. I estimate that I caught the other side with too many men a dozen or so times a season. I saw it as yet another way of making a contribution from my little cubicle on the bench.

I didn't see it that night, but Larionov did, *in spite of the fact that he was the puck carrier*. Igor had uncanny vision when he played. He was completely aware of everything around him, 360-degrees. Everyone on our bench, and theirs for that matter, was stunned.

Paul Coffey was sitting next to me on the bench as the play unfolded. "Have you ever seen anything like that?" I asked Paul.

"Yeah," Coffey said, "I saw Gretz do it a couple of times."

It was a treat to be a member of such a talent-laden team. Watching Lidstrom was like watching a master craftsman ply his trade. He was almost always flawless. He wasn't like Coffey, who could take the puck from end to end. He wasn't like Konstantinov, who could blow up an opponent with a ferocious hit in open ice. Lidstrom played the game with his head as much as his body. He could solve any problem by out-thinking his opponent. He always made a good decision with the puck and without, the highest percentage play. He was also always the calmest player on the ice. I'm not sure the word *panic* was in his vocabulary. He had incredible hands. Not many in the league were as skillful as Lidstrom was at keeping a puck in the offensive zone on the power play. His shot was really accurate; he had a quick compact release for a bigger guy, and he was a very fluid skater. He made safe play after safe play after safe play. At the end of almost every game, you would have said, "Nick was perfect tonight."

The Red Wings were fun as well as talented. Darren McCarty was one of my roommates, and we hit it off because we found humour in the fact that we were exact opposites when it came to our travel habits. We were like Felix and Oscar from *The Odd Couple*. I was Felix. As soon as we checked in, every piece of clothing that I brought with me ended up on a hanger or in a dresser drawer. Meanwhile, it always looked as if a hand grenade had exploded inside Darren's suit bag. The blast sent clothes all over our room.

In that era, Detroit was a destination where players wanted to go because the Red Wings were always contenders and owner Mike Ilitch paid his players well. The Red Wings always boasted one of the NHL's highest payrolls. Detroit players' spending habits reflected the higher salaries they were receiving. The team's Super Bowl pools had higher entry fees and they weren't as conservative with their money as I was.

I discovered that on my first road trip with the team. Eleven of us were eating at a high-end steak house in Toronto. When you added in the drinks, the bill was approaching $2,000.

Defenceman Bob Rouse suggested that we play the "credit card game." I would come to appreciate in time that "Rouser" loved the credit card game. Someone had to explain to me that each of us would place our credit cards in the empty bread basket. The basket would get passed around the table and cards would be pulled out one by one in a blind draw, and the last card left in the basket would be used to pay the entire bill.

I had never played the game before. But, hey, I'm a team guy. I would never consider not playing.

As the basket makes its way around the table, guys like Yzerman, Lidstrom, Mike Vernon, and Chris Osgood are all relieved as their cards are pulled from the basket.

You know where this is headed. It comes down to McCarty's card and mine being the last two remaining in the basket. And it's McCarty's turn to draw out a card. (Darren told me later that from the time the third or fourth card was pulled, he was thinking to himself, *Please don't let it be Stu.*) He pulls out his card, meaning I'm stuck paying the dinner tab on my first meal with my new team.

That stung but I didn't mind paying. I found that there's no better way to endear yourself to new teammates than by buying them dinner! As it turned out, this group was one of my favourites to have been part of over my career. The Detroit players were very close.

Goalie Mike Vernon was the only Red Wing I knew before the trade. Although he was two years older than me, Mike and I played against each other in the WHL. He was also with the Calgary Flames when I broke in with that team, but the story I liked to tease him about took place after I had walked away from the Flames' camp back in '85.

When I met her, Pam worked as a server at the Keg restaurant in downtown Winnipeg. It was about a block away from the Westin Hotel, where most NHL teams stayed. One night, I arrived at the Keg to pick Pam up after her shift and I spotted several Flames players at the bar. Because I had been at Calgary's training camp the year prior, I knew most of the guys seated at a table near the bar. Mike Vernon, Kevan Guy, Perry Berezan, and Gary Roberts. I caught Pam's attention and realized she had been waiting on the Flames.

Initially, I felt a little awkward. After all, I'd walked away from something they were doing really well at. The Flames were on top of the world. On the other hand, I was still unsettled about my decision to leave. I went over and said hello, and they put me completely at ease. Vernon seemed particularly happy to see me.

But his demeanour seemed to change when he realized Pam and I were a couple. He seemed sheepish, like a high schooler caught cheating on a math test. I suppose I should have figured it out at the time, but it didn't click until after we left the restaurant. Pam told me Vernon had been hitting on her from the moment he entered the bar. This was no great crime. Vernon had no idea that Pam and I were together and Verny was unattached at the time. But it made for a great story I could tell when Vernon and I were together with teammates or friends. I enjoyed having a reason to needle him tucked away in my back pocket.

We could laugh about it, but there was a more serious side to that chance encounter. It was actually a pretty cool moment, walking into the restaurant and being welcomed by a tight-knit group of guys who were playing at the most elite level in the world. I came away thinking, *That could be me.*

—

That Wings team was a very confident group. We finished the abbreviated regular season with the league's best record of 33–11–4. We led the NHL in goal scoring and were second in goals-against. We were dangerous offensively and we didn't give up much in our own end.

We took down the Dallas Stars in five games in the first round of playoffs and then swept the San Jose Sharks in the second. We expected a tougher match-up against the Chicago Blackhawks in the 1995 Conference Final. The Blackhawks were the only team that gave up fewer goals than we did. The Hawks had Ed Belfour in net, and a very talented group of skaters. Bernie Nicholls, Jeremy Roenick, Joe Murphy, Tony Amonte, Gary Suter, and more.

It was a much tougher series than the first two. Game 1 went to overtime before we won 2–1 on a Nick Lidstrom goal. The Blackhawks led 2–1 in Game 2 before we tied it on a Doug Brown goal and then won it on a goal by Kris Draper with 1:45 left in regulation. That game could have gone either way, and our usually reliable goalie nearly cost us the lead.

After the Blackhawks pulled Belfour in the final minutes of that game, we kept them bottled up in their own end. Time was ticking down and we owned the puck. With three seconds remaining, Vernon decided it was time to celebrate. He left his crease and started toward our bench with his hands in the air, already celebrating.

The problem was we had just lost the puck. Chicago winger Tony Amonte ended up with it on his stick and fired a desperate 150 foot wrister from inside his blue line. I don't know whether Amonte realized that Vernon had vacated the net or not. It's possible he spotted Vernon out of position near the hash marks before he fired.

Realizing his mistake, Vernon made a late lunge at the puck, but he wasn't even close. The puck clanged off the post. Vernon escaped embarrassment by millimetres. When our bench emptied and the players gathered around Mike, he was white as a ghost. The full weight of how close he had just come to costing us one was only beginning to sink in.

—

Pam and I went out to dinner that night and we brought our oldest daughter along to a restaurant in suburban Detroit. Detroit had not yet adopted the nickname Hockeytown, but the team was all that anyone was talking about.

We certainly heard about it, sitting in our booth in the restaurant. The people in the booth behind us were clearly hockey fans, and I could hear every word of their conversation. I half-listened and agreed with most of what was being said. They thought Scotty was a genius for acquiring Fetisov for a relatively low draft pick. Very true. But the one thing the most vocal member of the booth behind us couldn't figure out was the trade for Stu Grimson.

"Why on earth would Bowman go out of his way to get a player like that?" he said.

I looked at Pam and asked, "Did you hear that?" She had not.

For the moment, I said nothing to the guy. But when it was time to leave, I stood to my full height and turned to face the guy's booth as I put on my suit jacket. I opened up my posture in the way I would if I were talking to a fellow heavyweight. I could see the light go on in the guy's eyes. He had to be asking himself: *What are the chances that this hulking human leaning into our booth heard the nasty comment I just made a couple moments ago?*

I put my left hand on the back of the seat, and held out my right to shake his. "Just so you know," I said, "I am going to do everything I can in my power to make sure this trade works out for you." This guy's eyes were as big as saucers; he had no idea how to respond.

Naturally, all the guys got a laugh when I told the story at the rink the next day.

—

With the series shifting to Chicago, I knew Bowman would want a more physical lineup. I was still in and Bob Errey was the healthy scratch.

I played only one shift in the first period of Game 3. In the second period, Bernie Nicholls scored on the power play to give the Blackhawks a 2–1 lead. Trailing never bothered us. We were a pretty poised group. We knew we could score when we needed one.

But that usually meant the physical guys would be on the bench so the skilled guys could go to work. I wasn't expecting to be on the ice much in the second period, and I didn't leave the bench for the first five and a half minutes. But Scotty was always full of surprises. Without warning he calls out "Primeau, take Taylor and Grimson with you!" Tim Taylor was my regular centre but Scotty wanted to shake things up. This was a good way to get Primeau some extra ice against some lesser competition depending on who Chicago sent out. Clearly, it didn't bother Scotty that Taylor and I had been sitting for the equivalent of a full period of hockey.

He's putting us in now? I'm thinking as we pile over the boards. Don't get me wrong; I was thrilled to get the nod but this was a weird moment to be deploying a couple of stone cold skaters from the fourth line.

Cold or not, Taylor and I are in top gear as soon as we hit the ice. Tayls takes an outlet pass in our zone and he and I are on a two-on-one break through the neutral zone.

Steve Smith is the only Chicago defender back.

This looks promising, I'm thinking as I cross the blue line—a half-second offside.

The play is whistled down and I'm thinking . . . *Damn, I just botched what could have been a really good scoring chance.* Even though we've only played a few seconds, I worry Bowman might change lines. But he doesn't. Primeau wins the neutral zone draw back to our defenders and we regroup as a unit back near our own blueline.

The exact same play seems to be coming together again. Taylor catches a pass on the regroup and here we are heading toward the Chicago end two on one. And Smith is, once again, the lone defender back for the Hawks.

We're gonna get a second crack at this!

This time we're onside. I drive the net, thinking Taylor will either shoot or slide me a pass. If he shoots, I want to be in the perfect spot to jam home a rebound.

Looking at Taylor, I see his pass slip past Smith's stick. I don't attempt to settle the puck. I just bang it as hard as I can toward the net. The puck then threads through the gap in Belfour's pads. To make the play, I have to drag my right leg to meet the puck square with my stick. I'm off balance and, as a result, I crash hard into the end wall behind the Chicago net. Feeling no pain whatsoever! Moments ago, I'd been sitting on the bench as one of the highest-paid spectators in the building. And fast forward 30 seconds of play, I have just scored the tying goal in the Western Conference Finals!

I was stunned. I remained there behind the net kneeling with my arms raised. Taylor and Primeau raced over to congratulate me. I was still on my knees. I was numb. I had never scored a goal this important before. I was soaking it in. Probably fifteen or twenty seconds passed, but it felt longer.

Primeau finally had to snap me back to reality. "Uh, hey Stu," he said. "We should probably get back to the bench."

Everyone loves to see the fourth line score. Maybe it's because we like to see the hardworking guys get rewarded. Maybe the feeling is that if the hardnosed guys can do it, then the skill guys can too. In any case, it's always electric.

When I got back to the bench, I took my seat next to Chris Osgood. Chris leaned in and said, "Hey Stu, what do you think the guy from the restaurant is thinking right now?" All of us within earshot of Ozzie cracked up. Good point!

We ended up winning 4–3 on Vlad Konstantinov's goal in double overtime. But the reporters were still buzzing about the 2–2 tying goal I had scored and the circumstances around it. One writer pointed out that it was just my second shift of the game. I quipped, "Two shifts are all I need."

—

We won that series in five games to earn Detroit's first trip to the Stanley Cup Final since 1966. The Red Wings hadn't won the Cup since 1955.

The hockey world had been scratching their heads over the New Jersey Devils' neutral zone trap the entire season. New Jersey coach Jacques Lemaire's defensive system definitely worked; there was no denying that. But fans of run-and-gun hockey felt that the trap took the speed and skill out of the game. Still, we had our own novel defensive system called the "left-wing lock," and we had given up fewer goals than the Devils.

The systems were similar, but the trap could be more aggravating because you faced the pressure in the neutral zone. New Jersey didn't bring an aggressive forecheck. They were built to counter-attack off turnovers. Under our system, we created turnovers in the opposition end. If you could break out quickly, you could beat our lock. But you had to be pretty fast to be faster than the Wings. And we didn't believe for a minute that the neutral zone trap was going to slow us down. We were 12–2 in the playoffs going into the Final, and we truly believed there was no way the Devils could beat us four times.

I remember talking with Ray Sheppard in the trainers' room about how the Devils had plowed through the Eastern Conference playoff field, posting a 12–4 mark. I think there was an overall sense in our group that we would have our way with the Devils the same way we handled the Stars, Sharks, and Blackhawks.

However, when Bowman made his final address to the group on the eve of start of the series, we wondered for a moment whether *he* believed we would win it. Scotty stood on the perimeter of our dressing room, facing the fitness room. And with his back to the entire group, he started into a vintage Bowman ramble about the neutral zone trap.

"Here's the thing about the trap," Bowman said. "You think you are breaking out of your zone, you play into open space, and then you get to that space, they close it down, and you are trapped. That's the thing about the trap. You don't think there's a trap until you play into it . . . and then you're trapped!"

Every player in the room had a perplexed look on his face. We kept waiting for Bowman to tell us how we were going to conquer the trap, but that answer never arrived.

"You don't think you are in the trap, and then you are," Scotty continued. "I don't know how you're going to beat it. I don't know what you're going to do."

Then he was finished and he walked away. We all looked at each other as if to say, *Are you kidding me? That's all he's gonna say?* With Bowman, you often had to search for hidden meanings. Was he trying to instill a sense of urgency in us? Was he just issuing us a challenge? Was he saying it was up to us to show the neutral zone trap wasn't foolproof? Was the confusion we felt just the collateral damage that came from being pushed to find a creative solution?

When the Devils beat us twice in the Joe Louis Arena, we were stunned. During the regular season, we had lost only four games at home in regulation. Panic crept into our camp for the first time that season. Our high-powered offence generated only three goals in the first two games.

We were getting shut down, but in no way was our leadership group to blame. In fact, I thought it was one of Steve Yzerman's best moments. In our first practice in Jersey after Game 2, Stevie called us all together after the coaches left the ice. Players only. He rallied us by going around the group, one by one, and highlighting what each of us was good at, what each of us had to do to beat the Devils. He singled me out for the goal I scored against Chicago. He challenged us all to be better. He did everything a captain could to galvanize us.

Coffey was vocal in that meeting too. When Coffey was traded to the Red Wings, Yzerman had been in the NHL for close to a decade. But I believe that Paul's experience with the Edmonton Oilers during the dynasty era rubbed off on Steve. Paul was a close friend to Steve while they were teammates, a great ally and adviser. I watched Stevie's leadership skills grow by leaps and bounds over the parts of three seasons I was on the Wings, due in no small part to Coffey's influence. I have great respect for the player and the person.

Yzerman was vocal if he needed to be, but he was primarily a soft-spoken captain. He and I often talked about our families; we were both raising young children. My observation: it's uncommon in sports for superstars to be caring and thoughtful. Not so much because they are aloof or self-absorbed but rather because they constantly have people pulling at them for different reasons. Yzerman was an exception in that regard.

I found him to be a really humble person. Stevie had time for everyone.

But he didn't have an answer for the neutral zone trap. The Devils swept us and we managed to score only seven goals in the four games.

—

Six weeks later, it looked like I had played my last game for the Red Wings.

I was a restricted free agent the following summer, and the Wings and I couldn't come to terms. New York Rangers general manager Neil Smith made me the first restricted free agent to receive an offer sheet under the terms of the new collective bargaining agreement. Smith stunned me by offering a five-year contract worth $540,000 per season, plus a $250,000 signing bonus. The Red Wings had seven days to match the offer or lose me and accept a third-round pick as compensation.

The strategy of making an offer sheet is generally to structure it in such a way as to discourage the former team from matching the deal by including some element that the former team would find objectionable. The salary was in line with what enforcers were receiving at that time. However, nobody was handing out long-term deals to 30-year-old enforcers. And the signing bonus was the final twist of the knife.

Smith, who had been the Red Wings' director of scouting before landing the Rangers job, predicted the Red Wings would match the offer. But my experience sitting on the bench told me that Bowman couldn't want me *that* much. Not five seasons and a signing bonus. I told Neil there was no way Detroit would match. I didn't believe they would. We bet dinner on it.

To my surprise, the Red Wings matched the offer. Apparently,

Bowman did appreciate what I had to offer. I owed Neil dinner. I called his assistant and got the name of his favourite restaurant in Manhattan (the Pen and Pencil Steak House, by the way), then called the restaurant and had them forward the gift certificate to Neil at the Rangers' offices. It had been weird talking to a GM from a different team during the offer sheet negotiations, but it would have been illegal tampering to sit down and dine with Neil after I'd re-signed with Detroit.

The contract seemed life altering to me. The deal provided significant financial security for me and my family. It was almost too good to believe. As an officer for the Royal Canadian Mounted Police, my father earned $2300 per month to serve and protect Canadian citizens. He never made more than $58,000 per year before he retired. I had just landed a contract worth $2.75 million to protect a bunch of hockey players. That was somewhat hard to reconcile.

—

Shocked by the loss in the 1995 Stanley Cup Final, the Red Wings tore through the 1995–96 season with hopes of getting it right the following year. We downed the Winnipeg Jets in the opening round and were in a tight battle with the St. Louis Blues when Bowman announced a unique plan to use my talents.

During a team meeting at the Adam's Mark Hotel in St. Louis, Bowman announced some personnel and line changes. Bob Errey was drawing back in. Paul Coffey was going to get a new defensive partner.

"And Stu will be on the bench," he said.

The phrasing of that sentence left me wondering what exactly that meant. Am I dressing but not going to play? Or did he mean I was being scratched?

I wasn't the only player puzzled by the meaning of those words. In conversation with a couple of my teammates, all I got was shrugs. Finally, I went to Dave Lewis; Louie had to know what was going on.

"What does 'Stu on the bench' mean?" I asked. "I'm dressed, but he's already decided I'm not playing?"

"No, you're going to coach," Lewis said. "Scotty wants you on the bench."

In the Winnipeg series, Kris King had been injured, and the Jets had looked through the NHL Rules and discovered there was actually a rule that allowed for a rostered player to be on the bench in street clothes as a quasi-member of the coaching staff. Bowman liked the idea so much he was going to try it with me. In one sense I was somewhat pissed that I was coming out of the mix as a player. On the other hand, I was flattered that Bowman valued my presence to that degree.

Coffey thought it was hilarious. "Good thing you wore your 'A' suit on this trip!" he said after we figured out my new role. He was right. I left Detroit in a sharp navy suit with a tie that popped. There were plenty of "road suits" in my closet back home that would have made for a very average presentation in my debut as an NHL bench boss.

It was surreal, standing on the bench with the crowd behind me. The tension of the game is very different when you can't go over the boards to do anything about it. I believe a lot of guys would have had a hard time not dressing, but I tried to see the upside in it. My game had evolved to the point where my role was very specific. If standing on the bench is what's being asked of me, I'm going to be the good soldier. And I'm going to contribute in whatever way I can. I believe that kind of thing makes a difference. The way you carry yourself, the words you choose, all these things add up. Keeping that in mind is part of what leadership means. So there I was, patrolling the bench beside the most successful coach in the history of the game. There were lots of moments when I'd lean over and tell a guy what I was seeing. But mostly I just tried to be an encouragement. Coaches value a player who can be a source of energy on the bench as well as the ice. That was an important part of my game as a player. That was what I attempted to provide as a coach.

But the really strange part of my new gig came during the intermission. Because I was a player, the coaching staff didn't want me in the coaches' office while they were discussing adjustments for the coming period. At the same time, I felt really out of place sitting in my stall, wearing a suit, looking more like some Wall Street stock trader, while my teammates were in hockey gear.

After we downed the Blues in that series on Steve Yzerman's memorable double-overtime goal, Bowman decided to keep me behind the bench in the Western Conference Final against the Colorado Avalanche. That time off the ice turned out to be quite a bit harder than watching the St. Louis series from the sidelines.

The series ended up as one of most talked-about in Red Wings' and Avalanche history because of Claude Lemieux's ugly hit on Kris Draper in Game 6. I was beside myself. I could see the whole thing unfold right in front of me. Coffey was struggling with a puck that was bouncing up the right boards and then squirted into the neutral zone. He chopped it up to Draper, who had moved back quickly to help him out. Drapes swivelled to face back up-ice, and calmly moved the puck up the boards. It never occurred to him that Lemieux, who had been pressuring Coffey, would circle back and blast Draper into the boards from behind. It was sickening to watch. The Wings were a little slow to react because they couldn't believe what they'd just seen. And none of us knew until after the game just how bad the damage was: Kris had a broken jaw, a broken nose and eye socket, and five teeth had been bent back. Draper's face needed extensive surgery to repair. I had flashbacks to my own surgery six years earlier.

It also stung that it was Drapes. He was a friend to everyone on that team—and that was the most famous third line in the game. We should have retaliated by winning the game, but we didn't. And because we didn't, we were out. It was a tough way to end the series.

People said Lemieux turned the series around given the emotional impact of that hit. Maybe he did. I don't know if there's anything I could have done. Looking back, the question I ask is whether my presence would have made a difference had I been playing that night.

It's not an easy answer. What I provided on the ice was accountability. To that point in my career, no one had taken a run that cheap, that dirty at any teammate of mine. But, the series was already veering out of control before that hit, and Lemieux was already a thorn in our side having suckered Vyacheslav Kozlov earlier in the series.

Opposing players rarely behaved like that if a heavyweight like me was dressed on any given day. So my best guess would be that Lemieux would not have run Draper if I had been in the lineup. But that's only a guess because I can't begin to know what was going on in Lemieux's head through it all.

—

Although we lost that series, I still believed this team was going to win a Stanley Cup. We simply had too much talent. With a new contract, I was excited that I was going to be with this group for a long time to come.

Feeling empowered by our new-found wealth, Pam and I decided to buy our first "hockey home." We had a summer cottage at Lake of the Woods and our first house in Winnipeg. However, we had yet to buy a home in any city I played. I was thirty. We were overdue. Every stop had seemed temporary to that point.

Now, we believed we would be in Detroit for some time to come. We started looking at homes in Birmingham, Michigan, and found a terrific place on the same street as Paul Coffey and Mike Vernon. Imagine that, three Red Wings living within six houses of one another on a sleepy little street called Hawthorne in suburban Detroit. Our families would celebrate holidays and birthdays together.

We were excited to learn what life could be like when you knew you would be in the same spot for five years. We closed on our first home in March 2006. It was a beautiful place. Seven months later, I was playing for a different NHL team.

1 0

CALLING OUT
COFFEY

Once, when I was playing for Chicago, I bumped goalie Ed
Belfour during practice and we ended up in a shoving and cuss-
ing duel. It happens—more than you'd think. But players usually
leave any bad blood on the ice. NHL players have pretty thick
skin. If you can let go of a beef you have with an opponent during
a game, you can find a way to forgive a teammate for something
that goes down in practice. You usually end up laughing about it.

But Belfour had an eccentric personality as well as a short
fuse. When we got back to the dressing room, our argument
flared back up again. Hockey players can be pretty brutal on one
another in terms of the ribbing we'll give each other. If you can't
take a dig from a teammate, you're probably not cut out for life in
the NHL. But even in that context, it can go too far. At one point
during our back and forth, Belfour called me a "piner." His point

was that what I had to say mattered less because I played less. I rode the pine.

That stopped the conversation instantly. During my fourteen-season NHL career, Belfour was the only teammate who ever tried to insult me by pointing out that I didn't play as many minutes as regular players. The enforcer role was such a respected position in those days that it was just readily accepted that tough guys played less and that was the nature of the role. It was never a topic of conversation. To make fun of a tough guy by saying he logged fewer minutes would be like ribbing a designated hitter for not playing a field position.

When Belfour said that, I was caught completely off guard and I could tell by the expression on his face that he knew immediately that he had crossed the line. To Belfour's credit, he apologized to me the next day. But it did make me think about my job, and what a guy like me brings to the team. And the fact is, you can't judge all players' importance by their minutes. Sure, if your number-one defenceman is playing thirty minutes a night, you know the team is leaning on him heavily. But tough guys typically don't eat up big minutes. The tough guy's job is to make everyone else's minutes a little easier and a little safer to play.

The pursuit of team success is a partnership. No matter what your role is, if you've bought into the partnership you get a say. Tough guys included. I may have played only a handful of shifts each night, but I never viewed myself as a minor contributor. You have to view your role as important to the team, or it won't be.

I was never timid about voicing my opinion. Part of being a protector is being a leader. Much of that is just built into an enforcer's personality. They're not usually loud guys, but they tend to be a forceful presence. A lot of tough guys I've known are mild-mannered and often funny, especially away from the rink. But as game time approaches, they can dial it up to the point that the intensity is smouldering. It's critical that you get there in that role. You've got to push yourself to play on the razor's edge of adrenaline. In that spot between recklessness and aggression, if you can't find that line and straddle it, you're not long for the role. I was that way, anyway. People used to say they were surprised by how affable I was in public. But when I laced up the skates, the wires would touch and I would operate at a higher voltage. I became a very different person.

No one is more invested in the team than the tough guy. He's the player who puts it all on the line every time he drops his gloves. The average skater does run a risk of injury as part of every single shift. But the tough guy meets that risk much further down the path. Two fierce combatants weighing in excess of 250 pounds, in some cases, throwing bare-fisted punches with enough force behind them to crush human bone is a frightening proposition.

Taking a hit to make a play, battling in the corner against a bigger guy for a loose puck, blocking a shot—all these things can lift a bench. All these things can spur a team on to win when winning may have been doubtful. But for the tough guy, raising the level of his team's play and turning momentum is his primary responsibility. He has shown the team time and again that he is willing to lock horns, even if he'd rather not. If his team shows up flat, he's the one that answers for that; he's going to have to create the energy to turn things in his club's favour. So the tough guy has every right to speak. When he decides he needs the room's attention, he gets it.

Not that hockey players like getting called out. Especially future Hall of Famers. I felt that if something essential needed to be addressed, I had a platform to say it. Even if the guy who needed to hear it is Paul Coffey.

Paul and I were good friends when we played for the Red Wings in the mid-1990s, and we lived on the same street. Goalie Mike Vernon also lived on Hawthorne. Back then, the Red Wings owned a jet named Red Bird 1, which flew out of Oakland Airport. The three of us would always travel to the airport in one car. All of us are opinionated, always willing to speak our mind. I would say that, between the three of us, we always believed we had an answer for whatever problems the Red Wings were facing at the time.

But our carpooling friendship didn't last long. Maybe Hawthorne Street was jinxed for hockey players—all three of us were off the Red Wings' roster within a couple of seasons. I lasted just seven months after buying that house.

On October 9, 1996, the Wings got out of a contract dispute with Keith Primeau by trading Primeau, Paul Coffey, and a first-round pick to Hartford for Brendan Shanahan and Brian Glynn. In hindsight, it was one of the biggest blockbuster deals in the Red Wings' history. Shanahan and Coffey are legends and Primeau was a three-time thirty-plus goal scorer.

I wasn't part of the trade itself, but the trade did affect the lives of the Grimson family, which was now five strong. After the dust settled, the Red Wings needed another roster spot to make room for Shanahan. And I was deemed expendable. Placed on waivers three days after the trade, I was claimed by the Whalers on October 13.

Primeau, Coffey, and I had just gone from a Stanley Cup favourite to a team that was picked to miss the playoffs. I was disappointed. Coffey was livid. The last thing he wanted was to leave Detroit. Like the Grimson family, Paul and his family loved Detroit and life as a Red Wing. Add to that, Paul was upset by his suspicion that Steve Yzerman didn't try to dissuade the Wings from trading Coffey.

I have no idea whether Yzerman had that kind of influence, or whether he would even have been comfortable injecting himself into trade talks. But I can say that Coffey believed Yzerman could have, and should have, insisted that Coffey remain in Detroit.

Coffey was angry to the point that he didn't report immediately to Hartford. When he did finally show, it was clear he didn't want to be there. He made next to no attempt to hide it. He was a distraction from the moment he arrived. Paul was totally disengaged. And of course, that was on my radar from early on.

When you are a member of a team, you come to the rink every day and you attempt to build toward something. In Hartford, we were trying to build a playoff team. The Whalers had missed the playoffs for four consecutive seasons before Paul, Keith, and I arrived there. The mission was to avoid a fifth. And it was fair to say that Coffey had not bought in. It was starting to become a disruption to me and my teammates.

Coffey was thirty-five when the trade happened. He was a superstar, winner of the Norris Trophy two seasons before. He was still a dominant puck mover, a player who could expect twenty-two-plus minutes per game. I was a player who could anticipate only a couple of shifts per period, although Hartford coach Paul Maurice was playing me more than Scotty Bowman had in Detroit.

Not everyone would have felt comfortable calling out a guy like Coffey. But right or wrong, that instinct has always been part of my DNA. Veteran Kevin Dineen—in his second tour with the

Whalers—and I had been talking about Coffey and what a distraction he was becoming. If anyone on our club was going to address this it was probably going to be me.

The next day, we're back out on the ice. We're doing the classic "horseshoe" drill: one guy swings through the neutral zone, takes a pass from the opposite corner of the rink, and heads back to the end he started and takes a shot. It's obvious Paul is not taking the drill seriously. He's firing pucks into guys' skates, or just out of reach. This is the same defenceman who had broken some of Bobby Orr's records, missing passes a peewee makes regularly. It was not accidental. Finally, he sends me one of his grenades as I loop toward his end of the ice. Missed my stick by two stick lengths.

I'd had enough at this point. I broke ranks, stopped the drill, and got right into Paul's face. "Quit dickin' around Coff," I said to him. "If all you're gonna do is screw off all morning, show yourself off the ice. We're trying to accomplish something here. If you're not interested in being a part of it, pack up and move on!" No surprise, he was pissed. And he erupted.

We were screaming at each other. And our teammates understood that they couldn't allow us to start throwing punches. Coffey had a lot of assets as a hockey player, but he was never going to win a showdown with me. They had to pry us apart.

I never regretted dressing down Coffey, even though he was a friend. Some teammates thanked me for setting Paul straight. Maurice never said anything to me directly, but I had the impression that he was appreciative that a player took the initiative to address the Coffey issue. At age twenty-nine, Maurice was the second youngest coach in NHL history. That made him more than five years younger than Coffey. It could not have been easy for Maurice to deal with having one of the best defencemen in the history of the game undermining his coaching efforts.

The Coffey problem was finally resolved in December when the Whalers dealt him to the Philadelphia Flyers for Kevin Haller, a first-round pick, and a seventh. The Whalers also gave up a third-round pick. Coffey's career in Hartford lasted twenty games. Paul and I still get along, by the way.

One funny postscript is that Coffey ended up back with the Whalers organization two years later, although by then it had relocated to Carolina. The Flyers moved him to the Chicago Blackhawks, and the Blackhawks sent him to the Whalers for Nelson Emerson on December 29, 1998. Maurice was still the team's coach. Awkward.

—

Coffey wasn't the only Whalers player I got crossways with. After the Whalers moved to Carolina, defenceman Enrico Ciccone played fourteen games for us and somehow managed to alienate me and everyone else on the team.

At the time, our captain Kevin Dineen was coming back from surgery to repair an abdominal tear and he had recently been cleared to rejoin the team in full practice. He had been practising for a few days by this time, and our hope was that he would be returning to the lineup soon.

It's a normal practice until we are skating line rushes and Ciccone decides to explode Dineen with the heaviest hit I've ever seen in practice. It came out of nowhere. Sometimes you see a big hit in practice because two guys have been pushing and jawing at one another for the entire practice. Nothing happened that day that gave anyone any warning that this hit was headed Dineen's way. He had no reason to be keeping his head up. There was no context within which a hit this hard on Dineen made any sense.

Until that point, I had gotten along fine with Chico. But I snapped when he blew up Dineen. This was our captain; this guy was heart and soul to our team. I skated over to Ciccone and cross-checked him to get his attention. I threw my gloves to the deepest corner of the end zone and I was about to tear into Enrico. The entire crew on ice saw this coming and in seconds there was a sea of 'Canes between the two of us. No question, this one was well on its way to escalating into a major fight. The thing of it is, nobody told me to confront Ciccone. It's what tough guys do.

While playing with the Los Angeles Kings a few years later, I called out teammate Bryan Smolinski for different reasons. The Kings were a team teetering on the edge of the playoffs. Sportswriters and fans were writing us off, but we had faith in the room that we were a playoff team. I was fully invested. L.A. was a great fit. Great guys, great city and a coach, in Andy Murray, who seemed to appreciate what I brought to the mix.

In an important game down the stretch, Smolinski was taking a critical faceoff late in our zone. As he was lining up for the draw, I spotted Smoke making casual conversation with the opposing centre. Better still, as they were preparing for the puck drop, Smolinski tapped the other guy's shin pads with his stick. I don't know how you go into a draw that important—your season hanging in the balance and you're trading niceties with your counterpart.

I snapped. Kelly Buchberger was sitting next to me, and Bucky saw it the same way I did. "What on earth is Smoke doing?" I asked loud enough for everyone on the bench to hear. When you were fraternizing with an opponent during a game, Darryl Sutter used to call it "cuttin' a deal." Maybe in Smolinski's world this was a time for deal-making, but I wasn't having it. Bryan was too important to us and this was too important a moment.

As we were heading off the bench and back to the room during intermission, I blasted Smolinski. I pulled no punches. I told Bryan there was no way he went into a draw that important with that kind of "soft" demeanor. It sends the wrong message about him. More importantly, it sends the wrong message about us. We were hovering between eighth and ninth place in the conference. Soft was not going to get us a berth in the post-season.

Smolinski turned white. He was shocked that I would tear into him in front of the entire group. It probably didn't occur to him until later that the public nature of the rebuke was by design. If they hadn't already, this was a good opportunity for the rest of the group to receive the message that we were making the playoffs come hell or high water.

It's fair to say the scene made the dressing room a little on the uncomfortable side through the intermission. But afterward, several teammates told me they agreed with my appraisal of Smolinski's actions. It should be noted that Smolinski and I remain friends to this day. I considered Bryan an exceptional player and a great person, but we couldn't accept anything less than his best under the circumstances. Sometimes you've got to have hard conversations.

Our Kings clinched a spot that year. Knocked off the heavily favoured Red Wings in an absolute stunner of a series. We took the eventual Stanley Cup Champion, Colorado Avalanche, to six games. It was a great series and many said that no one gave the Avs a series that year quite like the one our Kings did.

When an NHLer tries to hold other players accountable or tries to keep the group on task, it can be tricky work. It can blow up in your face if your timing is off or if you're just wrong in the first place. You need to be careful that you don't come across like you believe you know more about winning than the rest of the group. I tried to not overdo it. If you go to the well too often, the impact of your words can lose their value.

During my first pro season, with the Salt Lake Golden Eagles, some of the veterans on the team didn't appreciate how vocal I was. Coach Paul Baxter called me into his office and told me that a couple of players had spoken to him about me. A defence-man named Darwin McCutcheon was one player in particular who thought rookies should be seen but not heard. Word got back to me that McCutcheon was calling me "Boy Scout" behind my back. According to Paul, Darwin was complaining that I was off the mark when I was vocal in the room. Baxter's response to McCutcheon was to "tell him yourself if you think he's wrong. You're the one in the room, not me." No such conversation ever took place while Darwin and I were teammates. In all honesty, I thought he and I got along well until I began hearing the stories of him lobbying Baxter under the radar.

McCutcheon ended up being traded to Indianapolis. When we were scheduled to play them, another teammate of mine, defence-man Rick Hayward, warned me that "Cutch" was gunning for me. Hayward had been with him the day before the game while we were in Indy during one of our many long IHL road trips.

I was grateful for the heads-up, but I was thinking McCutcheon needed to be careful what he wished for. I was pissed that he had gone to Baxter rather than doing me the courtesy of talking to me face to face. This is a rare moment for me when my personal feelings carried over onto the ice. I usually had respect for my opponents—but not this day against Indianapolis.

Late in the game, we tangled. There weren't many moments in my career when I went into a fight with this anticipation of anger. Too much anger can be a dangerous thing. But adrenaline does add 10 or 20 percent to what you would have under normal circumstances. When McCutcheon and I squared off, I just waded in. I was throwing before I even got hold of him, swinging from way back. It was a very one-sided fight. I clocked him repeatedly, and he ended up with a broken nose. McCutcheon and I were dead even in terms of physical size. Both stood 6'6" and weighed roughly 230 pounds. But one of us had much more on the line than the other as this one got started.

McCutcheon's complaint was the only time in my career where I got backlash from a teammate for my attempts to have an impact in the room. Addressing it in the way that he did called my integrity into question as far as I was concerned. And I was pissed over that. I was no 40-goal scorer, but I had a pretty good sense of how to manage a room full of hockey players even as a rookie.

My former roommate Keith Primeau used to get some of that same backlash. Preems wanted badly to win and he worked his tail off. Keith played hard every night; I had a great deal of respect for him. Everything he did he did to raise the level of the group. In Hartford and Carolina, he was constantly challenging us to do better. I always liked his approach. Because we have such a small window as pro athletes, making the most of your opportunities is critical.

But some guys started to resent his style. He had a reputation for being a ball-buster. I didn't realize how widespread that reputation was until we were playing the Montreal Canadiens in 1997–98. Those Adams Division rivalry games were always heated—generally one heavy hit or a fight away from total mayhem.

The Canadiens had just acquired belligerent forward Mick Vukota in a trade that sent Darcy Tucker to the Tampa Bay Lightning. At one point during the game, Primeau was dropped into my line for a shift while we tried to get back into our regular rotation after a penalty kill.

We were out against their fourth line, and as we were heading back to the bench, I heard Primeau going back and forth with Vukota. Vukota was mostly silent until Primeau stopped talking. "Okay, Keith, you're right. You're the only one who wants to win," Vukota said matter-of-factly. His deadpan tone made the words even more biting. As I said, tough guys can be pretty funny. I think even Primeau laughed at that one that day.

—

In those days, it was more acceptable than it is now for NHL teammates to argue, confront one another, or even fight. Hockey is a physical sport, and frustration can creep into a team for a variety of reasons. Personalities clash. People boil over.

Craig Hartsburg was my coach during my second tour in Anaheim; he always made life difficult for his players when the team was playing poorly. Hartzy liked for his veterans to take ownership in making sure everyone was pushing hard to be at our best. It's well documented that playing for the likes of Darryl Sutter, John Tortorella, Ken Hitchcock, or Mike Keenan could be very hard. But Hartsburg was highly underrated in this respect as a coach. He was just as crusty and short-tempered as any of those other guys. He made sure you understood what he wanted from you, and what he wanted from you wasn't always easy to deliver.

Hartzy could make the rink a miserable place to be when things weren't going well.

He preferred high-intensity practices. He liked veterans to police practices to make sure everyone was invested in his process. Under Hartsburg, I felt as if one of my jobs was to push the pace at practice and keep everyone on high alert. When you had a hard-edged coach, such as Hartsburg or Sutter or Keenan, you were likely to have confrontations in practice. When everyone is feeling the pressure, even in practice, it doesn't take much to launch World War III on the ice. An ill-advised comment, a heavy hit, or a perceived lack of effort can have dire consequences.

One day, we were playing three-on-three small-area games down inside the tops of the circles in one end zone during practice. I was matched up against Teemu Selanne. We were battling for a loose puck, and I slashed him hard. Not on the hands. Right across the chest. He looked at me like, *Are you kidding me?*

He had good reason to be mad at me. I was way over the top that day. But the Ducks were struggling at the time, and this was my misguided way of attempting to ensure that everyone was practising at a high level. You play the way you practise. Hartsburg hadn't ordered me to stir up trouble. But keeping everyone on their toes was one of my implied duties while playing under Hartsburg. He had an old-school view of his enforcer being the team's policeman, protecting players during games and keeping them in line at all other times.

Selanne isn't a mild-mannered player. He's got a little warrior inside him. He didn't slink away quietly. He pushed back and went nose to nose with me. But others again stepped in quickly and cooler heads prevailed.

In today's world, where social media makes reporting instantaneous and far-reaching, my confrontation with Selanne would have been broadcast widely within minutes. In my era, it happened often enough that a reporter might not even ask about it. I won't be the guy saying the old way is better. I appreciate the need for accountability, and I understand teammates shouldn't be trading punches with one another.

But I *will* be the guy who says leadership is complicated. It's not as simple as standing up before a game and saying, "We have to get pucks in deep and get traffic in front of their goalie." Sometimes it requires a tough love approach. Sometimes it takes a teammate's advice to get a player back on track. Sometimes it takes a teammate getting in another teammate's face to make sure he understands what's expected of him. Sometimes teammates need to argue just to clear the air.

At times, being a leader means putting yourself or someone else in an uncomfortable situation for the benefit of the team. Plenty of strong, healthy, lengthy marriages have known awkward moments that the couple wouldn't want the rest of us to see. The same is true with professional sports teams. Plenty of strong, successful teams have times when a team leader has said something, or taken action, that makes the members of that team uncomfortable. That's a part of leadership. If players are not performing in the best interest of the team, a leader needs to set them straight. I believed that when I was in the NHL and I still believe it today.

11

THE RIGHT HAND

Early in my career, I was out for dinner with Pam in Chicago. Boogie's diner was in the Gold Coast district of the city. I was playing for the Blackhawks at the time, and we were in the middle of a playoff series against the Red Wings. It was an off day for us, so Pam and I were enjoying a moment of solitude between games.

That is, until I heard this voice booming from across the restaurant: "Hey Stu!"

It came again when I didn't find the source of the voice at first.

By now, everyone in the restaurant was looking at the big man walking toward me, and many of them undoubtedly recognized him as Bob Probert.

As I turned to greet him, I really didn't know what I was supposed to do. We had fought four times during the regular season. At that point in my career, I wasn't yet clear on what kind of relationships NHL tough guys had with each other off the ice.

I wondered if I was going to have to fight Probert in the restaurant in front of my wife.

He seemed more friendly than menacing as he strolled toward me. But would it be wise to let down my guard with Bob Probert bearing down on me? *Should I stand back and get ready to throw or should I shake the man's hand?* That's what was running through my mind before Bob reached me and held out his hand. I was braced for a replay of the Kamloops movie theatre episode circa 1982. This turned out not to be that.

For a good ten minutes, Bob and I chatted like a couple of buddies from high school or former neighbours who hadn't seen one another in a while. It was clear to me that Probert didn't care that we might be trading punches the following night. He could not have been friendlier. We were just a couple of guys standing there with our fists jammed in our jeans trying to figure out why my Blackhawks were up in the series (3–0) when his Red Wings had got the better of us during the regular season that year (5–1–2; they nearly ran the table on us in 1991–92).

Bob had kind of a sheepish look on his face, which I am tempted to interpret, as I look back, as an acknowledgement that even though we had never spoken before, we knew each other in a way that the people we cared about never would.

That meeting helped me realize that most NHL tough guys probably see their role the same way I did. It's our job, but it doesn't define who we are as people. Probert was an intimidating, monstrous force on the ice. But he was a pretty engaging guy off of it.

I didn't hate Probert, and I don't believe he hated me. When things boiled over on the ice for us, it was merely an extension of our roles within the context of the game. We were trying to give

With my sister, Sam, circa 1969. She's two years old here, and I'm just four. We were a very close family. We still are.

Waiting tables once a month as a team promotion in Regina, circa 1982–83. I was involved in more than my share of mayhem, but I was always a team player.

Checking Rocky Dundas in Junior, circa 1982–83. Part of my job has always been to make sure no one enjoys playing against me.

Skating against Dave Manson while I played with the Blackhawks. Hockey is a small world. "Charlie" and I have been teammates and opponents, going back to junior.

Fighting Kelly Chase. "Chaser" was not just a teammate—he's a good friend. One of the hardest parts of the job we did was squaring off with people we truly respected.

With my biggest fan in Chicago, Joey Ligas, Jan. 6, 1990. On the back of the photo is written "Dear Stu, Thanks for memories. You will always have a special place in our hearts. Chicago and the Ligas family miss you!"

I was proud to wear the "A" while I skated for the Ducks (circa 1993–94).

At a Christmas skating party in Anaheim with Kristjan (age 2). I was very popular while employed by the "mouse." It's nice to play the good guy in a Disney production.

Western Conference champs, 1994–95. This was Detroit's first trip to the Stanley Cup Final since 1966. Playing with so many future Hall-of-Famers was a highlight in my career.

It was hard to put down roots knowing that NHL enforcers are often traded. My first year on the Carolina bench, 1997–98, with Steve Chiasson (RIP) to my right. Raleigh was my seventh NHL city.

Fighting Marty McSorley, circa 1998–99. One day a you're watching a guy like Marty make a name for himself in the NHL. The next, it seems, you're squaring off against him.

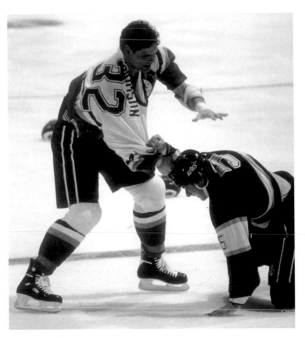

Fighting Troy Crowder. Part of the tough guy code: you never go for the knockout when the other guy is vulnerable.

Wade Belak battled depression and sadly died at just thirty-five years old. RIP. Wade was a great example of the reluctant warrior—he was a warm, funny, thoughtful guy.

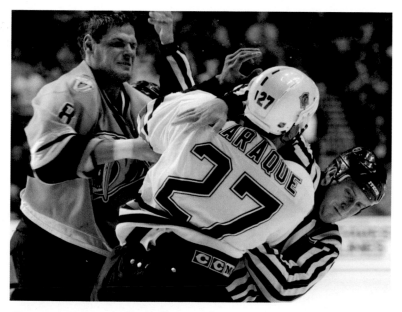

Georges Laraque clipped me with one in Dec. 2001. The straw that broke the camel's back. I retired several months later due to post-concussion syndrome.

Jennifer and me with my sweet, loving parents in Kelowna summer of 2018. Our grandson Atticus Roy tagged along for the pilgrimage home.

Among my greatest joys in life is seeing my children together and observing how much they mean to one another. Whenever (left to right) Erin, Kristjan, Hannah, and (horizontal) Jayne get together, the energy coming off of these four beautiful people is electric. I love them so.

With Jennifer at the Predators Christmas party 2016. Our one and only date on ice. She said she could skate.

Me and Jenn at Lincoln Memorial, May 2017.

In the press box during intermission at a 2015 Predators game. The best part of life after hockey is meeting—not fighting—some of the toughest humans to have walked the planet. From left to right: Dave Brown, me, Jody Shelley, and Jim McKenzie.

"Nearly 10,000 career PIMs assembled in a single photo!" Me, Bob Probert, Chris Nilan, Troy Crowder, and Dave Hutchinson, on tour in Afghanistan meeting the troops.

our team a competitive advantage by protecting our teammates. We were just doing our jobs.

I didn't fully understand this the first time we chatted, but I did sense that he and I were on different paths. I mention this because our careers ran parallel in so many ways. We were the same age and nearly physical replicas of one another. We were drafted together to Detroit in the same year. We retired the same year. We played for the same teams. We went toe to toe many times, which creates a very unique level of intimacy. At a minimum, we were part of the same brotherhood.

But brothers don't always walk the same path. Within the game, it was known that Probert was a much scarier fighter when he was drinking and on cocaine than he was when he was sober later in his career. Deep down, Probert was probably more of a nice guy than he was a fighter. He may have been a reluctant warrior like me. Was his substance abuse intertwined with his role as a tough guy? I didn't know him well enough to know the answer to that but it appeared to be the case.

Playing the tough guy role comes with considerable pressure and anxiety. These are things you learn over time. One day you're a green rookie, just trying to prove you belong. At some point you realize you've made it. Later still, you're the guy the rookies are measuring themselves against. No one comes along and tells you when you move from one category to the next.

I did slowly come to see that I had been wrong about a lot of the true heavyweights I'd fought early on. My biggest mistake was the assumption that they had their fear under control, and that they could see right through mine. I thought that when I looked at a big, tough guy, that was all there was to him. I suppose that's an easy mistake to make, because that was all that mattered to me at the time. I assumed they were all meaner than shithouse rats, just judging by the looks of them. And that's probably what I looked like to them. It takes us all a while to realize that the guy you're about to tangle with probably slept restlessly the night before the game same as you. What I mistook for the icy calm of an assassin, in many cases, was just the look of a guy tamping down his own emotions the same way I was.

For that reason, tough guys are always looking for a way to cope. Some self-medicate through alcohol or drugs. Maybe more than "some." It may be closer to "most." I'm not going to list all the guys who dealt with their issues that way. I'm not going to list all the enforcers who died premature deaths, some by their own hand. That list is too long, and too troubling. There is no escaping it: the job we do takes a heavy toll. That's not to blame anyone, or excuse anyone. It's just a simple statement of fact. The saddening statistics tell us that it can be hard to keep going, night after night. Whether you take up that burden willingly or have it jammed into your hands. Whether you handle it wisely or in ways that come back to haunt you and those who love you, it can be a heavy burden. And some guys leaned on solutions that kept them going for one more game, or one more sleepless night, but it caught up with them in the long run.

When twenty-seven-year-old former NHL enforcer John Kordic died alone in a seedy hotel room on August 8, 1992, the hockey world started to discuss, for the first time, whether NHL fights were having a long-term impact on players' health. Twenty-seven years later, we are still trying to sort out the health hazards that come from fighting, or playing a physical game, in the NHL.

On the night Kordic died, he was stomping around his hotel room in an uncontrollable rage. According to *Sports Illustrated*, it took nine police officers to subdue him. He died in the ambulance, ranting until he gasped his last breath. An autopsy revealed that he died from lung failure due to heart malfunctions. Needle tracks ran up his arms. Vials of steroids were discovered in his room.

Quebec Nordiques coach Pierre Pagé told *SI* that it was like Kordic "had a time bomb inside of him." Stories emerged about the struggles Kordic had with drug abuse, and the mixed feelings he had about being a tough guy. A few months after his death, Canadian television did an extensive report about his life and troubles. His former teammate Ryan Walter said Kordic couldn't make peace with how he had to play to stay in hockey. From 1985 to 1992, according to hockeyfights.com, Kordic had ninety-six fighting majors. That's roughly 43 percent of my career total.

I'm not judging other guys' choices, though I do lament them. It only makes sense that some of us are going to look for relief or help. Remember, guys in that job face down a level of fear that is probably far beyond anything athletes face in any other sport. A boxer or a mixed martial arts fighter may know well the sense of dread that hangs over you before an upcoming fight. But the boxer goes through that process just once or twice a year in an average year. For an NHL heavyweight, you go through the preparation daily; you never get to let your guard down. Every other night you could be called on to step into another bare-knuckled brawl. Try to imagine what it would be like to be a top-ranked MMA fighter, knowing the day after a title bout that you might have to fight again, at any time.

Goalies have a tough job too. Someone once observed that you don't know real pressure until you try to do your job in front of twenty-thousand people who are alerted by a loud horn and a red light every time you make a mistake. That's tough. But now imagine a job in which, when you make a mistake, you get punched in the face and knocked to the ground in front of the people you're supposed to be protecting. Imagine the threat of pain and humiliation every time you pile over the boards. Tough guys deal with a rare form of pressure. I'm not complaining. After all, I chose that life, it did not choose me. But if this book is to serve any purpose at all, we owe it to these guys as human beings to attempt to understand what they endured.

A lot of them are more reluctant than you'd think. Remember, most of them were skill guys growing up. I may have scored only a handful of goals in the NHL, but you have to be a pretty good hockey player to score even *one* in the best league in the world. Deep down, hockey players want to be the guy who scores the big goal. Every player on the bench wants the puck on his stick in the last minute of the game, and knowing it's never going to happen can be hard. You will never hear me complain about the job I had. But for some enforcers, I know they felt like they had ended up doing something they hadn't signed on for.

Then there's fear. These are the bravest guys you're going to meet, but they're not stupid, and they're not reckless. They know the risks they take. Georges Laraque was one of the biggest, strongest guys I ever faced. He used to intimidate other players by smiling as they were squaring off, as if he was planning to enjoy the fight. But he's on record saying that he was terrified. He didn't sleep the night before games if he knew there was a legitimate heavyweight in the lineup. If you stare down fear like that night after night, year after year, it takes a toll.

In my estimation, there is no harder role to play in all of professional sports than NHL enforcer. The pressure is immense. It's tectonic. Most of it is probably self-imposed. No one wants to win more than a tough guy. He really does want to take the team on his shoulders. He is more than willing to sacrifice to give the bench a lift. He doesn't begrudge it. But you're not going to win every fight. Sometimes you're going to come out on the wrong side of it. If you say to your teammates that you've got their back, and you end up lying on the ice, looking up at the guy who just put you there, you can end up beating yourself up more than the other guy did.

Never mind the fact that if you lose enough, you may be out of a job.

I shouldn't generalize too much. Every tough guy walked his own path. But I will say this. From the time I first started using my fists in high school, part of what drove me was some awkward attempt to find myself. What I eventually learned was that, if you're not careful, it can lead you to lose yourself.

—

As reapers go, I was never actually all that grim. Unless I got crossways with someone on the ice, I generally was—and am—a very positive guy. That helped me a lot during a career that was no walk in the park. But that's not just naturally in me. It's not just a lucky accident, or good parents. I had something going for me through my entire pro career that helped me immeasurably.

I met Pam at a time in my life when I tried to solve a lot of problems with my fists. I drank a fair bit too. Fighting and booze tend to end up in the same places a lot. When you try to solve your problems by adding another problem, there is nowhere to go but down. I left a lot of problems in my wake. And my fists were the cause of a lot of those problems.

A lot of people cared about me. But the people who saw what I needed were Pam's parents. Meeting them changed my life. I'm really not sure what they saw in me. I lived my life trying to impress people with my recklessness and toughness, but I doubt that's what they saw. The thing is, if you're going through life trying to control what other people think of you, what perceptive people are going to see is a guy who is trying too hard. If those people are also caring, thoughtful people, they may help you see that the answers you're groping for may be right in front of you. Bill and Doris Tibbs were caring people.

I was brought up in a Lutheran household, and early in my childhood, religion was very important to our family. My mother made sure we went to church every Sunday, and my sister and I completed the catechism program. But as we grew older, religion became less and less important to us as a family. It was no longer even a once-a-week event; it became more something the Grimson family did on just religious holidays like Christmas and Easter. Which was fine with me; I never really got much from it as a young boy anyway.

The Tibbs family was the first family I had ever met whose faith seemed to permeate every aspect of their lives. Theirs was a seven-day-a-week relationship with God. There was a peace and a calm to Pam's family that was in stark contrast to the wild life I was living. And it didn't take long, even for a brawler like me, to see that their serenity came from their personal relationship with their creator. As a young adult who had spent most of his life to that point anxious, restless, and unsettled, I was intrigued by the peace I observed in the Tibbs family. I wanted to know more about that kind of faith because in it was the peace that I craved. They ministered to me in a really quiet, caring way. Through them, I began to understand that Christianity isn't a badge you wear on your sleeve. It's a relationship you enjoy with your creator.

I get it. People don't expect to hear that from someone like me. It seems like a contradiction: the guy who made a living intimidating other professional athletes? A *Christian*?

Not only do I see no contradiction, had it not been for my faith, there is an excellent chance I would never have carved out a career in the NHL. Back in 1987, when I went to my second Flames training camp, I was very nearly as anxious as I had been in my first camp—the one I walked away from. But I was about to learn an important difference in the way I would navigate my second attempt at a pro career.

I remember being sick in bed in my dorm room unable to participate in a power skating camp Calgary had sent me to prior to main camp in 1985. Out of equal parts boredom and desperation, I started reading a book that Pam's mom had given me before I went off to camp. It was called *Breakaway*, published by a group called Hockey Ministries International, which serves as the official chaplain to the NHL and other pro and junior leagues. Many Christians see sharing their faith as essential to faith itself, and this gift was Doris's way of doing that. People tend to turn their noses up at the word "evangelizing," because we tend to be uncomfortable talking about faith. But to a Christian, it means sharing something precious to them. That's what Pam's mother was doing.

The book contained a collection of short stories or vignettes, three to five pages long, about Christian athletes in the NHL. Laurie Boschman, Mike Gartner, and Bob Froese were some of the players I remember reading about in that collection. What made the book so relevant to me is that each of those players had experienced some of the same anxiety and stress I was feeling that day.

You can appreciate why the book struck a chord with me. It was an important realization. The guys I was reading about all enjoyed a contentment that was so foreign to me as I wrestled with the question of whether being a tough guy was a career path I could follow. I knew immediately that this was the understanding that I had been craving. A relationship with God is what I didn't have and needed most. I understood immediately that this would change my life.

I was sick as a dog, confined to bed. Probably just sick with worry. Physically sick from the anxiety and inner turmoil I was experiencing. When I look back at this pivotal moment in my life, I believe I never would have read that book if I hadn't been sick in that dorm room. It was meant to be.

A few days later, I was contemplating what I'd read as I drove home to Kamloops to visit with my parents before the start of Flames training camp. I pulled off the Yellowhead Highway somewhere between Edson and Hinton, Alberta, and stopped the car. I closed my eyes and I prayed, mimicking something I had read in *Breakaway*.

"God," I said, "I want to turn from the decisions I have made and the way I have been living my life. I choose to place my faith in you. I want to go in a different direction. I'm releasing all of the bullshit that has gone on in my life to this point. I want the peace that I believe I can find in you."

No lightning bolts came from the heavens. There was no providential sign that what I had just done was resonating in the skies above. But I knew from that moment that I was going to make greater space in my life for my creator. I knew I was going in a different direction.

I also knew that, with this new-found sense of peace, I may

have removed one of the key obstacles standing between me and a career in the NHL. Odd as it may sound, it was the peace that comes from faith that allowed me to step into the fray and forge a career as an NHL enforcer. A little like "there are no atheists in foxholes" perhaps?

Stress is just the worry that things won't work out the way we want. We all face that. But a guy who puts it all on the line in front of a packed house of cheering fans faces it more than most. From that moment forward, I sensed that the stress would be different. I sensed that the stress would be more manageable. I'm not saying that fighting became easy. If you're not at least a little anxious about a fight against Dave Brown, you're not going to last long. But once I carved out a greater space in my life, I knew I could afford to be less anxious about the results along the path. All I can control is how hard I work.

With my faith at the centre of my life, a lot changed for me, though not overnight. In time, my faith made me a better husband, father, and person. I learned to be less self-absorbed. I quit drinking, not because I believed that my faith didn't allow it but because I wanted to model something different for my children as they grew up. I wanted my children to see that you could find respect and acceptance in the world without alcohol and all its trappings. My faith helped make that clear to me. And perhaps most importantly, it brought me to an understanding that I didn't need to act out in order to find friendship, acceptance, or respect.

Over the years, there's one piece of scripture that has become an anthem in my life. Isaiah 41:10 reads: "So do not fear, for I am with you; do not be dismayed, for I am your God. I will strengthen you and help you; surely I will uphold you with my righteous right hand." What could be more comforting than the idea of resting in the righteous right hand of the God of the universe? That's where that peace came from.

I'd like to think my right hand helped others too, though in a far less providential way. Not everyone could reconcile that I was a Christian whose job involved hurting others. But I never had an issue balancing my faith with what I did on the ice. I see no contradiction in that at all. In fact, I have always seen my role in hockey as an extension of my faith. Who better than a Christian to take on the role of protector?

When I saw someone getting taken advantage of out there on the ice, I knew it was on me to set things straight. I have never believed that my job was a compromise of my faith. If I punched people out in everyday life, it would be a different story. Fighting came within the context of the game. For me, it was always a cut and dried issue. Either a Christian man can play a physical sport or he can't. And I believed that he could. I was not compartmentalizing my faith or my playing style. I was a Christian man when I fought. I had rules and lines I never crossed.

Through the years, my pastors supported my unusual mix of a Christian lifestyle and a profession in which violence is a given. Being Christian didn't make me perfect. I am the first to admit that I made bad decisions at times. You're prone to cross the line when you play an aggressive role and your adrenaline is constantly running high. Many times, I've wished I could go back and change decisions I made. But Christian or non-Christian, who among us doesn't feel the same way? Christianity doesn't guarantee a perfect life—just a forgiven one.

My position: if there has to be a player in this sport who sticks up for the smaller man, the less physical athlete, or who makes it easier for the skill players to do what they do best, why shouldn't it be a Christian? Why shouldn't it be a guy like me who rushes to the aid of the smaller or the more skilled players?

My teammates will attest that I was never one to bring my faith inside the room. I was never comfortable initiating that conversation, or even steering it in that direction. All I can do is believe what I believe, live my life the way I choose to live it, and if others want to know what makes me tick, they will ask. For me, sharing my faith does not happen without the other person in a conversation inquiring about my spiritual side.

And finally, this *is* just a game. Christian athletes play physical roles across a wide range of sports. My teammates understood who I was and what I believed. But they also knew I was no choirboy. It's no secret that when you talk about faith you risk being seen as soft. No one becomes a Christian to be cool. Having made that a lifelong choice, though, I'd like to think that I reduced some of the stigma associated with being a Christian in pro hockey. Although, to be fair, I may have been a little harder to pick on.

As a Christian, I know I am not going to convince anyone who is not open to being convinced. That's not how faith works. It's not like the law, where sound legal reasoning carries the day. You don't get talked into faith if you're not leaning in that direction to start with. Either you're open to it or you're not. From the moment I opened myself up to it, I came to know a freedom I'd never known before. It was no longer important to try to impress others. I quickly came to see the flaw in that thinking and how empty that life could be. Faith allowed me to have peace around the fact that life is messy and inexact; I could fall short of the mark and still wrap myself in the unconditional love of a caring God. Faith allowed me to shed the burden of other people's opinions; all I had to abide by was what I knew to be true.

12

HONOUR AMONG TOUGH GUYS

In my IHL days, I could count on my gear being sabotaged whenever I played on the road in Peoria. I'd show up before a game and my laces would be cut, or my gloves would be filled with shaving cream. Something would always be amiss. And I always knew who to blame.

Tony Twist played for Peoria, a St. Louis Blues farm team then, and Tony put the touch on our trainers so he could sneak into our room and send me a "hello." Twister and I grew up together in Kamloops. We were friends long before either of us made the NHL. Our fathers were both in the RCMP. I knew the on-ice Twister and the off-ice Twister, and I much preferred dealing with the off-ice Twister.

He was barrel-chested and was impossible to knock down even if you landed a hard one. He threw cinder blocks at you from both sides and had a unique gunslinger personality. He was spirited, mischievous, and belligerent. "He's smart enough to own the bank, but he'd rather rob it," as fellow tough guy Kelly Chase used to put it. That is, Twister was categorically not a reluctant warrior. He was the exception to the rule.

I remember once I was talking to him about Dave Brown. Back when Tony was breaking into the league in Quebec, Brownie came to town and was doing typical Brownie stuff. He was looping over the Nordiques' side of the ice during warm-up, the same tactic he used to intimidate me. Twister decided he wasn't going to take that bullshit and looped over the red line going the other way to engineer a collision with Brown. There was almost a heavyweight bout before the game even started.

In the end, the two were separated and Twist ended up being scratched before the opening faceoff. Twister was genuinely upset that he wouldn't get a crack at Dave Brown that night. I remember thinking, *Yeah, I'd be disappointed getting scratched on any night. But was it really all that bad if the coach took a date with Brownie out of your hands?* Need we revisit Chapter 6, dear readers?

Tony Twist was a genuinely scary guy. He was one of the few guys I fought who truly liked what he did. And he was really good at it. I fought him just once in the NHL, and it was a reluctant encounter even for the least reluctant tough guy I knew. The game was getting lopsided and my Ducks were nearly down and out. Twister and I fought that night purely out of obligation.

We didn't hate each other. We didn't even want to hurt each other. Fighting is not easy. Fighting someone you actually like is even harder.

Of course, we all still had a job to do. One of the many aspects of the fight game that caused me anxiety was the probability that

I was going to have to fight a close friend. After Kelly Chase and I were teammates in Hartford, both he and I talked about the likelihood that we would have to battle each other down the road.

Chaser is one of my all-time favourite people in hockey. He was barely two hundred pounds, but he would fight anybody in the NHL. He always had a full tank of passion and energy, was never short on piss and vinegar, and he was one of the funniest, wittiest guys I played with or against. He had the heart of a lion. I loved him as a human being, and I dreaded the possibility that we might have to fight when we both left the Whalers. And we would have done it too, because we were both professionals.

Fortunately for both of us, that scenario never presented itself. But I wasn't as lucky when it came to my good friend Jim McKenzie.

McKenzie and I became really close when we played together in Anaheim. It was my second tour of duty with the Ducks. Our families grew close, especially the kids. But there is nothing quite as temporary as a roster spot for a heavyweight, and both McKenzie and I had moved on within a couple of years. McKenzie was traded to New Jersey and I signed with the Los Angeles Kings.

Since we were in different conferences, and our teams didn't meet very often, that should have meant we likely wouldn't end up fighting each other. But in the back of our minds, we knew the possibility existed. Eventually, one night at the Staples Center in L.A., it did.

The Devils were leading in the game and I had just taken a shift. I liked Kings coach Andy Murray because he played me more than most coaches had in my career. But Murray mishandled this situation. Much of Murray's experience came at the college level, and occasionally that led to a questionable decision in the NHL. This was one of those instances. When Murray saw McKenzie go over the boards, he sent me back on the ice even though I was out of gas having just taken a turn.

Big Mack was a beast; he could hurt you. Jim and I had tangled plenty before we ever played together in Anaheim. I knew I had my hands full and I knew I was in a bad spot as soon as Murray sent me back out. McKenzie didn't want to fight me, but we both knew what Murray expected of me. We were trapped, and there were eighteen thousand people watching. Including my wife and all four of the kids, who were eager to see Mack after the game.

A hockey fight may take only thirty seconds, but it can feel like an eternity, even if you're starting fresh. I was running on empty and Mack knew that; he would have gladly let me off the hook if I had steered it that way. In retrospect, I should have laid off and just played. I should have told Murray I was in no position to take on the other team's heavy until I got a breather. Instead I decided I had to go. I don't remember what we said to each other, but it was clear that neither of us wanted to be in that position. I shook my gloves off first.

McKenzie got the better of me in that one. I was just trying to tie the man up but I had little strength to do even that. Mack is really effective with either hand and he got a sharp one in. He hit me so hard that it left a hole in my cheek wide enough that I could stick my finger through my cheek to the inside of my mouth. My son Kristjan was just old enough to realize that his dad was fighting his friend. That kind of thing was really hard for a boy of five to understand. McKenzie was so angry that Murray had put us in that spot that he trashed the Devils' dressing room after he was escorted off the ice.

Later, he was even more upset when he heard about Kristjan's reaction.

Like McKenzie, I blamed Murray. In my era, more than today, most coaches knew how to use their enforcers effectively. It was as important as a Major League Baseball manager knowing how to effectively execute the double switch. If Murray didn't know that McKenzie was good at what he did, he should have. At the end of the day, the tactic did nothing for our Kings.

Ours was a job. But it was never *just* a job. We managed adrenaline and emotion for a living, and if you are going to try to channel powerful forces like that, there will be spillage. In that line of work, you simply can't be professional without being emotional.

—

Fighting may be emotional, but it doesn't just happen. It's something you have to do right or you won't be doing it for long.

Back in the golden age of heavyweights, everyone in the rink knew when a scrap was about to unfold. If the fans up in the nosebleeds knew it, the tough guys certainly did too. If the score was lopsided and the fourth lines hadn't been playing much, I didn't have to say anything to the guy I was about to fight. Just the fact that we were both on the ice at that moment told him everything he needed to know. If I said anything, it would just be to suggest we wait a few seconds after the puck dropped, so that we could avoid taking a penalty for "staging" the fight. I rarely dropped the gloves right off the draw. The only exception would be if the other guy had done something pretty egregious to provoke the fight.

But the usual way to get things going was to time it so we collided early in the shift. I would open up my posture. No one could fail to understand that body language. It's the gauntlet going down. If the other guy squares up, then the gloves come off, and away we go.

What happens next is not the mayhem it may look like. If you've ever seen two non-fighters try to go at it, you have a sense of how hard it is even to stay on your feet, never mind keep your defence up and look for your spots. Tough guys know what they're doing. Guys who do it for a living have their strengths and weaknesses. They strategize. There aren't many guys I would have fought if I didn't have a book on them.

If I was fighting a right-hander, as soon as the gloves came off I was measuring the distance between us. I wanted to do two things at once. I liked to tie up my adversary's power hand with my left. That means getting a fistful of his far sleeve, around his right shoulder or even a little deeper. And I wanted to fire a right at the same time. I could grab and punch simultaneously. It's more difficult than it sounds—but it's effective if done right. If you clutch someone's shoulder while delivering a punch with pay-load, you may get him off balance. A quality first punch can end a fight early, or at the very least set the tone. I did that many times in my career.

Probably the quickest one I ever recorded came in a fight against St. Louis Blues tough guy Reid Simpson on December 28, 2000. Simpson was a light heavyweight who fought in the heavy-weight division. He gave up four inches and forty pounds when he tangled with me.

I had no reason whatsoever to fight Simpson when he challenged me late in the third period. In fact, I had earlier fought up-and-comer Reed Low in that same game. It was a great fight, pretty even at the end of the day. Reed was a big, strong man. But

I was all set for the night. Besides, my Kings were up 5–2 late in this one. There was no good cause for me to go.

On the other hand, because we had a comfortable lead, I also didn't have a competitive reason *not to* fight him. Still, even when he was running around the ice being a nuisance, I was willing to let it go. But when he suckered me in the side of head with his gloved hand, I decided I'd had enough. We were both penalized for the short conversation we had after that punch. If the ref was trying to cool things down, it didn't work. When we came out of the box, I told him we were going to sort things out right there and then.

I pointed toward the centre of the ice, but we ended up fighting near the St. Louis bench. The bout has plenty of views on YouTube. I sized him up for only a second, measuring in my mind the distance I needed to launch a right. Then I packed everything I had into my first shot. Three seconds after the fight started, I landed a right that dropped him like a sack of potatoes. The video shows me stepping over his body and skating away like it had all been in a day's work. Simpson had to be helped off the ice. He was so wobbly that I was concerned he was in real trouble. I sent our dressing room attendant over to check on Simmer and was relieved to hear he was doing better after he got into the dressing room.

Both Low and Simpson have become good friends in retirement. Lowsie was able to provide me with the back story from the Blues' perspective. After Low and I fought in the first period, he and Simpson discussed the bout during the first intermission. According to Low, the conversation goes something like the following:

Simpson: "I'm going to get that fucking Grimson and here's how I'm going to do it: I'm going to wade in and I'm gonna one-punch him."

Lowe: "I just fought him and he's a handful. I don't think that's a good idea."

Simpson ignored Lowe's advice and ours ended up being a very short fight. The postscript of this story is that Simpson and I became teammates the following season. The Nashville Predators brought him in after I was injured.

We became friends. Any time he would introduce me to friends, Simmer would say, "Hey, meet Stu. Stu and I fought when he was in Los Angeles and I was in St. Louis; I got third place in that one."

Lefties were something completely different.

My weakness was my inability to sort out the unique challenges of facing a left-handed fighter. No matter how much I tried to adjust, southpaw fighters always gave me trouble. If you asked NHL fight fans who my nemesis was, they would probably say Bob Probert. But I would say it was Dave Brown, and that Georges Laraque was a close second. Brownie's left hand could wreck you. After what happened to me in my early fights with Brown, I always made it my first objective to get hold of his left hand. I was content to tame the dragon—I didn't need to slay him. Brown was the hardest puncher I ever fought (although Joe Kocur was also in his category; Kocur was known to shatter helmets).

If I was fighting a left-hander, I would go in with my left across my body to grip his left. The more dangerous the fighter, the nearer the grip I'd try for. The closer you are to his hand, the safer you are from him—but the safer he is from you too. Though at least you're not getting rocked by a shot you don't even see coming.

I liked to stand back and throw—but then, I have long arms. Shorter, thicker guys tended to be smart enough to try to stay out of range. Tie Domi was the classic grappler. He was strong but not tall, so he would try to get you to spend your energy wrestling with him, striving for leverage and struggling to get your right hand free, and then he would come on strong in the second half of the fight. Wrestling a guy like Tie is probably more tiring than throwing punches. So the strategy can be effective, because often by the time you're set up you don't have much left in the tank. A smart fighter can come away with the win by keeping his head out of the range of the really dangerous punchers. Kelly Chase and Darren Langdon were great strategists. Craig Berube, too, was pretty savvy.

Donald Brashear was a challenging opponent, because he never fought the way you thought he should fight. He was a big, strong man, weighing about 240 pounds. But he never wanted to stand in there and exchange haymakers. He preferred to grapple with you in close, trying to subdue you, before he started hammering you with his left. Every fight with Brashear started like it was going to be a Greco-Roman wrestling match.

My one lasting impression about Big Brash was that breath. I mean, breath that could make a freight train take a dirt road. Fighting in tight worked to Donald's advantage for many reasons! It's the little things you tend to remember.

Other guys were impossible to wrestle, because there was nothing to hold on to. There was a brief period when guys like Rob Ray would have their sweaters and shoulder pads off before anyone had thrown a punch. Ray never pulled that stunt on me, though Probert did. It's just damage control at that point. You can't control your opponent's power hand, so all you can do is try to push his shoulder back so he can't tee off. But you can't throw either, because you can't pivot and throw across your own body. If you're not anchored to the other guy, you're just going to fall down if you try to punch with any power. (Try it; it's tricky.)

Eventually, the linesmen arrive. If both guys are satisfied it's over, it's an easy break for the linesmen. Both guys are happy to break clean. But if one of us has a wounded ego, he may try to keep the fight going. Linesmen and tough guys have a pretty good rapport, though. The guys in stripes get it. They know how to calm down the one of us who feels he may have come up short—but they can also get pretty assertive. There are some big, strong linesmen out there. It's a lot easier to manage an enforcer's body if you can manage the personality first. Ray Scapinello was one of the guys that managed both aspects of the fighter well. His sheer strength made him somewhat of a legend. He was probably a foot shorter than me, but on that night in January 1992 when I lost my mind against Toronto, Ray took me down when no one else could. Hats off to Ray.

Sometimes my relationships with the officials could get comical. When Scott Parker came into the league, he had a beard that came down six or eight inches below his chin—Scott was on the leading edge of the whole beard scene. The first time we squared off, the sticks and gloves were strewn all over the ice and we were measuring each other off, and I heard one of the lineys yell, "Stu, I know what you're thinking, but don't you dare do it." He figured I was thinking about grabbing Parker's beard (which would earn me a match penalty). Although we added a serious layer of difficulty to their jobs, I'd say the tough guys got along great with the guys in stripes. We got to know each other pretty well. Every fight ends with some sort of physical interaction with a linesman (or two).

Though it would seem that an eternity had passed, I'd be on

my way to the box only a couple of minutes after I'd gone over the boards. Emotionally, I'd gone from one end of the continuum to the other, from the anticipation and anxiety over the very real possibility that I'd come out on the wrong side of a fight, to a huge release of tension, especially if I had shown well. If I had to do it again, the fighting would happen out of pure emotion. I wouldn't have to worry about it, so I could just focus on playing hockey.

Just as importantly, after receiving a penalty I'd be feeling a great deal of satisfaction. Three quarters of the time, when you get into it with another guy, you have created a surge for your team. When my teammates come over to bring my gloves and stick, when I see guys on the bench on their feet, tapping their sticks on the boards, I feel I've made my contribution to the team. A goalie making a huge save that brings the crowd to its feet, that changes a game. When Paul Kariya scores a clutch goal, that play can completely change a game. When I'm in the box, I'm usually feeling pretty good, because I just changed the game in my way.

—

One night when I was playing for the Blackhawks, I was in an intense scrap with Basil McRae of the Minnesota North Stars. On that night, I was getting the better of Basil. We were both rearing back and throwing punches when I started to get Basil backpedalling. His blade may have got caught in a rut, or maybe he just lost his balance. Whatever the reason, his leg buckled and he crashed awkwardly to the ice. I knew immediately he was severely injured.

I backed away because I knew Basil was in trouble. As it turned out, McRae had a spiral fracture in his leg. The early rumours were that his career might be over. Feeling horrible about what had happened, I asked our team services director, Steve Williams, if he could ask his Minnesota counterpart for McRae's phone number.

When I reached McRae and tried to identify myself, he was sure somebody was playing a joke on him. "Who the fuck is this really?" he kept asking.

Finally, I convinced him I was who I said I was and we talked it over. He told me at the end of the conversation that he appreciated that I had called him. As it turned out, the injury healed and McRae was able to fight another day.

Paul Stewart, a former NHL tough guy himself, was the referee the night of that fight. "I respect the way you handled that Stuey," Stewart said to me after McRae left the ice on a stretcher. While I appreciated the thought behind his comment, I didn't believe I acted any differently than any other heavyweight would have in my situation. We all understood what our opponent had to endure to be an NHL heavyweight. We understood the pressure he faced to do his job well enough to stay at the NHL level. But, on this night at least, it came down to one very simple premise. You don't strike another man when he's obviously in trouble.

The professional respect we gave each other was no different than what you might see in other professions. As people, we all want the respect of our peers. We extend professional courtesy to others because we want it extended to us. That's true of doctors, lawyers, general managers, CEOs, and NHL tough guys.

As NHL enforcers, we have a code that we follow. You won't find it in the NHL rulebook. It's unwritten, but anyone who fills this role knows it and appreciates why it's important. It's really just a series of common courtesies based on fundamental fairness.

If another player is banged up, you don't force him to fight. If an opponent is down and clearly out of the fight, the fight is over.

And . . . you don't jump a guy.

Ryan VandenBussche wasn't really a heavyweight. I can see why he might not have wanted to wait until a bigger guy was ready. But he jumped me a couple of times, and the second time he did he made me look bad in front of my home crowd. I was so pissed off, I couldn't even talk during intermission. I sought him out in the second period and settled the score convincingly. I had people at the game and they said VandenBussche was unrecognizable as he left the Arrowhead Pond of Anaheim that night. His nose was right sideways on his face; it was lopsided from the start of the "fair fight."

One player who had very specific ideas about his own code was Krzysztof Oliwa. When I tangled with him for the first time, he was playing for the New Jersey Devils. I knew former NHL goalie Glenn "Chico" Resch well, and he was serving as the Devils' colour analyst on television at the time. Chico warned me that Oliwa was on a mission that year.

"Stu, just a heads up," Resch said. "Our boy Kryz is fighting everybody. He's probably going to want to tangle with you tonight."

Wonderful news. Adding another snot-nosed rookie to my dance card was not high on the list of things I had hoped to accomplish during that night's match. Fighting a rookie was something that happened more often in the pre-season. The regular season is hard enough what with all the fights with existing tough guys. If you can avoid an unnecessary fight, you're going to avoid it. But there is always some kid looking to make a name for himself. I had been there myself, so I usually obliged. That's part of the code too. But I didn't care for it.

As Resch predicted, Oliwa came looking for a fight as soon as we were on the ice together. Oliwa was one of four NHL players ever to come from Poland, and his thick accent was unmistakable.

Big Kryz and I are shoulder to shoulder before the draw in our first shift on ice. He leans in and says, "Stu, my team must vin zis game. We fight now."

"What did you say?" I asked, unable to make sense of what he had just said.

"Stu, my team must vin zis game," he said again. "We fight now."

Gloves flew off and haymakers were thrown fast and furious. He was a tough kid. But to me, the funny part of this story is that we had the same conversation every time we fought.

"Stu," he said, "my team must vin zis game. We fight now." Every time we fought, the same simple phrase. We fought six times during our careers, and each fight started with the same words. Clearly, Kryz found the one phrase of the English language that would allow him to do his job and he mastered that phrase to his advantage. It made me laugh then and still does today.

Oliwa was an underrated fighter. He was 240 pounds and he could be a handful. Because he wasn't a heavy puncher, he wasn't a fighter that I worried about. But I respected his ability. He was also a real pro when it came to the fight game and would become angry if he didn't believe that his opponent lived up to his version of the Code.

That happened one night when I was playing for Los Angeles. My Kings were in Pittsburgh, where Oliwa was playing at that point in his career, and it was a rare night in my dealings with him—he didn't want to fight early in the first period. It looked like we wouldn't fight at all that night. But the Kings got down by a couple goals and I was looking to get into it with Oliwa with the hope of giving my team a lift. I wanted to change the momentum.

We end up on the ice together. I give him a shot—a cross-check on the hips—to let him know that I need to get into it. But he's being disciplined. He ignores me as if to say this isn't the right time for a fight. But from my viewpoint, it's the perfect time for a fight. He's waving me off but I'm not giving up. Later in that same shift, I give him another shot. Still no response. I decide I'm not taking no for an answer. As he is chasing a puck back into his own zone, I track him down and I cross-check him hard enough to send him sprawling to the ice and crashing into the boards. At this point, he has no choice and the gloves come off.

It was a pretty good scrap and we both headed to the penalty box. I knew as we skated over that Oliwa would want to talk. He always had something to say. I couldn't help but laugh as Oliwa leaned over the penalty box partition to address me.

"Stu," he said, "I am not asshole. You are not asshole. If you wish to fight, you just say, 'Kryz, we fight now.'"

I knew Kryz was offended by how this had all played out. I tried to listen respectfully to what he had to say, but it was difficult not to laugh. He was so serious. This was the world according to Kryz. He wanted to tell me there was no need to do what I did. He was probably right.

—

While Dennis Vial was never considered a top heavyweight, he was a really tough guy. I did have a couple of memorable fights with him. Neither fight was great, but I remember them because of the unusual circumstances.

One night, when I was playing for Chicago and Dennis was with the Wings, I was fighting Vial and our sticks and gloves were strewn all over the ice. We had to navigate through a field of debris as we battled. At one point, a stick ended up between us. I felt it with my skate and I pointed down to it while never taking my eyes off Dennis. Instead of just filing away the information, Vial looked down for the stick.

In a hockey fight you take whatever advantage comes your way. When Dennis looked down, I connected on a really solid uppercut. I mean, this was the stuff of the Three Stooges. "Hey Moe, looky here!" Boink!

Vial got to pay it back, though. When I was with Anaheim and Dennis was a Senator, I scuffed him up pretty good in a fairly one-sided fight. But at some point during the bout, he caught me with a left that broke my nose.

I never told anyone; you never want anyone to know that another fighter got in on you. Nobody noticed because the mark he left was really small. Fortunately for me, the fight happened near the end of a period. Instead of heading to the penalty box, I left for the dressing room. I wanted to get in there before my teammates so I could reset the bone in my nose.

He clipped me on the right side, breaking a bone that pushed a little bit out the other side of my nose. The bone was pointed west, and I was sure it should have been running north and south. Those bones are small. You had to look close to notice it. I reset it in the privacy of the dressing room, pushing the bone back into place. I never said a word to the trainer.

If you're a tough guy, you never want to admit an opponent hurt you. It was the only broken nose I ever suffered in my career and a doctor never looked at it. It was sore the next day. But I had other fights before my nose was fully healed.

Part of the code is what tough guys impose on themselves. It's like the scene from the movie *Fight Club* when Brad Pitt's character, Tyler Durden, says, "Welcome to Fight Club. The first rule of Fight Club is: You do not talk about Fight Club. The second rule of Fight Club is: You DO NOT talk about Fight Club."

The first rule of being an NHL enforcer is that you don't admit when you are hurt. The second rule of being an NHL enforcer is that you never waver in living by the first rule.

Fighters in my era didn't confess to injuries and pain because they were worried about their roster spots. From the day I started in the NHL, I heard that fighting was on its way out of the game. Nothing brought that home more than my first contract negotiation with crusty Blackhawks general manager Bob Pulford in 1992. As we haggled over a few thousand dollars, Pulford implied he was taking a risk by even signing me. "Stu, I don't even know if there will even be fighting in the NHL next season," he said.

While I realized Pully was just negotiating, it didn't change the fact that I was day-to-day an NHL tough guy. There are more tough guys in the world than there are roster spots. I was fairly confident in my abilities. I believed I was good at my job. But I also understood I could be replaced with one phone call to our minor-league affiliate. I also knew I was being paid well in comparison to my non–hockey playing peers, and I wanted to stay on NHL pay for as long as I could.

That's the simplest explanation for why, in my time, tough guys didn't disclose their injuries. But pride was also mixed into our thinking. We never wanted to admit that anyone could hurt us.

The only person the tough guy code who allowed you to tell was the heavyweight on the opposing team. It was normal to ask a fellow heavyweight not to challenge you if you were nursing an injury. Most of the time, a rival would agree to hold off, mainly because he wanted the same courtesy extended to him when he had an issue.

Several times in my career, I received three fighting majors during a game. But I fought four times in a game only once, while participating in a Calgary Flames training camp in 1988. The Flames' rookies were playing the Vancouver Canucks' rookies at the Father David Bauer Arena in Calgary.

This was during my second season with the team. We had a big, tough team and the Canucks had an equally rough bunch. This was more of a street brawl than a hockey game. After two periods, I had already accumulated three fighting majors. I remember fighting Jim Revenberg and, I believe, Ronnie Stern, though I can't be sure. It was a chaotic game.

Paul Baxter had been my coach in the IHL the prior year, and he was also coaching this game. When he was finished delivering his intermission speech, all the players started filing out for the third period. But I hung back in my dressing room stall, with no helmet and gloves on, believing that I'd been ejected because of my third fight. I was ready to hit the showers.

"What are you doing?" he asked.

"I've fought three times—I was gonna grab a shower," I answered, knowing that in any pro league, three fighting majors means you're gone.

"Uh, Stu this isn't exactly sanctioned NHL hockey," Baxter said. "This is an exhibition game. There's still twenty minutes left to play. Let's get back out there, champ." I had another fight in the third.

What's amusing to me about that memory is that once I became an established fighter, I never wanted to fight in three consecutive games, let alone four times in one game. Fighting heavyweights drains you, and my energy level seemed to dip after I fought two games in a row. Whenever I fought in three consecutive games, especially once I was in my thirties, I wasn't as effective in that third game. So I did everything I could to avoid that third fight until my body got the space to rest and repair. I believed I was at a significant disadvantage.

That logic is no different than an MLB manager opting to shut down a closer for a day after he has pitched a couple of days in a row. Could he pitch that third day? For sure. But his fastball probably won't have the same zip and the slider might not break as sharply. Could I fight in three consecutive games? For sure. But I was never going to be at my best in that third fight.

Of this much you could be sure, I was going to do everything I could, within reason, to avoid that third fight in a third consecutive game. That scenario happened during the 1998–99 season, when I was playing for the Anaheim Ducks and I encountered a young Calgary Flames heavyweight named Rocky Thompson.

The Flames had just called Thompson up from the Saint John Flames, probably for the sole purpose of fighting me and some of the other heavies on the Flames' tour of California. Even though he weighed only two hundred pounds, Rocky could handle himself. With only fifteen games played over two seasons, he was still technically a rookie. But I knew his reputation.

So it was shaping up to be an unfortunate night. It wasn't only about fighting in three games in a row. I didn't like fighting smaller fighters and I didn't like fighting rookies.

As I've mentioned, no coach ever ordered me to fight someone. Craig Hartsburg was the lone exception. Hartzy had a way of pushing my buttons and he was not shy to do so. I fought a lot under Craig.

If we were going to Vancouver, he would say, "Stu, I need you to be thinking about Brashear. We may need that from you early."

In two seasons under Hartsburg's command, I had forty-two regular-season fights. I had five seasons in which I fought twenty or more times in the NHL, and two of those were with Hartsburg. He saw my role as being more important than other coaches did. He squeezed as much as he could out of me those two years—the pressure was noticeably different.

Still, I had made up my mind that I would not fight Thompson that night. I was thirty-three and he was twenty-one. If I'd been fresh, I would have engaged him without hesitation. But I could see no upside in breaking my own rule about three fights in three nights.

The trouble was, he had made up his mind to fight me. He challenged me early and then landed a couple of quick punches before I reacted. It evolved into a pretty good tilt. Maybe it was a draw, or maybe I won it late. All I know for sure was that I was pissed when it was over.

I thought Rocky had crossed the line by jumping the gun. Also, I didn't like that he had clipped me in this one. I ended up chasing him around later in the game and told him I wanted another bout. He refused to give me one. That did nothing to calm me down. Another code violation: If you're going to put me in a spot where I had to fight you, you'd better return the favour. If somebody wants a second shot for whatever reason, you better give it to him. Especially in Thompson's situation; this young punk had just jumped me off the draw and landed a couple before I could get started. I had done it before many times. I did it with Dave Brown. Thompson didn't last long.

The rule about taking the same medicine you dish out applies to everyone, not just tough guys. If you're going to run around out there, you'd better answer for it when someone calls you out, no matter who you are. When it came to hockey fights, I stayed in my lane. I didn't challenge non-fighters. The one exception was superstar Eric Lindros.

Never did I feel guilty trying to coax Lindros into a fight. He was my size—six-foot-four, 240 pounds—and he seemed to enjoy running people over. People don't appreciate the skill that goes into a good hockey hit. The sheer skating ability, timing, and athleticism required to execute a big hit make it an art form. It's an elite skill, and it's often not the big guys who pull it off. The big open-ice hitters are usually more athletic than brawny. That elite timing and predatory instinct in a guy the size of Lindros made him a freight train. He could, and did, hurt guys. He knocked Ulf Samuelsson and Martin Ručinský out of the 1991 Canada Cup when he was still in junior. They were seasoned pros representing their countries and should have known to keep their heads up.

Eric blasted more than one of my teammates, so I felt I had a right to call him out whenever it happened. It would have been entertaining, had he ever been willing to fight me. He wasn't. Multiple times I asked Big Eric to drop the gloves, and each time he showed no interest.

On the one hand, I didn't blame him for saying no. He was one of the league's best players. It would have been a win for me just to get him off the ice in a five-minute major penalty. I'm sure his coach wanted to keep him away from me. On the other hand, I think he would have earned a little more respect around his game had he answered for it from time to time.

—

Matthew Barnaby had a reputation for being somewhat of a pain in the ass. However, for most of my career he never bothered any of my teammates and he sure never pulled his act with me. So I left him alone. Well, that all changed when I got to Hartford the last year the "Mighty Whale" was in existence.

You see Matthew was in Buffalo at the time, and the Sabres were a great Adams Division rival to my beloved Whalers. Well, on this one particular game day the Sabres were in Hartford early in the year. In fact, I had just been picked up by the Whalers on waivers and I was still pretty new to the team.

Kelly Chase was my partner in crime back then. We played on the same line and we terrorized some teams. He was also an awful prankster.

Chaser comes in the room sometime before we go out for morning skate that day and sits down beside me in my locker. He says, "What's the deal with you and Barnaby?" I said, "Nothing, why? What do you mean?"

Chaser says, "He's out there in the hall doing an interview with Whalers TV and sayin' stuff like . . . 'I don't get why Hartford traded for Grimson. Is he really that tough? I just don't see how he's going to help them.'"

I said, "You're not serious! You don't say crap like that." It's true: players *don't* say stuff like that. But I figured this is my first time playing for an Eastern Conference team and maybe the culture is a little different on the other side of the league. In any event, I'm not having it. I don't think I slept all afternoon before the game because I was so keyed up to straighten out Barnaby that night.

Warm-up rolls around and I am looping over to Buffalo's side of the centre redline glaring at Barnaby and he's got this goofy unassuming look on his face. Paul Maurice was our coach back then and to start the game Mo had Kevin Dineen on left wing opposite Barnaby's line who had started for the Sabres. The play goes down to Buffalo's end right off the draw and then the play starts to migrate back toward the Whalers' end of the ice. Dineen is my cross shift as I'm on left wing also. As Dino is skating by our bench, I grab his jersey and haul him toward the bench. "Dino! Get off!" I say as I pile over the boards and head directly to Barnaby.

With absolutely no regard for the play going on around us, I skate over to Barnaby and I give him a shot. "Let's go punk, shake 'em off!" He's looking at me thinking something like *I want no part of this and, by the way, it's like the first shift of the game!*

Once I realize that Barnaby isn't the least bit interested, I more or less play out the rest of the shift and then head back to our bench. I end up sitting next to Chaser when I arrive. He and I end up chuckling over what I assumed was a pretty humorous instance of me embarrassing and taunting Barnaby and his whole team for that matter. Paul Maurice leaned in between us both so he could make direct eye contact. "What exactly are you two up to? Why is it you take our first-line left winger off the ice so that you can jump out there?"

I explained, "Mo, I thought it'd be a great way to set the tone early if I went out there and tuned up Barnaby."

Mo replied, "*You* thought that would be a good idea? You don't think you ought to let your coach in on the plan? After all, this is kinda my bench to run, right?"

I shrugged my shoulders and sheepishly tried to laugh it off. The thought had not really occurred to me, strange as that sounds. I'm not quite sure why I thought it was within my discretion to start managing the matchups that night. There's no question that Chaser pushing my buttons early in the day had a lot to do with it.

That little exchange occurred early on in the 1997–98 season. It wasn't until ten years later that Kelly finally came clean and told me what really happened. Chaser and I are sitting in the stands at a morning skate before a Predators–Blues game that he and I were broadcasting. That's the moment he chooses to tell me he made the whole thing up a decade earlier. Barnaby never said anything like what Chaser had reported on that day. He fabricated the whole thing just to get a rise out of me. And did he ever . . . I may have been wrapped a little tight back then.

But Barnaby and I crossed paths again before I retired. I suspect our incident in Hartford left Barnaby thinking he should probably answer for the way I challenged him that night. My one issue was I just didn't like fighting smaller guys. For one thing, I didn't want to hurt a guy just because he'd bitten off more than he could chew. But also, there is almost no way to win that fight in a way that works to your team's advantage. If you win against a smaller guy, no one gets much satisfaction since the outcome is what everyone expected. And if the smaller guy does well, he gets points just for showing up. Barnaby got more of those points than he did wins, so I was happy on most nights just to let him be.

But one night Barnaby insisted. This was when I was playing with the Mighty Ducks. Usually Matt would run around, talking trash and singling out smaller guys and pounding them. He always had a smile on his face. He knew how to antagonize.

He tended not to play that way when I was on the ice. But on this particular shift, he took a run at me. Then he chopped the back of my legs with his stick. The officials missed it but that was no concern to me. It was Barnaby who was now the focus of my attention.

When the whistle blew, my line was supposed to go off at the end of our shift. But I noticed that Barnaby was staying on. I was beside myself over the fact that Matt clearly had something to settle with me. I motioned to the bench telling Hartsburg, "I'm staying on to take care of this punk."

Barnaby was going to pay a price for acting up. I pounded him pretty good, although I didn't hurt him. He controlled the damage by staying out of range of my right hand, but I tossed him around a bit to embarrass him in his own rink. Still, I left the exchange feeling less than satisfied; I wanted to tear that boy apart that night for behaving like he did. Did he think he was going to enhance his reputation by fighting me? I couldn't figure it.

—

If you were watching the 2016 All-Star Game, you would have seen heavyweight John Scott putting on a clinic. And you would have seen his teammates absolutely loving it. Fans went crazy for it too. And sportswriters couldn't get enough of it either, even if some of them were indignant that an enforcer was there in the first place.

The thing is, there is precedent for a heavyweight to be invited to the All-Star Game. During the 1992–93 season, the NHL was attempting to create a little more buzz around the All-Star Game. The league decided it would invite certain players, other than the All Stars themselves, who were particularly gifted at a variety of specialized skills. In order to identify those players, each NHL team hosted its own skills competition and the top four at each skill in each Conference would compete at the All-Star Game in Montreal.

Back in the days of wooden sticks, the Western Conference stacked up in the following way in the hardest shot category: Chris Chelios at 98.7 mph, St. Louis Blues defenceman Stéphane Quintal at 98.1, and Vancouver Canucks defenceman Gerald Diduck at 98.0. Coming in at number four in the Western Conference was yours truly at 97.7. I was going to the All-Star Game!

My newfound All-Star status was not universally well-received. *Chicago Tribune* reporter Mike Kiley said my invite to the gala was another case of the frog marrying the princess. "It may make a good fairy tale," Kiley wrote, "but it's tough to believe such things can happen in real life." But it did happen.

The guys gave it to me pretty good; I mean you see the irony right? I'm an All-Star averaging three or four shifts a night at the time. But I was proud to have earned the trip. I was looking forward to taking the entire family.

Unfortunately, it just wasn't in the cards. The last game before All-Star break I got into a skirmish with Detroit Red Wings forward Gerard Gallant. Gallant and I were just shoving back and forth after a stoppage. Awkwardly, he tried to punch me with a gloved hand and his thumb got me in the left eye, causing it to swell shut almost immediately. Because I couldn't see, I couldn't go to Montreal. One of the truly disappointing moments of my career. Competing against guys like Al Iafrate and others would have been a great experience.

A greater disappointment came in another form though. I never really established that I could play a regular shift at the NHL level. I left the game believing that I had more to contribute just in terms of the way the game is played apart from my role.

I aspired to emulate players like Sandy McCarthy, Bob Probert, Chris Simon, and Joey Kocur. McCarthy had a seven-season span when he averaged better than ten minutes per game. He proved he could score ten goals per season. Probert netted twenty or more twice. Kocur earned a reputation as a decent defensive forward, playing for a time on the Detroit Red Wings' Grind Line. He scored sixteen goals for the Wings in 1989–90. Chris Simon scored twenty-nine goals in 1999–2000. Going back a little further, Tiger Williams had thirty-five goals one season (1980–81), and a few more seasons in the twenties.

The truth is that I played that brand of game as an amateur, and even in the minors I was both skilled and tough. But there came a time as I entered the NHL that I began to invest more in the latter at the expense of the former. The shift was gradual and almost unnoticeable. But over time I found myself focusing far more of my attention on fighting than I did on simply playing the game. Ultimately the result was that my game being nearly one-dimensional for much of my career. To their credit, Probert, Simon, and the others struck a perfect balance in that playing and playing effectively was their primary focus. Apart from that, they were ready to do what needed to be done when the gloves came off. I had great respect for this category of players.

Mindset is important in competition. As a junior, I was a full-service player and I performed like one. I viewed myself as having a dual purpose. I saw myself as a twenty-five-goal scorer and an established heavyweight.

When I needed to fight, I did. But the other 90 percent of the time, I was thinking about being a quality hockey player. When I had that mindset, I had great confidence in my game. I was a Phil Esposito–style scorer in junior hockey. Deflections. Rebounds.

Quick wrist shots from the slot. I played the same way in university and was a point-per-game player.

Even as a first-year pro, I had faith in my abilities as a player. I found the net nine times in thirty-seven games before my season was ended by reconstructive knee surgery. I was on a twenty-goal pace before I blew out my knee. Even though I had almost a thousand penalty minutes in three seasons in the IHL, I still didn't view my role as wholly that of the tough guy. I saw myself as a reliable player who could be an effective fighter when it was needed.

The change in my perspective occurred when I reached the NHL. I don't know exactly when or why the change in my mind-set occurred. Again, it was subtle and went undetected by even me and those around me. I'm sure it had a lot to do with the fact that I was now tangling with some of the toughest men in the game, and these men could hurt you. See Dave Brown. All I know for sure is that at some point I became consumed by my role as a tough guy. I was no longer thinking like a player trying to earn more ice time. I was almost exclusively devoted to being the best NHL heavyweight I could be.

There was no single NHL coach who set out to pigeon-hole me. I pigeon-holed myself. I over-invested in the physical side of the game. Call it one of my character flaws. Instead of working on taking pucks off the wall effectively and contributing to our breakouts, I was always thinking about the next potential bout on my docket. I would be fixating on Probert or Brashear and their tendencies instead of concentrating on playing a hockey game.

During the summers, I wasn't working on my skating. I was in the gym. When I started my NHL career in 1988, I weighed about 225 pounds. And every team seemed to have two heavyweights my size. I remember my former Calgary Flames teammate Tim Hunter telling me that when he broke into the NHL in 1981 he was six-foot-two, 205 pounds, and that made him a big guy back then. But not for long.

Guys were making themselves bigger and bigger every season I was in the NHL. I bulked up right along with them. I topped out at about 250. You had to be to hold your own with 265-pound men like Georges Laraque. I transformed the boathouse at the cottage into a weight room. It was a great set-up, with free weights, a squat rack, Stairmaster, bench, and stationary bike. I'd work out every day, then jump in the lake to cool off. What I wasn't doing was working on the rest of my game.

—

When fans want to talk to me about my NHL career, they're generally looking for a Bob Probert story or what was going on in my head the night I went berserk against the Toronto Maple Leafs. They want to know what it's like to play for coach Mike Keenan or Scotty Bowman or seek my thoughts on who was the NHL's most underrated fighter.

I'm always willing to talk about the past. But when I think about my time in the NHL, my fight card isn't the first thing on my mind. I think about all the great people I met, the privilege I enjoyed being in an NHL dressing room, and all the fun moments I had as a player.

Some players remember how they scored the three hundredth goal of their career. I remember that my daughter Jayne was born September 2, 1999, right before I started training camp with the Los Angeles Kings.

On game days, Pam and I would drive to the rink separately. I came in my SUV for the morning. Pam and our four children would drive up later in the afternoon in our minivan to see the game.

One night early in the season, for reasons I don't recall, Pam and I switched cars post-game for the trip home. Because Pam's car had the infant car seat, I had baby Jayne with me as I drove up the Staples Center service ramp where the autograph seekers were stationed.

I stopped at the top of the ramp to sign some autographs for the Kings' faithful. Fans began to crowd around the vehicle and the fans toward the back of the pack had no idea which player was stopping to sign. One young fan worked his way closer to the vehicle and finally figured out that it was the Kings' enforcer inside and blurted out, "Hang on!! The Grim Reaper drives a minivan?!?!?"

I wonder what that guy would have thought if he knew the Grim Reaper could be bullied by a four-year-old. During the 1997–98 season, my Carolina Hurricanes were trying desperately to make the playoffs. Most of the guys had started playoff beards early with the hope of creating a little extra mojo. At the time, my daughter Hannah was four. She had mentioned to me that she didn't much care for the "dirt" on my face.

We lost our last five games, including our season finale at Washington, and didn't qualify for the post-season. The 'Canes flew home that night and everyone was asleep when I got home. Hannah had wormed her way into our bed and she was sleeping next to Pam when I got home late. She woke up when I climbed into bed.

"Daddy?" she asked.

"Yes, it's me, Hannah," I said.

The conversation woke up Pam, who asked if we were in or out. She hadn't stayed up for the end of the game.

"We lost—we're done," I said.

Hannah perked up. "Does that mean you're not in the play-offs?" she asked.

"Yes," I said.

"Does that mean you can take off the dirt?" Hannah asked.

"Yes," I answered.

"Thank you. Please take it off Daddy," she said.

"I will Hannah. First thing in the morning," I said.

"No, Daddy I want you to take it off NOW," she said.

Not only did the Grim Reaper drive a minivan, but he was a softy when it came to his daughters. I couldn't help but laugh while shaving at two o'clock in the morning.

13

MISTAKES, POOR DECISIONS, AND BAD LUCK

Hockey is complicated. When a hockey game begins, it is impossible to know exactly how it will end. Compare it to chess. Given the rules of the game, there are more possible outcomes in a chess game than there are atoms in the universe. Now consider how much more complicated hockey is than chess. Players can move in any direction, at varying speeds. Unlike chess pieces, hockey players don't have to wait their turn, and they're all moving at once.

Now factor in the coaches' input—unlike chess pieces, hockey players are all different, and coaches determine the configuration of skills on the ice at any moment. Then factor in chance—a weird bounce off the boards, a skate caught in a rut, a rough patch of ice that ruins a perfect pass. Then add in personality, emotion, and backstory. The fact is, though there are really only two possible outcomes (three if you include a tie), there are an infinite number of ways to get there.

The number of decisions that go into playing a game is incalculable. Not just large-scale decisions like whether to pass or shoot, whether to end your shift quickly once you get the puck in deep, or which guy to pick up on the backcheck. But little things, like choosing an angle as you close the gap, or adjusting your speed as you commit to a forecheck. Decisions so small you don't remember making them. You may not even think about them as you make them. As much as the outcome of a game is decided by the big save or the clutch goal, it is also determined by the accumulation of this infinite cascade of small and large decisions.

And if a game is that complicated, imagine how all those variables impact an entire career.

When I look back, I think about how the Chicago Blackhawks' decision to leave me unprotected for the 1993 expansion draft changed my life. I loved Chicago, but I would have had a completely different career if it hadn't been for a decision made in the Hawks' front office.

I also think about how the Red Wings' decision to put me on waivers in 1996 cost me a chance to win a Stanley Cup. I was happy for my former teammates as I watched the Red Wings win the Cup in 1997. But I would be lying if I didn't admit I was disappointed that I was not on the ice celebrating with them. It occurred to me while watching the Red Wings sweep the Philadelphia Flyers that I might not ever have another chance to win the Stanley Cup. That turned out to be true. I played five more seasons, made the playoffs twice, and never advanced beyond the first round.

I can't second-guess the decisions other people made. It was their job to make their teams better, and by definition that means making difficult decisions. Every year, every GM but one comes up short. No one can count on getting it right. In any case, it was never a GM's job to make me happy. That reality is just part of playing hockey for a living.

But I can second-guess my own decisions. It might have been a mistake to ask general manager Jack Ferreira for a trade during my first stint in Anaheim. While I enjoyed my time in Detroit and it gave me a chance to win, I didn't have the same stature with the Red Wings that I enjoyed in Anaheim. I was a leader in the dressing room. I was a crowd favourite. I was comfortable living in California. In hindsight, I may have been too impatient with coach Ron Wilson's decision to use only one tough guy per game.

By that time, I had been in the game long enough to understand that nothing is as temporary as an NHL coach's decision. If I had been patient, I could have easily been playing regularly again in a short period of time. My problem was that players like me had little leverage to push for the things that they believed were important to their careers. The only leverage I had was the willingness to move. To get what I wanted I had to be able to follow through on the threat of asking for a trade.

There is no question that the money impinged on my judgment. Salaries were rising significantly in that era, and my deal was expiring at the end of the 1994–95 season. One concern was whether the healthy scratches would diminish my value. The other issue was whether Jack Ferreira would offer me as much as I could earn if I were traded to a larger market.

Today when I look back, I believe I shouldn't have been as concerned about those issues as I was. Ferreira respected me and always treated me fairly. There was no reason to believe he wouldn't have taken care of me in the offseason. Likewise, there was no reason to believe my reputation would be eroded by being a healthy scratch now and then. Everyone understood how the tough guy system worked. Enforcers didn't dress if the coach didn't believe they would be needed.

The concern about my value dropping was also probably misplaced. By then, I had already registered more than a hundred NHL fights. It's not as if NHL general managers didn't know what I had to offer. But then the trade request wasn't crazy. Looking back, I can make a case both for and against.

But asking Carolina Hurricanes general manager Jim Rutherford for a trade? That's a situation where I definitely overplayed my hand.

Coach Paul Maurice played me more than any other coach ever had or ever would. He put me on a line with Kent Manderville and Paul Ranheim, and most nights Maurice would roll four lines and we'd end up playing eight or nine minutes. That may not seem like much, but those minutes were huge for a player like me. Double. I was accustomed to playing three or four minutes per game.

In this expanded role, I posted my best NHL season in 1997–98, playing all eighty-two games, and registering three goals and seven points with 204 penalty minutes.

Maurice appreciated what I offered as a physical player and a leader. He respected my dressing room presence. He viewed me as more than just a tough guy. This may have been the best fit I ever had in the league. I appreciated the expanded role. But I was midway through my five-year deal paying $540,000 per season, and my agent Larry Kelly pointed out that I was probably underpaid now. The market for tough guys was shifting and there were players making $750,000 and above. In Larry's view, my expanded role provided the leverage to redo my aging deal.

I discussed my situation with Pam, and she agreed with Kelly. The suggestion was that I ask general manager Jim Rutherford to renegotiate the last couple of years on my contract. Failing that, I would use the only leverage I had, which was to move. I would ask for a trade. I set up a meeting with him after the season and made my case for a reworked contract.

Rutherford is a straight shooter, a player's GM. He said he needed some time to mull it over. We agreed to meet again in a couple weeks' time. Ultimately, Rutherford told me he couldn't do it. "As a matter of policy, Stu, we don't reopen player contracts here."

"If you aren't going to do it, I need to go somewhere else," I said.

I regret that decision. It was a naive strategy, far too brash for someone in my position. Few contracts were renegotiated in those days, and probably none were done for players in my position. I'm not even sure it was permissible under the Collective Bargaining Agreement at the time.

The Hurricanes were also not a big-spending team. Rutherford's payroll for the 1998–99 season was just over $28 million, about $1.1 million under the league average. By comparison, the Detroit Red Wings were at $48 million. The Philadelphia Flyers and New York Rangers each spent more than $39 million. The San Jose Sharks and Chicago Blackhawks were both over $35 million.

What was I thinking? The Hurricanes were never going to renegotiate. Instead, when I asked they traded me to the Ducks.

The deal was Kevin Haller and me for Dave Karpa and a fourth-round pick. I was happy to be back in Anaheim, but my situation wasn't nearly as Grimson-friendly as it had been in Carolina. Hartsburg would never use me the way Maurice did.

—

The dream of being an NHL player comes with the hope for a Stanley Cup celebration moment on the ice. Sticks, gloves, and helmets litter the ice. Players overcome by emotion. Arms raised. Giddy teammates blanket the ice. Coaches and athletes embracing in a way that only they understand.

I missed that moment. In a career that spans fourteen years, you should know both the thrill of victory and the agony of defeat. But I did have the latter. I had the moment that I would just as soon forget and that moment came with the Ducks in 1999.

Hartsburg demanded plenty from me that season. He worked an enforcer into his strategy more than any coach I ever had. He believed a well-timed fight could spark a team, and he looked to me to deliver that on a regular basis. In 1998–99, I totalled twenty-eight fights in the pre-season, regular season, and play-offs. According to dropyourgloves.com, my record was 10–4–9 in the fights they scored. I poured a lot into being one of Hartsburg's Ducks that year. I battled for him and that group because that's the role. Especially when the coach puts a premium on that role.

Early in the season, I even recorded the only two-goal game of my NHL career to help us beat the Tampa Bay Lightning 5–3. That gave us a four-game unbeaten streak.

The goals I scored weren't exactly artistry on ice. An Antti Aalto shot from the slot struck my skate and snuck past Tampa Bay goalie Daren Puppa. That goal, the tenth of my career to that point, ended a twenty-game goalless slump. Less than four minutes later, I caught a pass at the top of the circle to Puppa's right and let loose an absolute muffin that squibbed off the toe of my stick and beat Puppa under the pads for my second goal.

Elliott Teaford's story in the *Los Angeles Times* jokingly referred to me as the Mighty Ducks' "new scoring sensation." It was one of the more memorable games of my career. "The best thing about scoring two goals in a game is that you want to go out and do it again," I told Teaford.

The guys, and the media, were all having fun with the story. One of the reporters jokingly asked whether I had any scoring bonus clauses in my contract.

"I don't think so," I said. "I've got to call my agent."

Under Hartsburg, I played an average of less than four minutes per game. But he believed in me. He saw me as a leader and as someone who could turn a game for us if I pressed the physical advantage in the right way.

That's why it hurt so bad when I let him and the group down on April 26, 1999.

—

Led by Paul Kariya and Teemu Selanne, the Mighty Ducks had a solid season that year, posting a 35–34–13 record to earn a playoff spot. We thought we could surprise the Red Wings in the first round of the playoffs, and we were disappointed when we lost the first two games of the series in Detroit.

We hoped it would be different in Anaheim. It was. We had a 2–1 lead after one period and were playing them pretty even in the second. Even after the Wings tied the score, we were still very much in the third game. Our crowd was buzzing. It felt as if we might climb back into the series that game.

It went bad for me and the Mighty Ducks when my old teammate Kris Draper, started running around stirring it up while I was out there. He took a cheap shot at our centre, Antti Aalto, and I snapped. As soon as Draper ran Aalto from behind, I cross-checked Draper up high. Draper dropped hard. Did he sell it? Yes, no question. But he knew me, knew my reputation, and knew that I was not going to get the benefit of any doubt. What I didn't see was that the ref had his hand up on a delayed call on my teammate Travis Green for elbowing Draper before he hit Aalto.

Don Koharski and the late Mick McGeough were the referees that night. They ruled my attack was "intent to injure" and I received a match penalty. That left us shorthanded five on three. Steve Yzerman put the game away. I had cost the Ducks the game, and maybe the series. We were down 3–0 coming out of Game Three.

Were we going to win that series if I had not taken such a misguided penalty? Not likely. Were we going to win that game? Maybe. All I know for sure is that my penalty could not have come at a worse time. These are the plays that a game or even a series can turn on. Two guys come together, both trying to win some small confrontation for their club's benefit. And when one of them makes a bad decision, it means everything is different from that point on.

That match penalty meant I was ejected. I could have showered and left the building. But if Stan Grimson had taught me anything, it was that I needed to stay and answer for the mistake I made. I needed to accept responsibility. And I wanted our fans to know how badly I regretted what I had done. This was the only way to communicate that to them.

The media gave me credit for showing up after the game to answer their questions. Reporters didn't have to press me about whether my antics had cost the team the game. I admitted my culpability immediately. It was my job to protect and defend Aalto, but I overreacted in this instance. I needed to go about that in a different way.

"This is not the time of year to retaliate," I told the media. "And, really, the game turned on that specific incident. Our guys had battled and played hard up until then, as well as we've played by far in the series. And then what I did made it pretty tough on us."

The future lawyer in me couldn't resist putting a finer point on the fact that I hadn't been charged with the proper crime. It wasn't intent to injure. Common sense made that pretty clear.

"If I'd wanted to hurt him, I could have," I said. "If I'd intended to injure Draper, he'd be injured. Someone submit the clip of that to the Members of the Academy. That was a fine piece of acting."

I was still guilty. But in my opinion, the proper call should have been a double minor at worst. None of that mattered, though. The Red Wings would have been on the power play regardless of what the referees called my infraction. I had reacted in anger. As soon as I connected with Draper, I knew I had hurt my team.

Because several of the Red Wings knew me from my days in Detroit, they didn't seem as angry about the hit as they could have been. "He kind of crossed that line, but you can't blame Stu," Detroit's Brendan Shanahan said. "That's his job."

None of my Anaheim teammates threw me under the bus either. But the penalty was all I could think about when I got home. I wasn't done accepting responsibility. The person I most wanted to apologize to was Hartsburg.

It was my habit to be early for every practice. But the day after Game 3, I arrived at the practice rink earlier than everyone except for the coaches and trainers. When I walked into Hartsburg's office I could hardly speak to communicate the regret I had over the night before. I was sobbing.

"I let you down and I'm really sorry about that," I told Hartsburg. "I know you understand where I was coming from and I probably don't have to explain." I couldn't stop sobbing, but I had more to say.

"It was flat out the dumbest thing I could have done in that situation," I continued. "I'm sorry it hurt us in the way it did."

Hartzy listened until I had nothing left to say. And then he offered some perspective. "We're trying to build something here, Stu. And these are the lessons we have to learn as a group if we hope to achieve anything."

He treated me fairly. That's more than I could have asked for. You live and you learn from it. In this case, I learned by making the biggest mistake of my pro hockey career.

—

My contract expired with the Ducks that summer and my best offer in free agency came from right up the interstate with the Los Angeles Kings at the same $500,000 salary. An important reason why I signed with the Kings was that I didn't have to move my family. It just made for a longer commute.

But the Kings were a good fit. We had a great group in Luc Robitaille, Nelson Emerson, Ian Laperrière, and others who remain friends today.

There was, however, a minor mutiny going on inside the Kings' room when I arrived. Several vets were not seeing the world in quite the same way as head coach Andy Murray. Again, out of respect for the chain of command, I got along pretty well with Andy. He used me a lot and valued me in my role. But Andy had a unique approach to the game that didn't square with a significant core of the Kings roster. Andy had no experience playing at the pro level and his coaching resumé was almost exclusively based in Europe. Right or wrong, that meant you were in an uphill battle from the day you set foot in the room during this period in the game.

The Kings were 38–28–13 in 2000–01, my only year there. And we had one of the highest-scoring teams in the Western Conference. It was a fun season. After the way I left Carolina, I didn't want to walk away from another good fit. But I was also inching toward the end of my career, and I was hoping to find some longer-term security at market value in free agency in the upcoming summer. That's why I was disappointed when GM Dave Taylor offered me just a one-year deal for $500,000, the same salary I had been earning the past several years.

I rejected the offer for two reasons. First, several of the tough guys were now making $700,000 and above. Second, I was hoping to sign another multi-year deal, just in case this was my last. Finally, I wanted to be with a team that had a better chance to win the Stanley Cup.

San Jose Sharks general manager Doug Wilson was in the ballpark. He offered a two-year deal at $650,000 per season. I was ready to put ink to paper with the Sharks when my agent, Larry Kelly, called to say the Nashville Predators were interested.

The family was back at the cottage when Larry called, and I remember the conversation I had with Pam.

"Nashville called," I said. "Larry says David Poile wants to sign me."

The Predators had joined the NHL as an expansion team three seasons earlier.

"You're kidding?" she said. "We're not going to Nashville."

"I feel the same way," I said, "but we should hear them out. No harm in listening."

Kelly liked to put me on the phone with managers that were interested because he always felt I did a good job of selling myself to a new club. He said I should talk to Poile.

Poile took my call the next day and made a strong argument for why I would be a good fit for his organization.

"David, I really want to win; I have come close and the window is closing," I told Poile. "No disrespect, but San Jose gives me a better chance of winning."

But Poile can be very persuasive. "We have an expanded role for you here. You'd be an important part of our leadership group," he said. "It's a great city and I'd like you to think about what a great opportunity this could be for you and your family."

I was pretty adamant about going to the Sharks but Pam and I agreed to play it the following way with David. And it proved effective. "David, here's the current offer from the Sharks. Two years at $650,000," I said. "For me to consider turning that down and a legitimate shot at winning, you need to blow that out of the water."

A couple of hours later, Kelly called to say Poile was offering two years at $750,000 per season, plus a club option for a third season at the same wage. *Well there's something*, I thought. The Predators had really put their best foot forward. Poile was communicating just how bad the organization wanted me by the strength of that offer. This was a lot to consider. If I went the distance on that deal, including the option year, I would be thirty-eight. This deal would probably take me to the end of my career. I had to accept it. It was that obvious.

And I did accept it, but the decision was complicated. More complicated than anyone involved could have known. It depended on what the GM of a team I would never play for was thinking at the time. It depended on how much guys I'd never met were being paid. It depended to some degree on the economy in Nashville, maybe even the weather in Kenora or my mood at the time. It's impossible to say how many factors large and vanishingly small went into that decision. But making it changed my life.

14

DAZED AND CONFUSED

I guess I wasn't thinking straight.

I was certainly being naive. I thought I could avoid fighting Georges Laraque. I had fought "Big Georges" several times before. I knew he could hurt me and I needed to just get through the night. Because I knew something wasn't right, hadn't been right for a while. I wasn't myself, and only a fool would fight Georges Laraque if he's not ready.

But as I say, I wasn't thinking straight. And the Oilers put me in a tough spot.

After a few shifts, it's clear they're trying to run the Predators out of our own building. They're running our guys, taking cheap shots. They're trying to intimidate us. As I see this playing out, I realize they're putting me in a position where I have to go out and fight Georges. So I do. I go out there and challenge him. That's my job.

It did not go well. I never really felt as though I was in it. His left hand got free, and he fired a few that landed. I went down.

It never occurred to me that the bout would lead to my retirement.

In the immediate aftermath, I was just angry. After the linesmen had stepped in, I broke the code. I got to my feet and got off a couple of quick rights before Georges could defend himself. I crossed the line. After the game I ran into him in the hallway, and the first thing he said was, "What the fuck, Stu? That's not the way." As if I didn't know. But he was right. I just wasn't myself. That was December 8, 2001.

The blows I took that night were no different from any other punches I had taken in the countless fights from before. Other fighters had hit me harder. Georges dazed me, but I regained my senses quickly enough. Still, something was different. Usually, my head cleared quickly after a difficult fight. Within two or three hours, I would feel better, and by morning I was normal. But after the fight with Laraque, I was definitely not normal.

My symptoms lingered. I felt pressure in my head, and by the next morning, the throbbing still hadn't subsided. Even on the second day after the fight, the pressure and the nausea persisted. But I said nothing. That's another way of saying I kept playing. Three days after my fight with Laraque, I played six shifts, 5:02 minutes, against the Los Angeles Kings.

Even though my symptoms weren't improving, I flew with the team to New York and played the following evening against the Rangers. My mind was still foggy. I felt queasy. But when Sandy McCarthy bumped my goalie, Mike Dunham, in Madison

Square Garden, I did my job. I immediately tracked down McCarthy. He saw me coming and gave me a shove as I arrived. Down I went. He could have jumped me then, but he didn't. McCarthy is an honourable fighter. He waited until I got up.

It didn't seem like much of a fight to me at the time. Given my condition, I was just trying to get through it. Watching the video today, it's clear Sandy was the busier fighter that night.

On the flight home that night, I finally realized I needed to tell someone that something was wrong with me. As strange as this sounds, I felt as if I needed permission from a teammate before I said anything to our medical staff.

I went to our captain, Tom Fitzgerald. It was a strange and even awkward conversation with a guy I knew well and respected a lot.

"Fitzy," I started, "I'm not feeling well. I've had these symptoms for a while now. Something's not right. I really feel like I have to tell [our trainer] Red [Dan Redmond]."

Fitzgerald looked at me strangely. "Why are you asking me?" he said. "Of course, go see him."

I understand now why that was such a strange conversation. From Fitzgerald's point of view he had to be thinking, *Is he serious? He's asking me if it's okay to see the trainer? About his head?*

Even a veteran like Fitzgerald didn't understand the code of silence tough guys impose on themselves when it comes to their injuries. I can guarantee that Fitzgerald played injured at some point in his career. But it was never his job to be invulnerable.

It was not easy for me to talk to Redmond about my symptoms. Today, the concussion protocol requires players to sit out until they are symptom-free. The doctor doesn't speculate about how long an athlete will be sidelined. He tells the player and the team that his return will depend upon his symptoms.

It was different in 2001. The protocol was to shut down a player for a specific period and then check his progress once it was up. What I recall is that Redmond, on the doctor's advice, shut me down for two weeks. But I can't be sure that's accurate; my memories from around that time are unreliable.

One thing I do remember was that at a point in my career when you'd think I had seen it all, it was still possible for me to experience something new. For the first time in my hockey career, dating all the way back to junior hockey, I was diagnosed with a concussion.

My resumé, by that point, included 393 fights if you take into account major junior, the minor leagues, and the NHL. Thousands of punches thrown and received, not to mention the multitude of encounters with sticks, pucks, boards, and Plexiglas.

But no documented concussions. Make sense? Hardly.

—

When I was diagnosed with this concussion, the sports world and medical community were just starting to get serious about the issue of brain trauma. It had always been there, but no one was addressing it systematically, and few people had any idea how serious the lingering effects could be. Not long before I played, if you got your bell rung, you scraped yourself up off the ice and did what you had to do to protect your spot on the roster. Players today, on the other hand, have their neurological responses carefully checked at the first sign they've been rocked by a blow to the head. Nobody plays until they've been medically cleared.

I was winding down my career just as the culture around head trauma was beginning to change. Did I have concussions before Laraque clipped me? Of course, I did. Maybe a dozen or more.

But they went undiagnosed and it was a badge of honour to keep playing even if you knew you weren't healthy.

Being ordered off the ice for two weeks was a major setback. Instantly, I believed that the cat was out of the bag. The heavyweights from around the league would know that I was vulnerable. I felt like a target as I first grappled with the news.

I realized early on that I had to set that sort of thinking aside because I had never experienced symptoms this severe before. Something sinister was going on where my brain was concerned and I now knew I needed to come clean about it and get help.

I was nauseous all the time, I felt constant pressure in a specific part of my head, and I couldn't get through the day without a nap. I also couldn't cope with brightly lit rooms, and I was highly uncomfortable in crowded spaces. The buzz of many voices in a crowded room really bothered me—my symptoms would flare up.

Post-concussion syndrome symptoms, which can last for weeks and sometimes months after an injury, include headaches, dizziness, fatigue, anxiety, insomnia, lack of concentration, blurred vision, ringing in the ears, and noise and light sensitivity. I had many of these symptoms. Carrying on with everyday life is pretty much out of the question, never mind playing sports at a high level. All you can do is manage the symptoms and let the brain heal.

I knew I needed to take some time to recover. Initially, I figured that after two weeks I'd be back on the ice. But after two weeks, Dan put me on an exercise bike at a prescribed heartrate and the symptoms came right back. So he shut me down again. Two weeks later, we tried it a second time. Same result. Symptomatic all over again. Two weeks became a month and a month became two months as the waiting and the process played out.

I decided to talk to my former Mighty Ducks teammate Paul Kariya, who had gone through his own concussion issues after Gary Suter cross-checked him in the face. He recommended I see Dr. Karen Johnston, a noted Canadian neurologist who had developed a reputation for being on the cutting edge of concussion research. He told me Dr. Johnston had helped him find a path to recovery.

I spent three days in Montreal being thoroughly tested by Dr. Johnston. She told me that, given the extent of the head trauma I had experienced during my career, it was possible that the next blow to the head I received could be debilitating. Dr. Johnston was the first person to speak the following words: "Have you considered not playing again?"

And I realized for the first time that my career might be over.

She explained to me that magnetic resonance imaging (MRI) showed atrophy on one side of my brain. Because I had no previous MRI to use as a comparison, Dr. Johnston said she couldn't draw any conclusion about the atrophy's progression. But given my history, age, and the MRI, she thought it best that I retire. I didn't see that advice coming. Maybe the possibility that I might have to step down had crossed my mind for a moment. But never did I envision a doctor telling me to do so in such a direct manner.

It was a sobering moment.

What was less well known a few years ago—what I didn't fully know, anyway—was that the immediate symptoms weren't the only thing I needed to think about. Dr. Johnston helped me understand that the cumulative impact of multiple concussions is the real concern, particularly if the individual doesn't allow his brain to heal. That description applied to me and most of the NHL's heavyweight fighters.

She also predicted that my recovery from this concussion would be slower because of my age. She gave me a lot to think about. Based on what I now know about my concussions, I view the Laraque punch as more of a last straw than the blow that ended my career. It was the punch that told me that my brain had received enough punishment.

Looking back at my final season, I realize I missed signs that my body was in trouble for a couple of months. In the third game of the season, on October 11, 2001, I fought Calgary's Craig Berube. The fight didn't go my way. He clipped me with one that dazed me, and the recovery from that fight took longer than usual. The headache didn't feel the same as with earlier fights. The fog was different.

Throughout that season, I felt as if something was wrong, and yet I wasn't sure what it was. I was more irritable, more on edge, perhaps even more stressed because I didn't know what was happening.

Once, during a morning skate, I snapped at assistant coach Paul Gardner over what was a really trivial matter. I'm skating through the neutral zone, puck on my stick, making ready to take a shot on our goalie, Dunham, when suddenly there's another puck whistling through my skates. I don't give it another thought until I get back in line and see Gardner stationed on the half wall. He has a stack of pucks near him, and he's zipping them at players as they're coming down to his end of the ice, trying to knock the pucks off players' sticks as they swing by . . . and he's having the best time doing it.

I thought it was odd that an assistant coach would be goofing off while the players are tuning up before game day. But I kept quiet for the moment . . . until one of those passes struck my puck as I attempted my next shot on Dunham.

I snapped.

Within seconds, I was right in Gardner's face. He looked completely shocked.

"Hey, it's game day," I said. "I'm doing my level best to get ready to play tonight. I don't need you snapping pucks at me. Don't do it. Understood?"

He had no idea how to react to my overreaction. He stammered out words.

"Uh, yeah. I get it. I guess," he said.

While I do believe it was the wrong time for Gardner to be clowning around, I look back at that episode and wonder whether it was somehow connected to what was happening to me mentally. Throughout my career, I had always respected my coaches. If I had something to say to them, I did it in a respectful way. I didn't confront them like some schoolyard bully. This confrontation with Gardner was out of character for me. But it fit the profile for someone with post-concussion syndrome.

The other sign I missed back then was the drop-off in my performance level as a player, not a fighter. No coach ever expected me to produce offensively. But in 2001–02, the quality of my play was poor, even by my standards. I had difficulty navigating through games without causing problems for my team—turnovers, bad decisions, mental lapses, ill-advised penalties.

One reason I signed with Nashville was because I believed, after reviewing the roster, that I could earn playing time on the fourth line. Instead, I found myself as an occasional healthy scratch. Coach Barry Trotz never said anything to me, but I didn't blame him for not playing me. I didn't like how I was playing, and yet I couldn't stop making mistakes. I couldn't seem to correct certain parts of my game.

Counting a pre-season fight with Chicago's Aaron Downey, I fought nine times from September 29 to October 9. I would say I wasn't myself in any of those battles. According to dropyourgloves.com, my October 30 fight against Los Angeles Kings bruiser Matt Johnson was the only fight that I clearly won during my final season. The website determined my record to be 2–2–4 that season in the eight fights that were scored.

In the four previous seasons, my record was a combined 46–14–23. It's impossible to know whether these numbers are accurate. Determining the victor of an NHL fight by video is a subjective thing at best. But if those statistics truly reflect how well I was fighting over those five seasons, they do raise suspicions that something was wrong with me in 2001–02.

Before fighting Laraque that season, I fought Vancouver's Mike Brown, Johnson, Chicago's Bob Probert, and Pittsburgh's Krzysztof Oliwa, and after each of those fights my recovery was longer than it should have been. I could have had post-concussion syndrome as early as October. It might have been the cumulative effect of fourteen seasons of head trauma. Looking back, Berube's blow may have been the first warning of post-concussion syndrome. And I ignored it. If I had been honest with myself, I would have admitted that I was in trouble very early in the season. I was just hanging on.

Then the fights against Laraque and McCarthy brought about the final confirmation that I couldn't be an NHL fighter anymore. I should never have been in those final two fights. I should have reported my symptoms long before I did. Based on a review of the video, I was outpunched 15–1 in those two fights. That's counting only the blows that landed. I can't imagine being that over-whelmed in two consecutive fights if I was fit to fight.

Because diagnosing post-concussion syndrome still requires both a mixture of judgment and science, it's impossible to know exactly when I had the condition and which blow caused it. But I've recalled enough anecdotal evidence to believe I had concussion issues far earlier than I reported them. That's my fault. I should have realized early in that season that my health was more important than my pride or the fighter's code of silence.

I could feel the price I was paying for keeping quiet, and Dr. Johnston had now confirmed it. The flight home from Montreal made me nauseous and left my head throbbing.

—

But I still didn't announce my retirement. In fact, after I had missed about twenty games, I told the Associated Press that I was still trying to come back. "My symptoms are going to dictate the best course of action as we go on—it's frustrating to be in this situation," I told the reporter. "Rest is the only remedy. My focus is just getting to where I am symptom free. I can't honestly say I've arrived at that point."

Tough guy to the end; unable even then to admit that I had been knocked out of the game by an injury.

Even as I dealt with my symptoms, I did my best to stay connected to the team. Through the rest of the 2001–02 season, I tried to go to the rink every day. By hanging out in the training room or players' lounge, I could stay current with team news and gossip. Part of my new routine was to meet Bill Houlder, Scott Walker, Greg Johnson, and Tom Fitzgerald for a pre-game meal at a Greek restaurant in the Nashville suburbs. We'd eat, laugh, talk about what was going on with the club and then we'd all head home for pre-game naps. Though there was no game on the other side of my nap.

Being able to feel as if I was still a Predator was important for my morale. My teammates went out of their way to make me feel included. Concussions have become a worrisome injury in hockey, and guys had questions about my treatment and the symptoms I was experiencing. Every day, they would ask how I was feeling. That question became more difficult to answer as time wore on.

It's normal for guys to play hurt—and not just tough guys. Persevering is partly about job security, but it's also about being part of a team. Playing through pain is part of the game. So it's always tough to sit out with an injury that isn't visible to the rest of the team like a broken bone or a separated shoulder would be. Not that anyone is going to call you out. But when you're injured there is some comfort in having an injury that others can see. Nobody questions the heart of the guy that comes to the rink on crutches each day. Head trauma can't be observed.

The effects of a concussion are even harder to communicate in ways that people who have been around hockey understand. The legends of the game are players like Bobby Baun, playing on a broken leg, or Patrice Bergeron, playing with a punctured lung. There is no real vocabulary for saying you'll rejoin the team when you feel like you can. It's not so much that other people don't want to hear it. It's that you don't want to say it.

That's true even when talking to doctors. If anyone wants the unvarnished truth, it's them. But I grew weary of having the same conversation again and again with the Predators' neurosurgeon, Dr. Carl Hampf. I saw him once a week, and it was like the movie *Groundhog Day*—a repeat every time. I was anxious to see and feel my condition improve.

That pressure to improve did not come entirely from me, however. I saw David Poile at the rink on one particular day. I'm sure he was feeling some urgency to get me back on the ice. After all, I was his big summer signing, and he seemed concerned that I might not play again. I told him, "David, I've come back from total facial reconstruction. I've played sixteen years on a rebuilt knee. If I can beat this, I'm jumping right back in there. But masking my symptoms is what got me in this jam to begin with."

To his credit, David realized that the words he chose could be taken as pressure to return too soon, and he was quick to clear the air. He wasn't asking me to take the risk associated with coming back when I wasn't ready. The only person contemplating that was me.

—

Although Dr. Johnston's recommendation to retire surprised me, I had given stepping down some thought myself if I'm being honest. I had thought about that option-year in my contract. I thought that if I could prove my worth well enough to get the third season on that contract, it might be the perfect way to end my career.

Pam and I had lived a relatively conservative lifestyle. We had saved our money and I was confident I had skills that were marketable outside the hockey rink.

My plan was to complete my undergraduate degree and then go to law school. I had already talked to the NHL Players' Association (NHLPA) executive director Bob Goodenow, about moving up to Toronto to work for the NHLPA. I really enjoyed the work I did with the union during my career. I could see myself making that my post-hockey vocation once I had moved on.

It was either the NHLPA or go to work for a team but I knew I wanted to stay in the game in some capacity. Hockey was all I had known through my first thirty-seven years. I had come to know a lot of great people in the game. I was confident that I wanted to be around the NHL after hockey was over for me as a player.

At the end of the 2001–02 season, I still wasn't ready to give up hope that I could play again. But when the 2002–03 season opened and I was still symptomatic, I was dreading going to the rink every day. I loved being around the guys. But it's difficult to answer the same question every day: "How do you feel?" Especially when the changes in how I felt, frankly, were unnoticeable.

The answer was invariably either "no better" or "miserable today." I was tired of the question and the answer. Progress was slow and I was frustrated.

I met with Poile and told him that I had not ruled out returning to play. But I wanted to talk to David about a "just in case" strategy. I asked for his blessing to enroll in college classes in the fall semester at Belmont University in Nashville. In the event that my condition didn't improve, I wanted to have a fallback plan. The plan being to complete my undergraduate degree rather than sitting around waiting for the water to boil where my symptoms were concerned. David said yes, but not before opening a discussion within which he offered me a coaching position at the Predators' AHL affiliate in Milwaukee. I hadn't seen that coming but I had to turn it down on the spot. In my condition, long bus trips, loud rinks, and the pressure that comes with a head coaching assignment at the pro level was far more than I could manage at that time. I was grateful to be considered in this way but I was in no shape to run a pro hockey program. I wasn't even sure I had what it took to take on a regular course load at school.

Despite still suffering from headaches, nausea, fatigue, and sound sensitivity, I signed up for a full academic load. Somehow, I made it work. I credit the fact that I was older and had fully developed work habits. I was far better prepared for higher education than I'd been when I was at the University of Manitoba in the mid-1980s. I was also motivated by my desire to study law. I needed an undergraduate degree before I could ever enter law school.

Crucial to getting through my one year at Belmont was the daily nap. That was the only way I could manage the workload while still suffering from post-concussion syndrome. Pam and the kids were incredibly supportive in allowing me the space to retreat when I needed a break from my new routine. It's not easy to create peace and quiet in a house full of four young children but we found a way to make it work for all of us.

The odd part about my time at Belmont is that I was fifteen to twenty years older than most of my fellow students. Plus, no one had any idea who I was. The Predators had just completed four seasons in Nashville and the team wasn't nearly as ingrained in the community as it is today. The players were still anonymous then, and we all enjoyed that. In Detroit, if a fourth-line winger walks into a restaurant, everyone knows who he is. In Nashville, back then, a Nashville Predator could walk around in complete anonymity.

My name just didn't ring a bell with anyone in my classes. The first time my background came up was during a Money and Business class that had only eight students. We had a three-day weekend coming up, and one of my classmates asked me if I had any plans.

As it happened, the Mighty Ducks were hosting a reunion to celebrate the tenth anniversary of the team. Pam and I had plans to take our entire crew back for the occasion. But I didn't go into that level of detail. I simply told him I was going to California.

"By yourself?" he asked.

"No, I'm taking my family," I said. "My wife and our four kids."

I could feel him doing the calculations in his head. *How does a college student afford to pay for six people to fly to California?* It wasn't adding up.

Finally, I explained that I once played for the Ducks. Then I explained what I was doing back at school.

From the look on his face, I could see that I had answered the question the whole class had been puzzled about up to this point: *What's this guy's story?* I had wanted to keep a low profile, but I suppose that as the only guy in the class with a good bit of silver in his hair and considerably more scar tissue on his face, it was always going to be difficult for me to remain anonymous.

It was a small, intimate class so everyone in the room was in on the conversation. It all made sense to them now. And the funny part was, it completely changed the dynamic in class from that point on. All of a sudden, the Predators had eight new fans and all my classmates wanted to hear the inside stories on the team and a breakdown on the game each morning after the club played. It was a lot of fun, and I made some good friends. From the other side, my teammates couldn't hear enough stories about my return to college. I was like a bridge to a foreign world for them. Bill Houlder would chuckle when I joked that, "at $750,000 a year, I was the best paid student at Belmont!"

—

When you spend your career as a fourth-line winger, you don't really decide to retire from pro hockey. Your body or the game decides that for you, and eventually you get around to admitting it's time. For me, what finally made things clear was not a tilt with one of my old nemeses, and not a conversation with a world-renowned neurologist or even an NHL executive. It was a trip to the mall.

That something so simple suddenly became so difficult for me tells you how debilitating post-concussion syndrome can be. In early 2003, I went to the mall with my family, including my mother-in-law and father-in-law, who were visiting from Winnipeg. We were just walking the stores, but after twenty minutes of being on my feet, I was nauseous. My head ached. We had to leave.

We came home and sat down to dinner, and I remember describing for Pam the way that brief outing made me feel, "I think I'm done." She nodded at me. I wasn't telling her anything she didn't already know.

Pam probably understood before I did that I likely wasn't coming back from this injury. She managed my care as much as I did, keeping the kids quiet when I needed a nap. She could tell when my head pressure was severe and when the throbbing was back.

In fact, probably my whole family knew my career was over before I did. When we were at the cottage in the summer of 2002, they saw me do nothing. They were accustomed to watching me work out two to three hours per day, every day. That summer, I didn't touch the weights. No physical activity at all—only rest.

I announced my retirement on June 1, 2003.

It was not the way I wanted to leave the game. As an athlete, you hope you can win a championship and ride off into the sunset with the Stanley Cup. You don't want to say goodbye holding a fistful of medical reports in your hand. Because I hadn't played since December 2001 and had not spent much time at the rink because of my college courses, my decision was very much an anti-climax.

I was an NHL player for fifteen years. It really didn't seem real that I was never going to play again.

I considered myself as prepared for that moment as anybody. I had plans for my career after the game; I had the better part of a degree under my belt, I'd done a series of internships with local businesses in Raleigh when I played there, and I had laid a foundation for the next chapter in my life. But until you actually step into that moment, when you walk away from the thing that you think makes you who you are, you don't realize how over-whelming it is going to be.

I had always been a hockey player. I had long ago devoted myself to being the best I could be at a very particular skill. Now that skill didn't matter to me anymore. I had built an identity around putting my body on the line to help my teammates. Now those teammates had someone else to do that. I was accustomed to travelling first class and eating in top-end restaurants. Now I would be eating at the campus cafeteria. I had taken satisfaction hearing fans chant my name. Now I would be just another guy. Which is fine; there were elements of "civilian" life that I was really looking forward to. But you don't make that shift overnight. Whether you're a banker, lawyer, doctor or a trucker, if you work in that role for your entire adult life and then you're forced to leave it overnight, there is going to be an adjustment. For you and those around you.

The reality hit me one morning when I was at the Brentwood Library in suburban Nashville. I was tucked away in a corner, working on a term paper, when an email arrived in my inbox with a ding.

The message read:

Retirement Party for Stu!!

Come join us and celebrate the close of this chapter in Stu's life and the opening of another. Please keep this quiet; it's a surprise. Please RSVP me at this email or on my cell number.

Pam Grimson

At this time, in addition to our own email addresses, Pam and I had a shared address that she mistakenly used for this message. She failed to realize that her invitation, intended only for friends and family, would also come to me when she hit the Send button.

I didn't have the heart to tell her that the surprise was spoiled. In fact, I kept this secret for several years before I let on what I'd known and how I'd known it.

In the days leading up to the event, it became clear that Predators forward Scott Walker had been enlisted to keep me occupied while Pam made the final party preparations. He had reached out and asked me to grab lunch and a movie with him on the day of the party.

That wasn't unusual. We occasionally met, and the routine included lunch and a matinee movie. Walker had suffered a concussion at the same time I had, and we spent a lot of time together rehabbing during our months of inactivity. A movie in the middle of the day was always perfect for me.

I was on to Scott's role in all this, so, after the movie, I was careful not to let Walker know that I knew about the party. When we pulled onto my street, I had to fake confusion about why there were so many cars lining the road. Then I acted as if I was starting to put two and two together to reach a conclusion that a party in my honour had been organized.

When I walked through the door, I did my best impression of a grown man being surprised at the fact that Pam had pulled this off without me knowing what was happening. Surprised or not, I was really touched by Pam's time and effort bringing everyone together to celebrate my NHL journey.

I had a wonderful time at that party. The entire Predators team showed up and we laughed and swapped stories until late that night. Pam gave me a really impressive collage, which the NHLPA had prepared. It was a timeline of the events of my career marked alongside other significant dates that occurred during Canadian and NHL history. Walker and team captain Greg Johnson presented me with a Rolex watch from the players. The inscription read: "Congratulations 729 Games."

I had played just two months with my Nashville teammates before I got injured, but we had bonded. This was a really caring group. It meant a great deal to me that everyone came to that party. It was just another reminder to me that the NHL is a culture rich with quality people. A critical aspect of team sport is the players' willingness to be there for the team. I learned that day that whatever investment you make in the group, it seems to come back to you many times over.

—

Adjusting to life after the NHL was a process. I discovered I was naive about how the real world, particularly the educational system, worked. I just assumed that being a pro athlete on a Nashville team meant I would be admitted into the Vanderbilt University law school.

That's not how it worked.

When I met with the school's director of admissions, I learned that Vanderbilt Law had received 4000 applications for 150 openings that year. In other words, being an NHL player wasn't going to help me as much as a perfect LSAT score. In fact, it probably wouldn't help me at all. That got my attention. Getting into Vanderbilt was going to be significantly more competitive than a battle for a loose puck on the ice.

So I applied to several law schools to ensure that I had options. As it turns out, Vanderbilt rejected me outright. The University of Tennessee waitlisted me, as did Samford University. When the Cecil C. Humphreys School of Law at the University of Memphis wrote to offer me a seat, I felt incredible relief. I had arrived at the point during the application process where I was beginning to doubt if I would get into law school at all.

The process was a reminder, maybe a much-needed reminder, that life after hockey was not going to be an easy lap around the rink. You'd think that a lengthy career in pro sport would have afforded me at least some advantage in law school. I'm not convinced that it did. I sat in class many mornings that first year of law school amazed and thinking two things. *These are some of the brightest minds I have ever been around.* And, *How the hell did I end up in law school in Memphis, Tennessee?*

If I did hold an advantage of any kind, it most likely stemmed from the fact that playing at the highest level of hockey in the world taught me discipline and the ability to manage my anxiety.

Challenging as life in the NHL had been, law school presented a challenge of another kind. We teach by the Socratic method in law school. Rather than a typical college lecture where it is the professor alone that speaks during a forty-five minute lecture, in law there is no lecture. Instead, a law professor spends the entire class asking individual members of the class a series of questions designed to tease out certain important aspects of whatever case the class is studying at the time. For example, my Constitutional Law professor might ask, "Mr. Grimson, could you please identify the basic premise of Justice Rehnquist's dissenting opinion in *Roe v. Wade?*"

And then, 75 classmates lean in to listen for your answer. Gulp. You had better have read the case before class and you better know what you're talking about.

There is nowhere to hide in law school. Everybody gets called on in that way. Classes are very calculated and very methodical. The prof will find you eventually. And you had better have an answer.

I feared Bob Probert less than I feared being called on and being wrong. Or worse yet, feared being unprepared. So you spend all your time out of class preparing for the time you will eventually spend in class. A rule of thumb for law school is that two hours of preparation are required for every hour in class. So do the math. If I have three classes in the coming day, that's six hours of reading. Law school was a full-time job and a half.

It was a lot of work and the work involved a great deal of pressure. Everybody felt that pressure, because not everybody would pass. We were graded on a bell curve, which meant that no matter what, some people just weren't going to make it. You didn't just have to be right. You had to outshine the person beside you.

The pressure and rigors of law school aside, I made a lot of good friends during my three years in Memphis. From the start, I was hoping to remain anonymous, so when we made up name tags during orientation, I used my first given name—Allan

Grimson. I've always gone by Stuart, but Allan is actually my first name. The first student I spoke with during orientation looked at my tag, looked at my face, no doubt taking inventory of the scars on my chin, and says, "Allan Grimson? Hang on. Are you the same Grimson that played for the Predators?"

So much for flying under the radar. Soon the whole group was on to me. But it worked out fine. Being a former NHL player can be an effective icebreaker in law school.

It broke the ice with my tort law professor too. In the American judicial system, tort law covers the settlement when one party has harmed another. It's civil law, not criminal. The professor was talking about a case that arose out of the sports world. The class was attentively taking notes on their laptops. Then Professor Case went out of his way to make an analogy to hockey. Everyone could tell he was trying to have some fun with this and that he was trying to draw me into the conversation.

What Professor Case couldn't see from the front of the class was that most of the students had clicked away from their notes and they were all now on YouTube replaying old clips of me in a former life. From my seat at the back of the class, it was a wall-to-wall display of some of my more noteworthy fights playing out on dozens of screens in front of me.

It was a rare but nice break from the typical daily pressure, and we all had some fun with it. Still, that moment gave me pause to consider that I had evolved, or even matured, in a way. As a teenager, getting in fights in Kamloops solely for the attention it brought me, I could never have imagined myself sitting in a law school classroom while other students watched me on their computers. Had I been able to imagine that, I suspect I would have thought it was pretty cool. That's the pinnacle for an attention-seeker, no?

But that day in torts class, I realized that I no longer needed or craved that attention. I had once lived for it. Now the attention that came from this past life seemed to have a proper place in my life. Now the attention was just incidental.

—

By the time I arrived in Memphis to study law, the pressure in my head and the nausea had mostly subsided. Eventually, I began to feel normal again. Less difficulty being around crowds. My energy level had mostly returned. The improvement was so gradual, so incremental, that it almost surprised me when I realized I was symptom free.

Not for a moment did I second-guess my decision to retire. Dr. Johnston's pronouncement that I had brain atrophy on one side of my brain had brought a sobering new concern. Instead of wondering whether I would ever return to play again, I was now concerned I was going to have health problems later in life.

Those worries took on new meaning as some of my peers began to die.

I knew Todd Ewen well and considered him a good friend. I don't want to exaggerate how close I was to Bob Probert or Wade Belak but we saw one another fairly regularly in retirement. Mark Rypien, Derek Boogaard, Steve Montador, I never knew at all.

But each loss of life was a tragedy and I was deeply sad after each was reported. Guys who did that job make up a sort of fraternity. It's difficult to describe the feeling that comes from learning that someone—a carbon copy of you, in many ways—has vanished before his time. We may clash on the ice, but *because* we clash, we know each other well. And once you've done that job long enough, you realize that few people in the world truly understand the unique fear that comes with it. A deep mutual respect forms over time. It's a brotherhood. And when a brother is lost the grief one feels stems from two things.

First, in most every case, these men were loving fathers and husbands. I sat in the pew as each of Bob Probert's four young children bravely described the depth of their loss. These lost tough guys missed the best years of their lives. In my view, the rewards of a career as challenging as the one we endured come well after you've left that career behind. The reward for me comes now. I am sixteen years removed from the physical and mental toil of the game and life could not be more enjoyable. Yet, these men are gone. They missed the joy.

Second, the shock and sadness resonates on a more personal level. *If that can happen to them, who's to say it can't happen to me?* We all take our licks, but I had always thought of those guys and myself as invincible on some level. To learn that someone very much like me could leave this earth so young and without warning was a sign that I was vulnerable too. Probie was, in many ways, my closest peer. Same age, same draft year, same size, same job. We both had young families. It was chillingly obvious that if he could fall, then I could too.

The families of Probert and Jeff Parker donated their brains to Boston University's study of chronic traumatic encephalopathy (CTE), and testing revealed the presence of the disease in both of them. Autopsies on Derek Boogaard's and Steve Montador's brains also showed CTE. Todd Ewen struggled with depression, as did Wade Belak, who died at age thirty-five.

The connection seems obvious for some: fighting leads to concussions, concussions lead to CTE, and CTE leads to depression and dementia. But I am not rushing to make that connection until the opinion of the medical community is somewhat more settled. And besides, each of these men died from causes that were unique to them. And the varied causes of death may or may not be linked to the roles we all held formerly.

I'm inclined to keep an open mind about any such connection. Gary Solomon is the clinical neuropsychologist who treated me through my own post-concussion period and Gary cautions me to read the research, not the headlines. He consults as an internal peer reviewer on the joint NHL/NHLPA Concussion Working Group. He's on the front line where the study of athletes and the effects of head trauma are concerned. Gary has become a great friend over the years and he's very tolerant of my monthly emails. Any time I have a question, Gary is the first place I turn.

What I have learned is that the connection between CTE and head trauma is an open question, although the link between head trauma and early onset dementia is a different story. And even if the medical community resolves one day that a link is clearly established, there really is no alternative course for me to take. I can't unwind decades of trauma to my brain.

At the time of this writing, there is no means of testing a live brain for evidence of CTE—let alone a treatment for a brain affected by it.

I don't wring my hands over what lies down the road for me. I am suspicious about what life will look like in my sixties, seventies, and beyond, but I control what I can control. I do what I can to live a healthy lifestyle. I keep an active mind, I keep abreast of the research, I eat a healthy diet, and I get regular rest and exercise. Based on the information available, I take stock of my life and I adjust where and when I need to. The rest is out of my hands.

—

But I refuse to mix the message about my decision to be an NHL enforcer.

Do I want the NHL to assist former players suffering from long-term medical issues?

Yes, I do.

Do I support the efforts to make the game safer?

Of course I do.

But am I willing to say the NHL promoted a culture of violence and hate and that no one should be playing under the current conditions?

No, I am not.

The truth is that I knew, and I'm guessing others did as well, that there was potential risk in doing what I did for a living. Common sense told us that. Most of the time I fought I didn't feel well immediately after the battle. The symptoms cleared up relatively quickly, but I always wondered whether that would manifest in health concerns over the long term.

Who wasn't aware that boxers experience long-term health problems from absorbing all that head trauma?

Here's the thing. Frankly, I don't believe the medical community knew enough about this area thirty years ago to provide any of us with definitive answers. But even if I had access to research that showed a potential for long-term health problems as a result of head trauma, I still would have played.

Something else to consider. Even now, given the scientific advances in this area, it's still a question of personal liberty in my opinion. Back in the 1990s, I was willing to accept the risk, some of it unknown, to play the sport that I loved. An important part of life in a free society is having the ability to make your own determination about the level of risk you are willing to take. There are careers we choose not to pursue or activities within which we won't participate because we choose not to accept the risk. Some avoid the military or work in law enforcement because of the danger. Some won't accept jobs where travel is required because they are fearful of flying. And some won't work in hospitals over a concern about germs and contagious diseases.

Yet others are willing to risk it all to scale Mount Everest or compete on the NASCAR circuit, or any other profession that comes with an element of great danger. Some would rather be firefighters than piano teachers, two jobs with two very different risk profiles. I'm guessing that, to some degree, those who prefer to fight fires do so *because* of the risks, not in spite of them. For better or for worse, we are free to take risks with our lives. Even in the 1990s, I knew there was danger in being an NHL enforcer. I did it anyway. I chose that career because, for me, the reward outweighed the known risk. I was entitled to that choice. It was mine to make.

Ever since Dr. Johnston told me about the atrophy on one side of my brain, I have wondered what lies ahead for me. After all, I had something in the range of four hundred fighting majors over the course of my entire hockey career. But even Dr. Johnston couldn't predict my future, or what my life will look like later in my life. Again, I take good care of myself and the rest is outside my control.

Just one regret in this area. Knowing what I know now, the one thing I wish I had done during my career was self-report what I was feeling. I now know that I should have told the medical staff many, many times when my symptoms arose. In failing to do so, I denied giving my brain the time it needed to heal. But that's on me. Nobody asked me to keep quiet about my injuries. I did it because I didn't want to lose my job by taking time to recover. The truth is, I enjoyed the lifestyle that a career in the NHL provided me and my family. And for that reason, I accepted the risks that I did. I understood the consequences well.

Now eighteen years removed from the game, I confess it's hard for me to reconcile who I was and what I did for a living back then. The further I get from that time in my life, the stranger that period and that person seem to me.

But this much I know . . . there's a remnant of that NHL tough guy still in there somewhere. Because, from time to time, I'm reminded of what Chris Chelios did to me at the NHLPA. And, to this day, I wouldn't trust myself if I met him in a dark alley.

15

UNION MAN

In March, 1992, the Chicago Blackhawks were gathered in Steve Larmer's hotel room. Every team had a union representative, and Larmer was ours.

We NHL players were threatening to strike that spring. We had gathered to hear Bob Goodenow, the newly appointed executive director of the Players' Association, give us an update by conference call. He painted a bleak picture. Negotiations were going nowhere with the owners.

Our decision to strike was nearly unanimous across the 500-player membership. The owners were threatening to grab total control of our rights to our names and likenesses. This struck at the core of the union. Without these rights, our ability to run a meaningful licensing program was next to impossible. It was the revenue that flowed from NHLPA-licensed products like hockey cards and video games that supported our union. It was a crucial moment for our group.

There was a good deal of testosterone in Larmer's room that day. You don't make it to the NHL if you're easy to push around, and we saw this as the owners' attempt to bust our union. We were pissed—to a man. So we all stood firmly behind Goodenow. Everyone voted to strike.

At the same time, there was a good bit of confusion in the room. No one said much of anything. After all, we were hockey guys. Who knew the first damned thing about licensing rights? The meeting was winding down and I motioned to Larmer that I had a question.

"What are the limits to Goodenow's authority?" I asked.

The room was quiet and seemed a little surprised that I had opened my mouth at all. I hadn't even played 100 games in the NHL. Despite being twenty-six, I was really just beginning to establish myself as an NHLer. Also, I could tell that not everyone understood my question.

"We've given Bob the right to call a strike for us but how far does that authority go? Does he have the authority to decide what terms are part of a new deal with the owners? Or are we going to vote again later?" I went on.

More silence as that sunk in. And then there came a lot of head-nodding and comments like, "Yea, Larms. What *exactly* have we authorized Bob to do?"

I wasn't doubting Goodenow's ability as a leader. I just believed we should discuss whether we were granting Bob carte blanche authority to take this to the finish line. Or were we, the players, going to weigh in on this as the process played out? This aspect of collective bargaining had not been explained to us. Long before I became a lawyer, I understood that details matter.

The players did end up striking, and our walkout lasted nine days. We won a significant increase in our playoff bonuses along with the retention of our licensing rights.

More importantly for me, those NHLPA meetings and the discussions around union matters sparked my interest in this area of the game. I discovered I enjoyed learning about and discussing the issues as well as serving as an advocate for the association. I was a player delegate to our union for about half of my career. I also served a term as vice-president on the NHLPA executive committee. And it makes sense in this way: as an enforcer, you're continually at work watching out for your teammates. For me, my involvement in union affairs was a natural extension of all that. Advocate. Protector. Comes from the same set of instincts, no?

—

Serving as a player representative in the sports world comes with risks. By definition, you're at odds with the people who sign your cheque. And sometimes you find yourself at odds with the people who control how much you play, and whether you play at all.

That was an issue for me more than once during my NHLPA career. I remember an instance during the 1995–96 season, when I was the Detroit Red Wings' player rep.

We were in Montreal for the third pre-season game in three nights, and a fourth in four nights was scheduled for the following day in Detroit. That would never happen in the regular season because the collective bargaining agreement doesn't allow it.

Before the game, coach Scotty Bowman had announced the lineups for the next two games, and some players were scheduled to play four nights in a row. I remember Darren McCarty was one of them, and that I wasn't. Players were buzzing about the taxing schedule, and everyone was confident it was not allowed. It was my job to call the NHLPA and get an answer from labour counsel in Toronto.

Minutes before the warm-up, I'm in the trainer's room on the phone with the NHLPA office. Bowman happens to walk by and immediately stops the procession of coaches headed out to the ice.

"Look at him," Bowman says to assistants Barry Smith and Dave Lewis. "Look at Stuey. He's calling the union. Yeah, that's what he's doing. He's calling the union."

Nothing ever happened in Bowman's dressing room that he didn't see coming. As it turned out, the CBA ruled against to playing on more than two consecutive nights, applied only to the regular season. The pre-season had fewer restrictions.

And of course, Bowman got the last laugh. He circulated a "revised" roster for the next game at home as we were flying back to Detroit. He had removed McCarty from the lineup for the fourth game. It would have been a small victory for me as a player rep if not for one fact.

The tweak to the roster was that Grimson was in. I would be the guy playing four consecutive games. Bowman and his staff thought it was a hilarious moment. I failed to see the humour.

—

It was as I became more involved in union matters that I began to think seriously about earning my law degree after my hockey was over. Labour counsel to the NHLPA became one of the post-hockey options I was considering. How could the NHLPA not hire a lawyer who had a fourteen-year career in the league?

When I told Goodenow, a lawyer himself, that I was thinking about going into law, he encouraged me to pursue it. He told me he would hire me after I passed the bar exam. But I wondered if he would follow through on that pledge after he and I butted heads while negotiating his new contract as executive director in 2001.

Goodenow and I got along reasonably well most of the time I was involved in the union, but that changed when we found ourselves on opposite sides of the table.

I was one of four vice-presidents on the executive committee when Goodenow's deal expired. Mike Gartner was working with the NHLPA as an adviser, and he informed us that Goodenow was asking to be paid more than the heads of the baseball, basketball, and football unions.

Goodenow's argument was that he was the only union head who managed to stave off the introduction of a salary cap or luxury tax. He was asking us to pay him a salary in line with what NHL commissioner Gary Bettman was making. Bettman was pulling down more than $3 million per year, whereas Goodenow's previous contract was based on the average NHL salary, which was $1.64 million. So he was looking for a raise of almost 100 percent. In Bob's words, if he was going to hold his own with Gary in negotiations going forward, he would need to "play in the same sandbox." That phrase would come up repeatedly.

That was some very expensive sand. As a union, we were thrilled with the job Bob had done for us over time. We knew he was entitled to a bump of some kind. However, our position, as a committee, was that Bob wanted to go to the head of the class in terms of what the other union bosses were making, in spite of the fact that our sport was dead last as a revenue producer. Historically, football, baseball, and basketball had always outpaced us at the gate, in cable television revenue and in the sales of licensed apparel. Goodenow wanted football money to run a hockey union.

Adam Graves, Vincent Damphousse, and Bill Guerin were the other vice-presidents on the executive committee; Trevor Linden was our president. To a man, we were all angered by Goodenow's demands. How could we justify paying him more than the directors of the other leagues' unions? And how could we justify decoupling his salary from ours? To us, it made sense for our guy's pay to trail that of the other union heads.

At the time, National Football League union head Gene Upshaw was paid around $3 million; National Basketball Association executive director Billy Hunter was making $1.8 million; and Major League Baseball union leader Don Fehr was at $1 million.

Early in the negotiations with Goodenow, Linden decided that leading our committee through this process was better suited for someone else. Because I had been vocal from the start of our negotiations with Bob, Linden asked me to take the lead. I accepted the job partly because I just enjoyed this stuff. But the real reason I did it was that I had strong views about where Bob's compensation should shake out at the end of the day.

Bob landed in Nashville during his fall tour in 2002, and we had earlier agreed to meet for lunch to discuss his latest proposal in our negotiations. Bob and I had been through several such discussions leading up to this point. It got tense quickly. Bob is a fiery guy, and I wasn't taking any backwards steps either. After all, there was a 700-plus member union out there who were counting on me to keep our executive director, but at the right price. What touched Goodenow off that day was not the membership's insistence on a number lower than his last offer. It was something I said.

At one point during our discussions, I referred to Goodenow's role as "union boss." His face got red and his shirt and tie seemed, all of a sudden, to tighten around his neck. As I learned that day, that red face was a tell of Bob's. If you saw that colour, you had just struck very close to home.

"Is that how you see me, Stu?" he asked. "You see me as a union boss?"

He was clearly offended by the job description. To me, it was just easier to say "union boss" than to keep repeating "NHLPA executive director." No different than referring to Barry Trotz as the Nashville Predators' bench boss. I wasn't trying to diminish his role. That's not how I operate, at least not at that moment. Plus, I, like the others, thought Bob had done a great job for us. "Union boss," in my mind, was an accurate way to refer to someone in Goodenow's position; it was not a derogatory term. We had a union, and Goodenow was the person in charge. Therefore, he was the union boss.

But Bob was offended. I had never seen his temperature rise like that in any previous meetings. While he didn't explain his reaction on that day, I found out later that he saw himself more as a CEO.

Sorry.

And we hadn't even got to the substance of our disagreement yet. I had to make it clear that I didn't believe we had to play him like Bettman to get Bettman to respect him. I didn't believe Bettman's view of Goodenow was influenced by how much money he earned. I told Goodenow I doubted MLBPA executive director Don Fehr had difficulty holding his own in negotiations with commissioner Bud Selig or any of the owners. He was the lowest-paid executive director at $1 million per year. Selig, on the other hand, earned $15.06 million in the fiscal year ended October 31, 2006, according to *Milwaukee Business Journal*.

With Fehr at the head, the MLBPA stood its ground against a salary cap. Even today, the MLB has no cap, due in no small part to Fehr's skills as a union head. Fehr trailing Selig by $14 million in salary was no hindrance to the basketball union.

The reference to Fehr didn't sit well with Goodenow. The colour rose in his face yet again.

But this was early in the negotiations, and we eventually found agreeable terms in a new deal for Bob. The rest of the executive committee and the entire membership weighed in on the new contract once we got close.

Goodenow received a lucrative six-year contract. But we managed to grind down the average annual salary to $2.5 million. The players could live with that number. He wasn't earning what Bettman was making. But his deal was in the range of those of the other union heads. Not the highest, certainly not the lowest.

In hindsight, I am reasonably sure that Goodenow didn't appreciate my role in those negotiations. When I was hired by the NHLPA in 2006, my co-workers on the executive level mentioned that Goodenow was often heard referring to me as the "pissant player" negotiating his deal during this period.

It's not a popularity contest.

—

After I retired, it took me three and a half years to finish my undergraduate degree, graduate from law school, and pass my Tennessee bar exam.

What that meant is that I was in class studying torts, constitutional law, and *Brown v. Board of Education* at the University of Memphis law school when the NHL locked out the players in 2004. I was on the sidelines (though I was studying labour law, and of course keeping in touch with guys I knew who were still in the game).

The primary issue during this work stoppage was the salary cap. The NHL wanted cost certainty, and Goodenow made it clear that this was the hill the NHLPA would die on. Both sides dug in and prepared for a long struggle. But it went on longer than either side wanted. Eventually, the 2004–05 season was cancelled. Millions of dollars had been lost, players were anxious that their productive playing years were slipping away, and owners were just as anxious that they were losing fans and revenue. Worried about losing a second season, NHL officials and the NHLPA returned to bargaining the following summer, and after some extensive backchannel negotiations, a deal was struck in July. It included a salary cap, the details of which were ironed out by Goodenow's right-hand man, Ted Saskin, and NHL chief counsel Bill Daly.

The fallout was immediate. Goodenow was asked to resign, and he was gone five days after the agreement was reached. He had been so aligned with a strategy to stand firm against a salary cap that it's not hard to understand why he had to leave when a cap was implemented.

This was supposed to be a time for healing, and the fiery Goodenow was not a healer. Goodenow was once described as a great wartime general and a terrible peacetime general. I think that's an accurate assessment. He was always ready to do battle, but he was not skilled in the art of diplomacy.

Looking at the game from the outside, all I knew was that Saskin was hired to replace Goodenow as executive director. That was an awkward situation for me, because it had been Goodenow who had promised me a position at the NHLPA.

What I didn't know was whether Saskin would follow through on Goodenow's pledge. I thought well of my chances though. Saskin had been at the union for most of my career and we got along well. We had worked closely on union matters during my time as a delegate and an executive committee member.

After I wrote the bar exam, Saskin did bring me on as a labour counsel. I headed up the player relations department, representing players in supplemental discipline in addition to working in the player grievance department. I was really excited about the new position; labour counsel seemed like a hand-in-glove fit for someone with my background. However, it was apparent early on that the fallout from the lockout was far from over.

I came on seven months after Saskin was hired, but it felt as though I had landed in a war zone. The NHLPA was fractured, the working environment was contentious, and every day I was busy trying to extract myself from yet another political quagmire.

The problems were multi-layered. For one thing, not every player was happy that Goodenow had been asked to leave. Goodenow was a fire-and-brimstone leader, and some players appreciated how he had stood up to the league. So we had pro-Goodenow partisans within our ranks.

We also had anti-Saskin partisans. Not everyone believed it was a good idea to hire Saskin, as he came with baggage. Had Ted done an end run on Bob by reaching a settlement behind his back? No one was comfortable answering that question. Whether Saskin was trying to do what was best for the rank and file or not, there were some who believed that Saskin had been disloyal to Goodenow and the union. To that faction, it didn't smell right to hire him as the NHLPA executive director without considering other options. And some players didn't want the man who accepted a salary cap running the union going forward.

On the other hand, there was a growing number of players who supported Saskin in spite of the contentions of the other side. After all, Saskin *was* the architect of the new salary cap system. And he had designed and negotiated the system with the league at the request of the executive committee. Without Saskin, and Goodenow at the helm, the sport could conceivably have gone dark for a second straight season. By hiring Saskin after Goodenow was removed, the union could retain the expertise needed to safeguard the players' interest in a new "cap world" as well as maintain important institutional knowledge. That made sense too. By the time I arrived to work at the NHLPA, this group represented the overwhelming majority of players in the league.

But there was more. The finer point of the entire divide came down to the following. The executive committee, in firing Goodenow and hiring Saskin, failed to follow the union's constitution. The executive committee, made up of four vice-presidents and the president, had essentially fired Goodenow and then appointed Saskin as executive director.

However, the NHLPA's constitution is quite clear on how the hiring process works. According to the constitution, it is the role of the executive board, consisting of one player representative from each of the league's thirty teams, to decide who sits as executive director. That didn't happen when Saskin was hired.

A group of dissident players, led by players like Chris Chelios and Eric Lindros, pushed this issue and demanded that Saskin be removed from the executive director's position immediately. Former players Steve Larmer and Trent Klatt were also in that group. Given that the constitution wasn't followed, this was not an unreasonable position to take. At the end of the day, I agreed with the reasoning behind that position. The process was flawed.

However, and this is where I parted company with the dissidents like Chelios, as a union, what do you want to do about it now? Fire Saskin and search out another executive director? Or keep Saskin, the new system's chief designer, as the new system is being implemented?

Chelios, a former teammate of mine in Chicago, called me several times after I started working at the NHLPA to enlist me in the drive to get Saskin removed. I told him that I agreed with his position, but that I believed he was lobbying the wrong person. I told him it was the players themselves who needed to act if they wanted changes. It wasn't up to in-house counsel to decide who served as director.

"I agree that the executive committee got it wrong," I told Chelios. "But three quarters of our members or more are prepared to move on. Saskin's a logical choice in a cap world. Unless the executive board is ready to do something, then let's move on, Chris."

I should have known that Chelios wasn't going to let it go. He played hard on the ice—why wouldn't he be just as stubborn off it? But I would have acted differently had I possessed the same information that Chelios had at the time. He owed it to me to be straight with me. And he wasn't.

Even before I was hired, Chelios had evidence that Saskin had unethically read private player emails during the time players were deciding whether to hire him as executive director. Chelios never shared that information with me.

At some point, rumours about Saskin reading emails started to emerge. In March 2007, I read an article in the *Toronto Star* that quoted Shawn McEachern as saying that Saskin had called him unexpectedly to discuss how McEachern felt about Saskin's hiring.

According to McEachern, the call seemed odd because he and Saskin had never spoken about the issue and yet somehow Saskin seemed to have some very specific information about McEachern's opinions. The conclusion McEachern reached is that Saskin had been reading emails he sent to other players on the NHLPA server.

Keep in mind that, at this time, email was still a relatively new innovation. The NHLPA had built its own server and the players were given email addresses on that server so that the union could better communicate with its members. For most players, the NHLPA email address was their only or primary email address.

The minute I read that article, the entire picture became clear. Saskin had done this. He had accessed the server and he read private player messages. I knew this to be true. How? Because I knew Shawn McEachern—not well—but I knew him well enough to know he was an honest guy. Players like McEachern don't say what McEachern said unless it's accurate.

Saskin was out of town when the article was published. It would be another two days before he returned to the office. For a good part of those two days, I wrestled with whether to confront him on this or not. I talked to two of the other attorneys on staff who advised me, "Stay out of it. Not your issue." And of course, I had Chelios in my ear.

At the end of the day, the decision was an easy one. It may not have been my issue. But I was a player long before I was a lawyer. And, as a player, I made my living in a very specific way. I wasn't about to bury my head and ignore the interests of over 700 players. Whatever the consequences were.

When Saskin finally returned to the office he was item one on my agenda that day. I was going to put this to him in a way that he had to either admit it or deny his involvement.

"Ted, if you did this I need to know. If you didn't, I'll stay on and it lands where it lands. But if you did do this, you gotta let me know. Because if you did, this union has a decision to make."

To my surprise, Saskin's admission that he had in fact accessed and read player emails came without much struggle. Words to that effect may have been the first thing out of his mouth.

After leaving Saskin's office, I contacted NHLPA consultant Mike Gartner, along with NHLPA lawyers Ian Penny and Roland Lee, and told them what Saskin had said. "He did it. He read the guy's emails to keep himself installed," I said. "This may be a fireable offence."

I suggested that we need to go to the executive board with what I had just learned. The others agreed. In just thirteen months on the job, I had gone from NHLPA associate counsel to whistleblower.

The tide turned quickly against Saskin. On March 11, the NHLPA executive board held a conference call and voted to place Saskin and Senior Director of Business Ken Kim on a leave of absence while an investigation was conducted. Saskin was not on that call.

According to the *Toronto Star*, even Ottawa Senators right wing Daniel Alfredsson, an interim vice-president on the executive committee and a long-term Saskin supporter, said Saskin's actions "were unacceptable."

Saskin was fired on May 11, 2007. What I didn't see coming was that the guy who turned him in would follow him out the door.

—

By that summer, Chelios had become the Detroit Red Wings' player representative, which meant that he had a seat on the executive board. Our relationship had always been amicable, but it started to deteriorate fast. Within months, we were butting heads routinely. In the days leading up to our annual summer meetings, I began to hear that Chelios now had me in his crosshairs.

I told him if he was planning to make the case for firing me, I wanted an audience with the board to answer for whatever nonsense he was telling them. Chelios was initially opposed to my presence in the meeting, but Penny was eventually able to get him to see this was the fair and reasonable thing to do.

Just being in that room was a surreal experience for me. The board is made up of all the team reps from around the league. In other words, the guys I was addressing were there in the same capacity that I used to be there, not all that long ago. Sure, I was a lawyer now. But I had been a player, and a player rep. I knew these guys. I was one of them.

But the mood in the conference room wasn't just strange. It was toxic. It was clear that Chelios was driving the whole thing. With the exception of Eric Lindros and Shawn Horcoff, the conversation was carried by Chelios and Chelios alone. He had decided I had to go, and he was prepared to use his full weight to sway the group against me. And I concede: he has a great reputation. He was a great player, and I respected him. The other players—most of whom were much younger than him—would have gone through a brick wall for him.

Chelios's reason for wanting me fired came down to the following. Early in my tenure as union counsel, he called and asked for mobile numbers for all the player representatives. I told him

I didn't have them but I would try to get them. After I hung up, I got up and walked into Saskin's office and relayed Chelios's request. Saskin told me that Chelios had asked for and received that information from him two weeks earlier, and that I shouldn't worry about it.

I explained to Chelios what Saskin had said; Chelios wasn't happy. He said that Saskin had not given him that information. I remember thinking, *Should I make an end run around my boss and get the information for Chelios because we were teammates?* Given that I was new to the NHLPA, I instead decided to tell Chelios to take it up with Saskin directly. I had no reason to doubt Saskin's motives at that time. If Chelios had reason to doubt them, he should have shared that with me. But he didn't.

So, in Chelios's mind, I was in league with Saskin. That was the case he was making, even though I was the guy who had blown the whistle on Saskin. He was driving the board against me over a bunch of phone numbers that he could have got elsewhere. There were thirty of my former peers all leaning in, all seemingly accusing me, and falling in step with Chelios. I couldn't believe it had got to this point.

There was a single thoughtful player who agreed with my point of view, and I have to admire his courage. If I had been in Dan Hamhuis's shoes, I would have found it very difficult to stand my ground in that room. Hammer was still a young guy, definitely not of the same status as some of the legends in the room. I knew him pretty well. In fact, I had invited him and his parents over for dinner when he was breaking into the league. He was a high draft pick of the Predators as I was winding down. I later learned that he was the one guy in a room full of reps who voted my way when the time came. Who else was going to publicly defy Chris Chelios?

I had a lot riding on this. I had been working toward this position with the union since the nineties. More importantly, I had uprooted my young family from a place we all really loved in Nashville because their father believed Toronto provided a stable new environment for us all. To watch that crumble in front of me at the behest of some jackass who knew just enough to be dangerous was both astonishing and infuriating.

But I had to keep my head. Realizing that Chelios had the juice to turn the board against me, I tried to be proactive by offering the board the opportunity for a do-over on my contract. Naive, I know, but Saskin's new deal ($2 million per year over six years) had bothered some players. His contract had turned many against him right from the beginning. It was part of why they pursued him until he left.

Through the grapevine, I had also heard that some players were grousing about my contract as labour counsel. Apparently, my three-year deal at $250,000 per year was far too rich for someone who had just passed the bar exam.

I understood that. It was more than most first-year lawyers would earn. However, this was a unique position. Yes, the law degree was newly acquired, but I had a significant background in the game at all levels. There weren't a lot of lawyers with seventeen years of professional hockey experience lined up at the NHLPA door looking for work.

Even so, I sensed that if I was going to come out the other side of this still holding a position as counsel to the union I needed to meet this group half-way. In an attempt to clear the air and start fresh, I told the board I was willing to revisit my deal.

The board seemed to seize on my suggestion. Lindros was appointed to negotiate for the board. We settled on a one-year contract at less than I made the previous year. It seemed as though the board and I had found a compromise.

Although I felt like I had done nothing wrong, I thought it was the right move to start afresh with the union. I wanted to demonstrate to the board that I could meet them where they were at. And for the time being, it appeared that I had accomplished that. At least until the new executive director was hired.

—

In October 2007, Boston attorney Paul Kelly took over for Saskin. He was best known in hockey circles for the work he had done as U.S. attorney for the District of Massachusetts in investigating former NHLPA leader Alan Eagleson for fraud and embezzlement. Eagleson had spent time in prison for his crime.

I didn't know what Kelly's hiring meant for me. He was in the office infrequently, and when he did show, he kept me at arm's length. I was suspicious that I was in trouble. I had the right read.

One day in November, Kelly made an appearance in Toronto and summoned me to his office. The conversation didn't last long. I was fired.

"You've been here a month," I said. "I'm not sure how you form an opinion of me after such a short period of time."

"It's not my decision," Kelly explained. "The board already took a vote to fire you."

Instantly, it was clear to me. The new contract was a charade.

"The board acted in bad faith," I told Kelly.

Paul turned white. He knew he had made a mistake as I left his office. He had said too much and what he did say made it clear to me that there was another fight coming.

Within weeks, I sued the union. I alleged that the executive board had committed fraud against me as they terminated my employment. The board members knew they were firing me and yet they engaged me in a negotiation to revise my existing deal. The NHLPA executive board withheld a critical piece of information as we agreed to terms in a new agreement. That's the legal definition of bad faith. I would have never entered into a new agreement had I known that a vote to fire me had been taken.

In time, we settled for the full amount of my original contract. I would not have accepted anything less.

To this day, I don't blame the other members of the executive board; these guys had no idea about the impact of the decisions they were making. Chelios drove them there. I can respect that Chelios had a Hall of Fame career on the ice. But what he did to me and my family during this period at the NHLPA was unconscionable.

He knew that the hiring of Saskin and his inappropriate accessing of player emails happened before I arrived. He also knew that I agreed with him that the process used to hire Saskin was improper. And if the executive board had voted to remove Saskin early in my tenure, I would have accepted that decision as a fair outcome.

Neither did the decision to fire me take into account that I was the one who confronted Saskin and forced his admission over the players' email accounts. I reported that within minutes of learning the truth.

In my short time as counsel to the NHLPA, I worked every day to advance the players' interests. I acted honourably. If you choose to question the decision I made to abide by my boss's orders and not give Chelios a bunch of phone numbers, okay. I guess I could have pushed harder for that.

But be sure to weigh that against the fact that this is the same guy who exercised the judgment to storm the executive director's office and force him to come clean on a very sacred matter.

Chelios went out of his way to get me fired. And I can't accept that he did it for the good of the union. Out of all that loss, no one benefitted. Not even Chelios.

Years later, when I was working as a broadcaster for the Nashville Predators, I saw Chelios as I was walking into the Red Wings' dressing room. As we passed in the hall, he said something about needing to hold a press conference to apologize to all of those who got caught up in the NHLPA firestorm.

That may or may not have been an apology. It was difficult to know what such vague words mean. In any event, I have no interest in building a bridge back to this particular former teammate. I'm not a hater. But I do choose to surround myself with people I care for and respect.

Life's too short.

—

Chelios did heavy damage to my life and my family. It had been a difficult decision to move to Toronto to take the position as counsel to the NHLPA. My family left Nashville kicking and screaming. At the time, my two eldest daughters, Hannah and Erin, were twelve and fourteen respectively. It was hardest on them to leave their friends and school to move to a different country. All of us had loved Nashville. But, in time, Pam and the kids began to settle into a new life in suburban Toronto. That was the summer of 2006. Seventeen months later, I had to turn around and tell my family I'd been fired.

The irony of all of this was that I took the NHLPA job because I believed that it provided the sort of security and stability our family had not enjoyed during my playing days. We moved a lot when I played. Coaching or working in hockey operations for a club seemed every bit as volatile as the player's life. I didn't want to subject my wife and kids to the threat of a move every two or three years. So I opted for a career at the union, where I have seen other lawyers work for decades. Now, just as my people had settled in, I had to tell them we were going to have to move again.

Because my father was in the RCMP, I went through that upheaval every three years, and I knew those moves are difficult on children because they were difficult on my sister and me. Moreover, during my NHL career, I had moved from Chicago to Anaheim, to Detroit, to Hartford, to Carolina, then back to Anaheim, and then to Nashville. Being an NHL enforcer was a nomadic existence in the 1990s. When you are playing in the NHL, many of your decisions are made for you. Pam and I did what we needed to do to keep me in the NHL. Sometimes we didn't want to move, but that was our only option if I wanted to keep playing.

But once I retired, we had more liberty to organize our lives. Suddenly, we could choose where we would live and what we would do next. From that point on, we were no longer living at the whim of an NHL GM. We made our own decisions. And that means taking responsibility for those decisions.

Pam and the kids made sacrifices for me. When my job at the NHLPA was snatched away, practising law back in Tennessee seemed to make good sense. We had enjoyed our lives there; I was licensed to practise law there. But that move too was another sacrifice my family made for me. The kids were happy in Toronto.

The move from Toronto back to Nashville turned out to be even harder than the move from Nashville to Toronto. Navigating that crisis was a terrific strain on the marriage.

We divorced in the spring of 2015 after twenty-six years of marriage. There was no single moment or event that caused our breakup. I have no one to blame—not Pam, not the NHLPA. This was death by a thousand cuts and I accept full responsibility for the end of the marriage.

The decision to divorce was mutual—one that was reached after a great deal of deep soul searching. From the start, I believed that I was marrying for life. I wanted that for my family, and I am deeply sorry over the impact the end of the marriage had on us all.

Our breakup was very difficult for our children. They were young enough to believe that their parents' relationship was immune to a breakup but still old enough to have very strong views about how wrong we were for failing to keep our family intact. But when the marriage ended, it was Pam that hurt most. Pam's world was defined by the roles of wife and mother. To their credit, our children cared for their mother well.

I was willing to play the villain if it allowed others to heal. But no one wants to be viewed that way by those they love. It was a harrowing loss to me. And it seemed to mark the end of everything that had made me who I am. My career as a hockey player had been snatched from me in a single moment. My career as a lawyer had slipped through my fingers just when it seemed to be taking off. My family had turned away from me just when I thought we could all finally be together. I felt like a failure. I didn't know who I was.

16

BACKGROUND CHECK

Until you're a parent yourself, it's impossible to appreciate all your parents did for you. Kids may adore their parents, but that love and appreciation only deepens once you know what it means to cherish someone else more than you do yourself. Hockey players are well known for thanking their parents on draft day and when they win a Cup. But it's not just hockey parents who deserve thanks for all the early mornings and sleepless nights. And in my case, it's not the rides to games on snowy Canadian highways I'm most grateful for. Not really.

What I remember most fondly are the times we were all together—my parents, my sister, and me. We owned a small trailer that slept the four of us comfortably, and we would set up camp at the Sukunka River, near Dawson Creek, British Columbia, or take a drive to Big Shuswap Lake while we lived in Kelowna, B.C. I have fond memories of fishing and roasting marshmallows with my family. I don't think kids need more than that.

I wanted for nothing growing up; Stan and Em Grimson raised me and my sister, Sam, in a loving and safe home. We never went without and we even enjoyed our share of luxury. My first trip to Disneyland came as a member of the Grimson family in the early 1970s, not as a player on the Mighty Ducks of Anaheim in 1993. The family even flew to Hawaii on another winter getaway. I enjoyed a rich and wonderful childhood, by any definition you care to apply.

And the most unique part about growing up as an adopted child in the home of Stan and Em Grimson? We were as normal as any other family, with one minor distinction. My sister and I were adopted. It was many years later that I even learned there was a stigma of some kind associated with adoption. My parents handled the psychological aspect of adoption as well as any family could. They consistently told my sister and me that we were special *because* they got to choose us. That's the way my parents framed it. From my earliest memories as a child, I was aware of my adopted status. There was no solemn sit-down to deliver the news of my origins. I was adopted and I was loved and that was just fine. I never felt shortchanged.

No doubt, I was a handful as a teenager, and my adolescence was rougher than others'. But all teens have a hard time finding their place. Who's to say that my teen years were made more challenging because I was adopted? I struggled with a lot of things at that age. My adopted status was not one of them. And of course, I can't compare my experience with one I didn't have. What I can say for certain is that we lacked nothing. Our parents loved us. We were lucky. No kid knows how lucky he is. But I know now.

—

I was playing for the Chicago Blackhawks when, in the summer of 1992, I received my first opportunity to learn about my biological parents.

At that time, the adoption laws in British Columbia allowed birth parents and adopted children to meet only if all parties agreed to it. If the Province of British Columbia was contacted for information, it would act as an intermediary. If an adoptee wanted to meet their birth mother, the province would contact her to see if she wanted her information to be passed to the person making the request.

If the mother didn't want a meeting, her name and contact information would not be shared. And it worked the same going the other way. If a birth mother reached out, the biological child could say "yea" or "nay" to a meeting. The Ministry of Children and Family Development in B.C. essentially acted as a broker of information and would only share personal adoptive information if both parties consented.

That's how it happened in my case. Through my parents, I received a letter from the province explaining that my birth mother wanted to meet me.

A complete stranger wanted to meet me. She had no idea what had happened to me after she'd given me up. I could have been anyone, but apparently I still meant something to her.

I had mixed emotions about the idea. On the one hand, I wanted to know my story. I had always been curious about my origins. My mom and dad were told very little about me when they flew to Stewart, B.C., then on to Vancouver to pick me up and bring me home in June of 1965. On the other hand, we had my family and we had Pam's family. I wasn't sure how I felt about a third.

Pam's concerns were even more practical: We didn't know anything about this person, just as she knew nothing about me. To Pam, it seemed complicated to invite a stranger into our lives. Plus, I was playing in the NHL at the time. How would my biological parent react to that news? She was trying to reconnect with a person she had carried into this world, but to what end? I suppose we felt that introducing someone new into our lives would be adding an element that we had little control over. At that time, our kids were young and we were careful to guard our privacy.

After weighing the pros and cons, I chose not to meet my biological mother in 1992. But her decision to reach out made me all the more curious about my background. Where had I come from? What did my biological parents look like? What were the circumstances that led to my adoption? I suppose the knowledge that she was looking for me stirred up emotions I had never felt before.

Adopted children tend to come with a bit of a mystery, especially in the mid-sixties. Back then, and certainly if they were using a governmental agency, it was uncommon for adopting families to know much about the origins of their adopted child. And being curious about this is just part of human nature. Seventy-two percent of adopted adolescents want to know why they ended up as adoptees. Sixty-five percent of those adoptees polled said they wanted to meet their parents. Ninety-eight percent want to know which of their biological parents they looked like. These are some fairly universal truths.

I've read up on it. Today's psychological literature states that searching for birth parents "is understandable, common and part of healthy adaption for adopted persons." (That's from "A Psychosocial Model of Adoption Adjustment," an article by

David Brodzinsky, Marshall Schechter, and Robin Marantz.)

There are practical reasons for adoptees to search for their biological parents of course. It's useful to know their medical history. With the advances in health care over the years, it's now highly beneficial for individuals to understand the risk factors they face from certain diseases. Anytime I had ever been asked about my family history in the context of a medical visit, I'd never had anything to offer.

But the primary reason why adopted children seek their birth parents is plain, simple curiosity. Once I'd heard from the adoption agency, that curiosity never really went away.

—

In 2010, I was heading to British Columbia for my parents' fiftieth anniversary. I flew from Nashville to Seattle, rented a car, and was looking forward to the drive back through the mountains to Kelowna. It had been a few years since I had been back home. Mom and Dad usually came to see us when the kids were young. It was easier for the two of them to get to us than for us to move the entire tribe of six to them.

I always get a little nostalgic going back home, especially when it's been a long time between visits. It's the mountains. When you grow up and the mountains are all around you it becomes a part of you, I suspect. This trip home wasn't just about my parents' anniversary. This was where life started for me.

Being back in B.C. for the first time in a while, I was struck by this feeling. *There are two people, somewhere very close to here, who are responsible for bringing me into the world. And I have never met those people.* I felt like I needed to know more. At that moment, it occurred to me that it was time to explore my history. I was going to seek my birth mother.

Soon after my parents' anniversary, I contacted the Ministry of Children and Family Development in B.C. and requested my birth records.

By then, the law had changed in B.C. The agency no longer acted as a broker of that information. Upon my request, I was sent a copy of my entire file, which included my biological mother's name: Judee V. Within a few hours of receiving that information, I was able to locate her on the internet.

Judee and I spoke and wrote several times in late 2010 before we decided to meet. In February of 2011, I flew to Vancouver to meet her for the first time. It was an emotional meeting. Without being asked, she began the story of how she became pregnant with me. We cried a lot that day. I hadn't realized how badly I needed to hear that story until she started to tell it. I still find that odd today. I had not known how much I needed to hear the one thing that affected me most—the story about how I came into the world—until Judee began. All I had really wanted to do was to meet her. To see what she looked like. Meeting her for the first time, I got much more than that.

She told me she had been in a relationship with a boy during high school. That he had gone off to Notre Dame University on a football scholarship and she became pregnant in his first summer back in Vancouver. According to Judee, he'd wanted to marry her but his family stood in the way.

I spent two days with Judee. Even though she had other children, she was clearly thrilled to be reunited with her first biological child. I was as honest as I could be. I told her I was not looking to fill a void of any kind, that nothing was missing from my life. I simply wanted to meet the people who were responsible for my birth. What I didn't tell her, but was thinking, was that I barely had time to keep in touch with my real family. I was concerned about compromising the time I could share with them.

"I think it's important that each of us needs to go at our own pace in this. And it has to be okay if one of us needs to go at a slower pace," I said to her. That seemed to resonate with Judee. She nodded to me.

———

Of course, I learned about my biological father that weekend too. My conversation with Judee was surprising on many levels. But she disclosed one detail I could never have seen coming: my father was former Canadian Football League player and former pro wrestler Mike Webster.

Judee had lost track of Webster over the years, meaning I was on my own to find him. It didn't take long. Surfing the web, I stumbled upon a pro wrestling forum where two writers were discussing Webster's wrestling career. I entered the discussion and explained that I was trying to reach Webster. To my surprise, one of them supplied me with his phone number.

My first attempt to reach Mike went to his answering machine. I left a somewhat vague explanation of why I wanted to talk to him. I told him my name and that, like him, I too had a background in pro sports.

"I'd love to connect with you—I believe we have a lot in common," I said at the end of the message.

Within a few hours, Mike returned my call.

Not quite knowing where to begin, I tried to elaborate more on the pro sports part of the message I had earlier left him. He interjected politely. "Stu, I know who you are," he said. "I followed your career."

I then caught him completely off guard. "There's more to it than that," I said. I told him about my conversation with Judee. I told him that he was my biological father.

Imagine getting that news for the first time in a cold conversation with someone you had never met before. "I knew you were out there and I always wondered if you would ever look for me," Mike said.

It was yet another very emotional conversation. I had a really hard time keeping it together as I spoke with Mike. As our conversation ended we agreed that we would attempt to meet at some point if we could find a way to sync our calendars. But something Mike said in our conversation that day left a strong impression on me. Among the first things he said to me showed something I really respected.

"Stu, I hope the mistakes I made as a young man have not caused you hardship in your life."

He could not have made a more thoughtful comment. He had no warning I'd be calling. And yet, Mike had the presence of mind to be that considerate. It felt to me as though those words had been front of mind for him for much of his life as he shared them with me.

After our initial conversation, we spoke a couple of times but mostly corresponded by email. With both of us leading busy lives, finding a time and place to meet was difficult. Eventually we were able to meet around the Christmas holidays in 2018. I was going to be in Vancouver during the holidays. On December 22, we spent two hours together at a Vancouver restaurant.

If you had walked in that day, you would have seen two very large men sobbing to one another over lunch. In the days before the meeting, I was beginning to feel some nervous anticipation.

I had already heard the story of how I arrived in this world but now I would hear it from Mike's point of view.

What I discovered when I met him was that my biological father had been feeling the same way. In all my anticipation, the one thing I hadn't considered was the possibility that he would be as emotional about this as I was. Yet there we sat, conversing and consoling one another through the tears. Early on we agreed that I look like Judee. Mike seemed to like that.

Mike's account of his relationship with Judee was generally consistent with her version. When he learned that Judee was pregnant with me, Mike wanted to marry her. Mike wanted her to come to Indiana and he wanted to start a life together. From Mike's perspective, his family had nothing to do with the fact that the two never married. His relationship with Judee had deteriorated for reasons completely unrelated to the pregnancy. By the time Mike returned to Indiana to resume school in the fall, he had made the decision that he could not be part of Judee's pregnancy. It was obvious that this was difficult for Mike to share sitting there with me on the day we first met. The guilt and shame he carried were obvious as he wept.

The irony in all this? I stepped into this area expecting that it would be me getting something that I needed. Something important to me. I had shown up looking for a glimpse of myself, but what I now realized was that I would learn much more about Judee and Mike than I ever would about myself. I failed to appreciate that connecting in this way might have important meaning for them also.

As we talked, it became clear to me that I had something to offer Mike far more important than anything I needed from him. Forgiveness. After he and Judee broke up, Mike moved on and eventually married. And as he later raised a family of his own, he carried with him the shame and guilt about the way he handled that moment in his life. I had never suffered from his absence, but it seemed that he had suffered from mine.

To look across the table from him, after all this time, and tell him that I forgave that and to have him accept that offer was a powerful moment for us both. The man faced perhaps the most difficult decision a young man his age could face. I was certainly capable of making the same decision under circumstances like those had it been me. I hope that, on that day, Mike Webster began a process of forgiving himself.

—

I may not look like my biological father, but I have learned that the resemblance between us is uncanny.

Just the fact that we were both professional athletes is a wild statistical outlier. The proportion of Canadians who have played in the NHL is under 0.0001 percent (for Americans, the number is more than an order of magnitude smaller); the number who have played in the CFL is even smaller. The odds that two people who have never met each other would both have played pro are vanishingly small. There aren't many guys big enough to be defensive linemen or NHL enforcers, and fewer still with the drive and ability to do it. And yet there we were. Webster had won a national championship with Notre Dame, and a Grey Cup with the Montreal Alouettes. He was six-foot-one, 285 pounds, by the way. Webster was no easier to push around than I was.

It's easy to trace heredity through physical traits but harder to do so with things that are less easily quantified, like personality. And yet there appears to be a straight biological line between Webster and me on that level also. I was involved in the NHLPA in one way or another for much of my adult life, and Webster became so involved in the CFL union that it ended his career. In his role as the player representative for the Alouettes in 1970, he organized a delayed arrival to training camp as a protest to the unfair treatment of CFL players.

The Alouettes responded by trading him to the Hamilton Tiger Cats. The Tiger Cats then asked him to accept a pay cut. Rather than do that, he quit football and moved into professional wrestling because former heavyweight champion Gene Kiniski had told him there was good money to be made as a wrestler. From that, "Iron Mike" Webster was born.

Long before he met me, Webster described himself as a "locker room lawyer" and a "shit disturber." Remind you of anyone?

If the percentage of Canadians who play pro sports is vanishingly small, the percentage of Canadians who play pro sports *and* achieve post-graduate degrees after their careers are over is nearly imperceptible. And yet, there was Webster, with his doctorate in psychology, specializing in hostage crisis behaviour. And there was Stu Grimson, attorney at law.

Concussions was another area of commonality. In 2016, Webster joined a class action lawsuit against the CFL for allegedly not providing players with enough information about the dangers of concussion. Webster told the *Ottawa Citizen* he was diagnosed with a traumatic brain injury a year before joining the lawsuit. He collapsed while working at a military hospital on Vancouver Island. Mike has been told that he suffers from CTE. We had a lot to talk about.

As a wrestler, Webster knew what it was like to be cheered by crowds, and he knew what it was like to be the bad guy too.

Webster teamed with "The Brute" on New Year's Day of 1973 to win the Canadian Open Tag team title, holding it for a year and a half. Iron Mike was a "heel." It was the heel's job to stir up the crowd by crossing the line with his disruptive behaviour. Heels are rule-breakers and evil-doers. But Webster put a different spin on the role during his time on the wrestling tour. He wanted to be a likeable heel. That's not a bad definition of an enforcer—a rule-breaker with a good heart.

—

I give considerable credit to my parents for handling my desire to meet my biological parents with compassion. They gave me space to do it without feeling as though I was hurting them. While I can't pretend to understand what they may have been feeling, I can guess they wondered why I needed to meet the people who'd given me up. I'm sure they wondered if it reflected upon the parenting job they had done. If anything, the search for my origins made me appreciate all the more what my real parents did for me.

In my case, it helped that my parents had already taken this journey with my sister, Sam. She had discovered her birth mother years earlier and developed a relationship with her.

I'm not sure that type of relationship was ever my objective. I simply needed to satisfy my curiosity and meet these people. Now that I understand there was guilt and shame around this decision made some fifty years ago, I'm also glad I've been able to communicate to Mike and Judee that I've enjoyed a good life. Ultimately, an unexpected pregnancy resulted in a very positive outcome.

I'm not closing the chapter on my birth parents. Frankly I'm not sure where that goes. Mike and I still stay in touch, mostly through email. I don't have much contact with Judee. And that's okay. I have no expectations here to be honest.

When you go looking for answers in something like this, you have to be open to the possibility that you may have been asking the wrong questions from the start. What I learned here was a lesson I won't soon forget. I wandered in hoping to get something and as it turns out, my role all along was to give.

At a glance, you look at Stu Grimson, and you look at Mike Webster, and you conclude that genetics can tell you how I became the person I did.

But look a bit deeper and it's a lot more complicated. Sure, it's doubtful I would have had the career I did if it weren't for the DNA I inherited. But there are a lot of guys my size who never got a sniff in the NHL. Maybe they didn't have parents like Em and Stan Grimson, who were willing to get their son to the rink and make sure he stuck with his dream when it would have been easier and less costly to do something else. Maybe they didn't have the kind of parents who could be tender when their children needed tenderness, and tough when they were behaving like idiots. You can have the physical gifts and not get far if you don't know how to make the most of them. You need role models for that, and I was very fortunate on that front. Nature only gets you so far. I couldn't have asked for better nurture. Mike Webster may have had a role in making me six-foot-six, but it was the RCMP officer Stan Grimson who brought out the protector instinct in me.

I'll make a larger point here. If you're asking the question "Who am I?" in the genetic sense, you're probably asking the wrong question. One thing that meeting my biological parents really brought home to me is that it's not who you are that counts.

It's what you do. The person you are is the person you become by making one decision after another. If you're lucky, you have people around you who make even hard decisions a little easier. Things could have gone differently for me if not for Judee V. and Mike Webster. They're responsible for creating the life. But no one shaped this life of mine more than my parents did.

The greatest gift Stan and Em Grimson ever gave me was they taught me how to work and they modelled the sort of determination that comes from hard work. There were times when I could have given up, or turned back—not making it would have been the easier path to take. Nature doesn't explain why I didn't. There were times when I could have given in to anger, or self-destruction—those are easy temptations to surrender to. Nature definitely doesn't explain how I managed to avoid the worst of that.

Nurture does, though.

CHERRYGATE

When I was sidelined with my concussion, Kelly Buchberger called me from Tootsies—the most famous honkey tonk in Nashville. The Phoenix Coyotes were in town and he and some teammates were downtown howling at the moon. He wanted me to come down and join them.

"Bucky, I'm sitting here in my pyjamas watching *Seinfeld*," I told him. "I'm not coming downtown."

"Get down here," he said.

I didn't really feel like it, but it's hard to say no to Bucky. We were together in L.A. for a year with the Kings and he was my kind of people. Tough as nails, heart of a lion, a throwback to a different time. So I gave in and headed to Tootsies.

When I joined the group, I ordered a beer. Buchberger was too preoccupied with the conversation to notice. But he almost fell out of his chair when he saw me take a sip.

People really are surprised when a non-drinker takes a drink. In my case, they seemed more surprised than they'd been when I gave up drinking seventeen years earlier. Having gone without for so long, I am very aware that drinking alcohol is a widespread practice in our culture. Most of us can't imagine a summer's day, a Friday night, a sweaty locker room, a Christmas party, or a dinner at a nice restaurant without a drink. Most everyone drinks. But the moment I held a glass of beer to my lips, many people were astonished.

I puzzled over that a little before I realized that not drinking had come to define me. You become the things you do. I suppose that makes sense. That's the way it should be.

But circumstances change, and we can change with them without compromising what we believe or who we are. I had reasons to quit drinking when I did—mostly that I wanted to model a different example for my kids. There's no obligation to follow the crowd. You don't have to drink.

As they got older, that view seemed less applicable. My kids had seen me abstain for years. They understood that lesson. Then, as they entered their teens and approached their twenties, I sensed my kids needed a different example. An example of how to consume alcohol responsibly. So, my behaviour changed but the motivation behind my behavior had not. Throughout the transition from abstaining to drinking socially, there was always a mindfulness of the impact it would have on my children. My circumstances had changed and my thinking evolved. That's just the way I'm wired.

When I meet people who don't know what I once did for a living, they're always astonished to learn that I spent fourteen years as an NHL tough guy. I suppose that today I may not seem like the sort of person who made a living with his fists. They say I must have changed.

And I have. Of course I have. Circumstances change for everyone; no one is the same person at fifty as they are at eighteen. We all learn and we all change. I've learned a lot of lessons, many of them the hard way. And, without question, I have changed.

But fundamentally, there are elements of who I am that have not changed. Does the Stu Grimson who used to get into fights in front of his hometown movie theatre still exist? Nope, not me anymore. Is the Stu Grimson who sticks up for others still around? Yeah, I gotta say, that's still me. Do I go out of my way looking for trouble today? No, I'm trying to be a little more discerning these days.

—

But when the moment calls for me to stand my ground, do I? Absolutely.

I am very resistant to being drawn into a debate on the side of those who want to blame the game and our role for taking some of the game's toughest players prematurely. Probert, Rypien, Boogaard, Ewen, and Belak. The circumstances surrounding their deaths were as different as the men themselves. Heart attack, suicide linked to depression, drug overdose, suicide linked to side effects from prescription medication, and accidental death, respectively. Were their deaths tragic? Without question. Is there a common denominator to all of them? Sure, the role. But does the role provide the explanation for all these untimely deaths? It's not that simple. Bob Probert died of a massive blockage to his heart. You want to blame the role for that? I understand the appeal of doing so. It makes for great headlines. But I don't make that connection. Maybe that's too nuanced a position for some but it's what makes sense to me.

And it sure seemed to ruffle Don Cherry's feathers.

It was the season opener to CBC's *Hockey Night in Canada* on October 6, 2011, and Don Cherry wanted to come on with a splash. The "patron saint of tough guys" was about to bite the hand that fed him and take a run at three such tough guys. Cherry singled out Jim Thomson, Chris Nilan, and me, and called us "pukes," "hypocrites," and "turncoats" because we said that the NHL should ban fighting. He said he was "disgusted" with us.

Somehow Cherry got the idea that I thought fighting should be eliminated from the game.

I'm glad our sport continues to refine the game and make it safer. But I've never said that the league should ban fighting. Quite the opposite; whenever I'm asked about this topic, I maintain there is still a justification for fighting even in today's game.

"[They say,] 'Oh, the reason that they're drinking, [taking] drugs, and [becoming] alcoholics is because they're fighting,'" Cherry continued. "You guys were fighters, and now you don't want guys to make the same living you did."

Not only had I never come out against fighting, I had also never battled drug or alcohol addiction. Cherry had the wrong guy. Nilan had his struggles with substance abuse, but he never blamed that on the role he played in the game and he never called for a ban on fighting. Thomson had openly admitted that he battled drug and alcohol addiction and had said he believed his role as an NHL enforcer had played a part in it. But that doesn't make him a hypocrite.

"[Cherry] has no idea," Thomson told CTV News. "I basically got a Ph.D. in this stuff because I've lived it. Has he even been down my road? Has he laid there the nights that I've laid there? It's shameful for him to attack the mentally ill and people with addictions."

Cherry had always gone out of his way to give tough guys their due. In fact, the man had built his own empire on our backs. For years, his "Rock 'Em, Sock 'Em" highlight tapes featuring NHL tough guys in their element had flown off of store shelves. Now he was attempting to humiliate three guys prominent in that role.

At the time, I was working for the law firm of Kay, Griffin, Enkema & Colbert in Nashville. The fact that I was a lawyer prompted widespread media speculation that my firm would be suing on behalf of the three of us.

As a first order of business, I called Cherry out on live air as to where he had heard the rumour that had touched him off. TSN was happy to give me a broad platform during "CherryGate" as I ran a one-man media campaign on behalf of the three of us. Through Cherry's attorney, I was told that Georges Laraque told Cherry that Nilan, Thomson, and I had been promoting a fighting ban. First mistake, Don. Georges is a lot of things. Well-informed is not one of them.

Eventually, Cherry apologized on air: "I've got to admit I was wrong on a lot of things," he said. "I put down three enforcers, tough guys, my type of guys, I threw them under the bus. I'm sorry about it, I really am."

To bring it all to a close, I issued a statement, through the firm, that we had accepted Cherry's apology and that we wouldn't be suing him or the CBC. All we ever wanted really was for Cherry to walk it back.

At the end of the day, this really was just a silly sideshow initiated by Cherry. But one where the three of us couldn't just let it lie. You can't use words like *puke, hypocrite,* and *turncoat* to describe people, not even for disagreeing with their point of view. (Which we had not even done.) And especially not on live television on one of the most-watched programs in all of Canada. I suppose the thing that bothered me most was the way Cherry had abused his pulpit and the impact that people like him are having on the public discourse today. You want to disagree with someone? By all means. But can you please do it with just a little civility?

The other realization I had was that maybe I hadn't changed all that much since that first training camp with the Flames, when I walked away from my first NHL contract. If I'm going to drop the gloves, it will be on my terms.

—

But while we're on the topic, I might as well make my thoughts clear on fighting. First, I've been hearing about an outright ban on fighting since before I started in the league. Would the league ever get rid of something that at least some fans love? They don't need to. Due to rule changes in other areas of the game, the game is faster and far more skilled than the days when heavyweights like me roamed the ice. That and a salary cap make it impractical to hold a roster spot for someone like that. So fighting has become marginalized. You still see it. You just don't see it as often.

With the game played at such a high speed today, I don't think the Stu Grimson of the 1990s could skate in today's NHL. Many of my peers would say the same about themselves if pressed.

Having said that, there are a lot of guys from my era that may have qualified for today's NHL. Probert, Kocur, Domi, Chase, McCarthy? I think so. Those guys could probably play today.

But I'll be honest—my game was optimized for a different NHL. There was a niche then for guys like me. I don't have any problem with that.

To be honest, I really enjoy the game the way it is played today. I marvel at the speed and energy. Players today do things on ice that players in my era never thought to do. Today's game is a marvel. It's in a good spot.

And I don't miss the arbitrary fights, those battles that occurred because fighters needed to justify their place on the roster. Fighting in the dying minutes of a lost game to "send a message." We don't need those fights anymore. Certainly not if we want to attract a broader audience to the game.

But two important justifications for fighting remain. First, there are few moments in a game more exciting than that moment where, if my team is flat, I go out and lock horns with a Probert. Inevitably, the energy on my bench is transformed and the energy inside the building becomes electric. And the way that typically plays out on the ice is that the momentum often turns in my team's favour. Anecdotally, time after time, I was amazed to watch my team as I served my fighting major from the opposite side of the ice as they pushed back against an opponent that had been imposing their will on us just moments before. Don't just take it from the guy sitting in the box. Statistician Terry Appleby analyzed 14,000 NHL games and came to the same conclusion the players and coaches have known intuitively since the game began. An astonishing 76 percent of fights produce an offensive surge for at least one team. And the other 24 percent of the time? *Both* teams pick up the pace. If you want a faster game with more scoring, don't get rid of fighting.

The second justification was much stronger in my era: if you don't dress someone on your roster who is capable of holding the other team accountable, that team may play you differently. And by differently, I mean that they may try to run you out of the rink.

After all, hockey remains a physical sport and dominating another team physically can still provide a path to winning. Again, this aspect doesn't hold up in the way that it did when I played. But intimidation still goes a long way in today's game. And the best way to proof your team against intimidation is to stand up to it.

Lastly, for what it's worth, shouldn't the players themselves have a say in how the game is played as it evolves? Of course. And especially today, when player salaries are linked to hockey-related revenue in a salary cap system. To that end, when NHL players are polled, nearly 98 percent support the idea that fighting should remain in the game.

18

ENTER THE RED QUEEN

The last meaningful battle I was in came up, oddly enough, in the broadcast arena. When I returned to Nashville from Toronto after leaving the NHLPA, I worked as a trial attorney at a Nashville-based law firm, Kay, Griffin, Enkema & Colbert, PLLC, but I still wanted to maintain a connection to the game. In talking with the Predators, they indicated they could use someone to do colour commentary on the radio for the Predators' home games. I was back in the game.

When the team was in town, I would jump up out of my attorney's chair at the firm at 5 p.m., head to the rink, and put on a headset to talk hockey for two-plus hours. What could be more fun?

Drawing on my experience as a player, I enjoyed more than I thought I would talking about the nuances of the game. I had more passion for the sport than I realized. The live on-air reporting gave me a buzz. My partner, Tom Callahan, had a real touch for creating the space for me to insert relevant insight. If anything, I talked too much.

While I was handling the radio duties, the Predators were grooming former Nashville player Wade Belak to have a role in the television broadcast. He would sit in the booth, wearing a headset, listening to Terry Crisp and Pete Weber in preparation for becoming part of the broadcast team. But tragedy struck on August 31, 2011, when Belak was found dead in a Toronto hotel. The loss was devastating—Wade left a wife and young children.

Several months later, Bob Kohl, the Predators' director of broadcasting, asked me to lunch. And lunch included an offer to be the lead television colour analyst on the team's flagship network, Fox Sports Tennessee. Believe it or not, I didn't see that coming. When I returned to my law office, I remember sitting at my keyboard staring at a blank screen dwelling on the offer that seemed too good to be true. I would be back on the hockey circuit. Had I missed it? Yes, I had. Would I miss the practice of law? Uh, no, not at all. Litigation was a great experience but I didn't have a lot of lawyer friends pleading with me not to leave the bar. Of course I said yes.

The transition from radio to television occurred over a few years. By the 2014–15 season I was on television full time. During that first season as the lead analyst on television working alongside the legendary Pete Weber, we experienced a technical glitch during a broadcast that people are still talking about in Nashville.

After the first period of a game in St. Louis against the Blues, Weber was checking Twitter when he noticed that there was a buzz about some racy unidentified audio interference that had bled into our broadcast. Viewers said it sounded like a woman in the throes of passion. Twitter was blowing up over the fact that some woman's outburst during sex was stepping all over our broadcast. "Porn Gate" was born.

Weber and I didn't hear it, nor did we have any idea how it occurred. But it created a firestorm. The Predators were unhappy because it reflected badly on them. Fox Sports executives were up in arms.

In time, we learned the source of the heavy breathing. An audio technician had left a laptop on and connected to our broadcast somehow. Inadvertently, the computer's browser played the trailer to a movie entitled *Wild*, starring Reese Witherspoon, that was soon hitting theatres. Witherspoon's memorable breathing pattern fits appropriately with the trailer video. However, if you're not watching the video, then it does sound like she's having great sex!

When the Twitterverse was still buzzing over it the next day, I thought the situation could use a little levity. I tweeted: "Our deepest apologies for the audio interruption on our broadcast of the game last night. The sound of my voice has that effect on women from time to time."

I later learned Predators executives were lining up to rap me on the knuckles over that tweet. Too soon to make light of it? Maybe. However, when the tweet generated thousands of retweets and interactions across social media platforms, I was spared punishment.

Lighten up, already.

It was around this time that I met Jennifer Ives. Life after my marriage to Pam ended was difficult initially. But, in time, everybody moves on. That's what people do.

Jennifer and I spoke by phone after we first connected by email. I was in San Francisco on business when I called her and we spoke for the first time. I was killing time one afternoon and decided to take in a movie. I decided to call Jenn before I walked in to the movie.

She sounded full of life. Really bright and upbeat. She asked what movie I was seeing and I told her I had been wanting to take in the new *Mad Max*. I'd seen everything else in the series to this point so I almost felt obligated.

As it turns out she had already seen it. She said she liked it but had one reservation . . . "There's one part that's really hard to watch. I had to hide my eyes. I'm not big on movies with a lot of violence . . ."

Hmmm. I thought. *This relationship may not get off the ground if she has a hard time with violence. Especially if her background research on me involves YouTube.*

"Tell me which scene you think I'm talking about after you've seen it," Jennifer said. We talked for fifteen minutes in all before we hung up.

I called her again the following day and told her I thought I had identified the scene she struggled with. There was a moment where a child is treated badly. "I suspect that's the one you struggled with right?"

"It was. Didn't you find it hard to watch?"

"I suppose so, but I probably have a different level of tolerance for violence than you." Understatement of the new millennium.

We set a lunch date. The Monday after I got back to Nashville we agreed to meet at Cafe Nonna in the Sylvan Park district of Nashville. We arrived at the restaurant around the same time and walked inside together. She was beautiful. Tall, curvy. A really warm smile.

I knew from photos that she had red hair but something occurred to me for the first time in this meeting. My longtime favourite musician was married to a redhead. Patty Scialfa and Bruce Springsteen married in 1991 and Patty—a great musician in her own right—immediately became a member of the E Street Band.

Shallow, I know, but the fact that the Boss was wed to a redhead gave Jenn this unique appeal in my mind. In fact, Bruce wrote a song in honour of Patty. "Red-Headed Woman" was never released on a studio album, and if you haven't heard it already, don't. It's filthy . . . in a good way.

Lunch was intimidating. Jenn is 5'11" and I'm 6'6" but she towered over me. There is a bench side and a movable chair side to most of the tables at Cafe Nonna. Jenn sat on the bench side, which happens to be a few inches higher than the chair side. I spent the entire lunch feeling like an eight-year-old having lunch with his mom. I'm not used to looking up at anyone.

We resolved at least one thing at lunch. We both liked Amy Winehouse and neither of us had seen the new documentary that was out. *Promising*, I thought to myself. Attractive. Tall. Good sense of humour. Likes movies. And movies that border on the dark side. Could this be going somewhere?

On date four, Jennifer said she wanted to go canoeing the next day. I said yes. I usually say yes . . . but I didn't really want to go canoeing. The next day, I called Jennifer and she was packing, getting ready to go.

I tried every excuse I could think of.

Stu: It's hot out.

Jen: Right, good thing we'll be on the river.

Stu: It's supposed to rain.

Jen: Good thing we'll already be wet. Do you even know how to canoe?

Stu: Are you kidding? I'm Canadian. We invented canoeing!

Finally, she said, "Well, I'm going canoeing. I'll give you a call when I get back."

I relented: "I'll pick you up in twenty minutes."

Jenn packed sandwiches and we had a small cooler of cold drinks all set for an afternoon on the river. The canoe excursion company transported us up the river and dropped us in the water. As we pushed off from shore, Jennifer was stationed up front with a paddle and I was in the back.

The second we pushed off from the dock, it started to rain. Not just rain but a heavy downpour, the kind that's hard to see through. Laughing, we made our way across the river and under the protection of some trees to wait out the storm. We were laughing and talking and then I noticed something that looked like white streaks running down Jennifer's back and shoulders. There was a pool of bronze-coloured water gathering at her feet. At the same moment, Jennifer realized the same.

I didn't know this at the time but, as a redhead with very fair skin, Jennifer keeps her "tan" in the bathroom cabinet. The rain was washing off that tan and it was puddling at her feet in the bottom of our canoe.

She was obviously embarrassed but laughed it off and told me that if I was gonna hang out with her, I should probably know her true colour.

I can't say for sure how most women would have reacted. But Jennifer's response communicated a lot to me in that moment. She had a great sense of humour and it was clear that she did not take herself too seriously. Soaked as we were that was a great day.

And a beginning to many great days. I found what I was looking for in Jennifer; I found my best friend. Jenn and I eloped in our own hometown; we married in Nashville on May 19, 2018.

—

When team president Jeff Cogen left the Nashville Predators in 2015, I should have seen the writing on the wall. Previously, at the NHLPA, I had already played the role of baby out with the bath water. It was Cogen who hired me away from the law firm; I was his choice to update the crew in the booth. However, incoming president Sean Henry reshuffled the deck and placed a new executive over our department. The new head of the broadcasting department and I did not see the world in quite the same way and that provided him the opportunity to put his stamp on the Predators' broadcast team. I was out.

Nothing good lasts forever, especially when the guy who hired you leaves. It wasn't until the first round of the 2017 playoffs that they finally got around to telling me that they were "going in a different direction."

I loved the job and I was baffled by management's reasons for firing me. The news came like a swift kick in the groin. I couldn't believe I was out. The timing couldn't have been more awkward— the Predators were in a march to the Stanley Cup Final and everyone in Nashville wanted to talk Predators. Except me. The last topic I wanted to discuss was hockey; I couldn't even watch the games. It was as though everyone in town was at this amazing party that I had no desire to attend or even hear about. Jennifer and I hunkered down and we laid low for much of the playoffs.

—

But by the time the Finals rolled around I was ready to jump back in the seat. Jennifer understood my love for broadcasting and, during my period of misery, she had done extensive poking around. Jennifer found me an agent in Tim Scanlan. Tim is with Octagon Sports Representation and he had a direct line to the decision-makers at NHL Network.

NHL Network's senior vice-president of production, Dave Patterson, agreed to use me on air when the 2017 Stanley Cup Final was in Nashville. It was an opportunity for me to audition on air with the possibility of joining the network in an expanded role in the fall. Working for the Predators, I had done live Arena Cam hits for the network in the past. Those appearances had always gone really well so stepping onto their air during the Finals was comfortable.

Apparently, everybody liked what they saw and heard. The network offered me a contract for a minimum of thirty dates working out of the Secaucus, New Jersey, studio. It was a perfect fit right from the beginning. Working as a studio analyst is probably a better environment for me after all. I get the space to elaborate more. I find that I'm able to offer a lot more insight in a studio setting as opposed to working in the booth on a live broadcast.

I work with talented people at the network and they are very good at what they do. It runs like a well-oiled machine. In a typical month, I fly in to Jersey every other week and jump on air for anywhere from three to five dates per trip. I love it.

My thirty-date minimum in my first year ended up being forty dates. And after the 2017–18 season, I negotiated another contract through the end of the 2019–20 season which saw my dates increase again. I was recently added to the team covering the 2019

Stanley Cup Finals. So the fit at the network seems to be a good one. I have been around the game all my life and I enjoy maintaining a strong connection to it.

The one thing I have come to appreciate most is the freedom I enjoy while working in a rotation with the other analysts at NHL Network. Working on the broadcast team for a single team like the Predators, on the other hand, can be all-consuming. From September to June, you're covering and promoting the team, in some way, every day of the season. Once the season starts, there is little room for anything else.

So now I'm able to pursue all the things for which I have a passion. Hockey among them. Jennifer and I also enjoy investing in real estate. And I worked hard to become a lawyer; the rotation at the network allows me to exercise that muscle also. I serve as corporate counsel and VP of Business Development at a company called ThirdHome in Nashville.

I have Jennifer to thank for that. Were it not for her searching out Tim at Octagon, I may have missed the opportunity at NHL Network. And missed something that Jenn had been saying all along. That they own you when you're working for just one team; there's got to be a better way to do what you love. I'm in a good spot now.

—

A lot has changed since that awkward, misdirected Kamloops native broke into pro hockey. I wear a suit now as I make my living. I rarely skate anymore. I haven't thrown a punch in nearly two decades but I'm still a tough guy in a lot of ways. My business is still the game I love. I still fill a niche role in the business; by no means am I the show's star. But every now and again the spotlight shines my way—and just like during my playing days when 20,000 sets of eyes would turn to watch me throw down—I need to be ready to do what I do. My circumstances have changed, and I have changed. But I like to think that, in many ways, elements of that same guy still exist today.

ACKNOWLEDGMENTS

Darryl Sutter. Darryl is a farm kid to the core. A man of few words but when he speaks you better be listening. Darryl was a hard case and a hard guy to play for. At times, he was too hard on us but I learned as much from Darryl as anyone I played for. I have always said that the voices of certain coaches resonate in the back of your mind when you're playing. Darryl's was one of those voices for me. "Don't worry about the score. Focus on winning your next battle and the score looks after itself." "It's not what happens. It's how you respond." Hockey truths and life truths.

Paul Maurice. Perhaps because he was younger than me, Paul treated me like a peer as he took his first post on an NHL bench in Hartford. But there's another reason behind his approach. I have spoken to Paul at length about this. He had no idea what to expect or even how to act coming out of a playing and coaching background that was formed exclusively in the OHL. So where did a twenty-seven-year-old rookie coach look for an example of how to communicate with the diverse members of an NHL roster? "I watched the alpha males. I watched the veterans of the group interact with their teammates," Maurice once confided to me.

Paul was mindful that players like Glen Wesley, Keith Primeau, Kevin Dineen, Kelly Chase, Sean Burke, and Stu Grimson were players first and foremost. But they were leaders as well. These were the guys who had taken ownership of that team and they felt an obligation to invest more in it than just their time on ice. And in doing so, they were very much an extension of the coaching staff. We took responsibility for our guys being prepared. Paul recognized the value in modelling his approach after the examples set by those men.

Additionally, we were not the most talented roster and Maurice and his staff realized that they needed to squeeze every drop out of the players they had. So Paul made it a part of my daily routine to sit with assistant coach Steve Weeks and to watch each of my shifts from the game before. Today this is a common and widespread practice across all NHL teams. Seeing yourself do it right or do it wrong is, in either case, an effective means of learning how to do it better the next time out. I saw the level of my play rise during my two years under Maurice. He invested a lot in me.

Again, I regret asking for a trade and forcing my way out of Raleigh. I had a good thing going under Paul Maurice. Paul stretched me as a player and a person.

Wayne Fleming. Wayne Fleming was a great hockey man. It's possible I learned more fundamentally about the game from Wayne Fleming than any other coach I had.

My first year in minors in Salt Lake City came directly after my sophomore year in Manitoba. I had just done a drill where my line goes on a rush to one end of the ice and then we race back to get a second puck and attack the same end for a second time. As we regrouped, I presented myself as a good option to the passer.

Rather than skate directly at him, I presented myself on a flat line in front of him. I had been taught this way for good reason. You are a better target for the passer and this path allows you to keep most of your speed as you transition.

My new coach Paul Baxter noticed this. As the drill was ending, he went out of his way to say . . . "the path you took there . . . you were coached well."

Wayne Fleming had a keen eye for the details of the game. And he was effective at communicating these details to us in a way that made us better as players. Moreover, in those two years of college hockey under Wayne Fleming I grew up a lot. Without that unconventional detour I may not have been able to take a run at a pro career in earnest.

Thank you Coach, you were instrumental to my development. Rest in peace.

Stan and Em Grimson. In life, with respect to some things, the choice is neither to like or to dislike. It is simply to do what must be done.

The greatest gift my parents ever gave me was they taught me how to work. My mom grew up on a dairy farm near Edmonton, Alberta. My father's family farmed wheat and other crops near Winyard, Saskatchewan. Growing up in the Grimson house you do for yourself. You don't hire a contractor to finish the basement at the family home when you can enlist your son as free labour and finish it yourself. You don't hire a professional to landscape the yard at home when you can go to a nursery, buy the sod and plants necessary to the job, and install it all yourself. Would you believe that my father dug, by hand, the opening for my grandmother's casket when she died?

When your parents model that sort of determination over the course of your childhood, the message takes. I have never been afraid of hard work.

The realization of our dreams does not come by accident. Our dreams are realized after countless hours of painstaking work. That was certainly the case in my life. I applied myself daily in junior hockey, college hockey, at the minor pro level, and finally at the highest level of hockey in the world in order to see the dream of a career in the NHL come to life.

The same can be said of a post-hockey career in the law. Earning a law degree was one of the most challenging things I have ever done in life. It was transformative for me. It reshaped the way I think. And it opened up a broad range of options for me after hockey. But a juris doctorate degree in law did not come without many, many months buried in the books.

Without the ethic for work my parents instilled in me, I would have attempted none of that. And I believe that I have been able to hand that gift to my children as they watched their father go back to school at thirty-seven years of age and reinvent himself.

Brian Wood. The idea of a book was so far from my mind when Brian reached out to me in 2013. From the start, Brian showed a deft touch. He made his point, which was that there was an audience for my story. But when I made it clear that I did not share the same view, Brian graciously stepped aside and waited patiently. We had other conversations over time and ultimately I came around to Brian's argument that I played a unique role in a unique time in our game. I am very grateful to Brian for planting that seed early on.

Kevin Allen. I have long admired Kevin's work. My opinion has always been that no one writes our sport better. In working with Kevin on this project, I have however come to hold a much deeper appreciation for his skill as a writer. In the countless hours we spent together, Kevin drew from me emotions and memories that were essential to the story, some of which I had nearly forgotten. Kevin has a very keen sense of the things hockey fans, sports fans, and readers, more generally, find palatable about this great game. There could be no other writer for this book.

Nick Garrison. The reason that Penguin ultimately published this book has everything to do with Nick. From our first meeting, Nick not only shared my passion for the project, he amplified it and he began to refine it. I rarely say this about anyone or anything: where this book and Nick are concerned, I felt an instant connection. Throughout the process, Nick has been a constant source of encouragement and a wealth of experience. Nick steered the production of this book in a masterful way. I count writing this book among the most memorable professional experiences of my life. Due in large part to Nick Garrison's influence over the project.

Jennifer Grimson. This book, and much that is in it, would not be possible without a woman named Jennifer. I met her in 2015, a time when I was in a pretty good spot. I was thoroughly enjoying my run as the Nashville Predators' lead colour analyst.

About two years after Jenn and I met, the sands started to shift under my feet. The Predators decided to go in a different direction. It was their decision to make but there is a right way to fire someone and a wrong way to fire someone. I got the latter and it stung for several weeks; I was not in a great place. Jenn was as good a friend to me during this period as anyone ever had been in my life. From the beginning, she had the vision that my dismissal from the Predators' broadcast team was a golden opportunity.

Jenn understood that I loved what I did and that I loved this as my connection to the game. But she believed there was another way to do it that would give me greater control of my life. She persuaded me to hire an agent. She found one in Tim Scanlan of Octagon, the same firm that represented me during the final years of my playing career. It was Tim who landed me the audition with the NHL Network which has turned into a role as one of the network's lead analysts.

However, because the network operates on a rotation basis it has allowed me to pursue another area that's important to my life. I worked hard to earn a law degree and working as a trial attorney was an experience I would not trade for anything. I no longer litigate but I enjoy a role that's a custom fit for me as Corporate Counsel and Vice President of Business Development for a Nashville company called ThirdHome. I wouldn't be here if it weren't for Jennifer's nudge.

This book wouldn't exist either. After I started dating Jenn, she convinced me to get back to Brian and I'm very glad I did. This book would never have happened without Jennifer's firm belief that the story is one worth telling.

There was a period of time in my life not that long ago where I doubted that I could be as happy as I am today. In Jennifer Grimson, I found someone with whom to laugh, to love, and to share my life. We are wired the same way. And she gets me.

There is nowhere on earth I would rather be than in the space right next to my Red-Headed Woman.

INDEX